OUTSiDE TiME

OUTSiDE TiME

A personal history of prison farming and gardening

HANNAH WRiGHT

Published by:

Placewise Press
Eightslate
Devon
EX15 3DR, UK

email: info@hanwrights.com
www.hanwrights.com

First published in 2017

Cover design and maps by Brian Dunce

ISBN: PB: 978-0-9957475-0-0
epub: 978-0-9957475-1-7

British Library Cataloguing-in-Publication Data
A catalogue record for this book is available from the British Library.

Typeset in Bembo by Streamline Photography & Design, Uffculme, Devon.
Printed and bound by HMPPS Prison Service Industries at HMP Coldingley.

With love and gratitude to my dad and Maurice,
champions amongst champions

A gem of a book

This is a gem of a book: a history of, tribute to, and eulogy for prison horticulture and agriculture. Staff who grow plants and livestock are exceptionally good at growing people too. Nature heals and instructs more effectively than courses. The prison service should 'get back outside'. A moving, informative, and personal tale.

Alison Liebling
Professor of Criminology, University of Cambridge, UK

An unexpected pleasure

This book is an unexpected pleasure – well-written, fascinating and full of heart. But above all it's a vital testament to the extraordinary power of gardening and growing food to heal broken lives. The prison service and the Department of Justice should take note.

Hugh Fearnley-Whittingstall
Celebrity chef, food writer and campaigner

Stimulating, warm and important

Outside Time is a stimulating, warm and important book. When you truly appreciate the healing power of nurturing the land and husbanding animals, and the life affirming nature of mastering the skills to garden and farm for transforming lives, you wonder at our culture and the quality of those charged with creating a roadmap to a prison system focused on seeing the end of a revolving door service. This book is an antidote to cynicism and, while focusing on prison farms, it provides lessons to all of us about reintroducing ourselves to the land and connecting to nature. *Outside Time* is a powerful reminder that the past has lessons to teach the future.

Sir Tim Smit KBE
Executive Vice Chairman and Co-founder of the Eden Project

Fearless and passionate

A fearless, passionate and deeply human treatise for rehabilitation by farming that makes perfect sense. Working the land, caring for livestock and producing nourishment reconnects hand, head and heart and should be revived throughout the prison service as a matter of urgency.

Miriam Darlington
Academic, journalist, and the author of Otter Country

A book worth reading

I do applaud your initiative: I have seen for myself the rehabilitative and redemptive effects of gardening in prisons: the pleasure in tending crops, the pride in serving them to others, and the confidence gained from the knowledge of and contact with the living world.

Rt Hon Baroness Jean Corston
Author of the Corston Report (2007) on women with particular vulnerabilities in the criminal justice system

A vivid and inspiring story

The author tells, from her own experience backed up with meticulous research, a vivid and inspiring story that deserves to be widely read. It has left me in no doubt that horticulture can and should provide prisoners with invaluable therapy as well as skills that are relevant both Inside and Outside.

Jane Fearnley-Whittingstall
Award-winning garden and landscape designer

CONTENTS

ILLUSTRATiONS

FOREWORD

Outside Time is a particularly appropriate title for a book about a little known element of prison life, as I will return to at the end of this Foreword. The aim of imprisonment is to protect the public by preventing prisoners from re-offending when they are released, by helping them to live useful and law-abiding lives. This is best done by assessing what it is that has prevented them from living such lives thus far, and identifying any potential that they have that could be exploited to ensure a better future.

Until 1877 most prisons were local, paid for by local taxes. More serious offences had resulted in transportation, firstly to North America, and then, following Independence, to Australia. It was not until 1843 that the first national or convict prison – Pentonville – was built, on lines like those adopted by the United States of America, following Independence. These had rehabilitation through work at their heart, every cell in the new prison having a loom in it.

Meanwhile, as should be expected in largely rural England, work in the rural prisons was essentially on the land. Many prisons had farms attached, which served two purposes – firstly they provided food for prisoners, and secondly they provided work. Over the years however, as we became a more urban nation, work tended to become urban-related as well. True an increasing number of prisons developed gardens, which offer horticultural work, but a large number of farms have been sold, some for the wrong reasons because, while food production and the provision of work still remain valid purposes, reduction in staff numbers mean that prisoners can no longer be escorted to and from, let alone at, their places of work, for fear of escapes.

Between 1877 and 1962, prisons were run by an independent organisation called the Prison Commission. Under the Commission, farms continued to flourish, because Commissioners saw the value of work on the land, both to the Prison Service and to prisoners on release. But, when the Home Office took over responsibility this ceased to be the case. Whatever their merits civil servants do not make good operational managers, and measurable targets and performance indicators are no substitute for the experience of experts who know what they are talking about. Furthermore, serving Ministers who come and go between as well as at elections, is not the same as servicing a long-term strategy. If only prisons had been left free of political interference they could have had a proper employment strategy, which based on their two useful purposes, could have included a long-term Farms and Gardens strategy.

That is the general overview of a former Chief Inspector of Prisons, designed to set the scene for this fascinating and informative book, rather than merely repeat some of what it says. *Outside Time* is a fascinating mix of personal anecdotes and stories, which describe the value of Farms and Gardens through the eyes of both prisoners and staff, interspersed with descriptions of different policy approaches and evolutions of practice.

To return to my opening sentence, I hope that *Outside Time* will be read by those currently responsible for a prison system, that is disfigured by the amount of time prisoners have to spend, locked up inside their cell, which is no place for picking up the skills that are essential if they are to live useful and law-abiding lives on release. Current fast-food habits are storing up long-term health problems. What better demonstration of purposeful rehabilitation than teaching them the value of good food, grown by fellow prisoners.

Lord David Ramsbotham,
HM Chief Inspector of Prisons 1995-2001

PREFACE

Managing work and rehabilitation within the demands of the prison regime is never an easy option with targets liable to change in response to political and reform interests. For many years, farming and gardening activities were seen as an outlet for supervised parties of prisoners to establish a routine to their day, foster a work habit and, through undertaking regular, useful and physically demanding work, develop self-respect. Working with animals brought a good response from seemingly uncaring individuals particularly teenagers. Although some prisoners attained industry qualifications the main purpose of the farming programme was rehabilitation rather than training for outside employment.

The Farms & Gardens group evolved over a 50-year period. It consisted mainly of civilian craftsmen expected to embrace technical advances whilst managing, motivating and training a diverse, unskilled workforce. From the 1960s through to the mid-1990s agriculture and horticulture was at the forefront of prison industries. Twenty years ago, HMP Farms & Gardens employed 2,000 prisoners annually and generated a profit of over £3m. They produced enough food to feed 47,000 inmates three times a day and thereby saved substantial Treasury funds. The success of the group was sustained not only through the hard work and dedication of the farms and garden staff with support from senior management but also the endeavour of the prison workforce.

However, a series of security incidents in the 1980s began to have a dramatic effect on the way the group operated. Categorisation of prisoners forced a re-think by management on their external employment. A reduction of category D prisoners and the introduction of community service sentences meant there was a declining pool of suitable prisoners to work on farms. Politicians and senior management had to focus on security and internal activities in order to sustain control of prison establishments and meet performance targets.

After heading Farms & Gardens from 1982-1991 my retirement from the service in 1996 coincided with the decision by the Prisons Board to examine the role of farms and gardens within the rehabilitation programme; it became obvious that the use of farms was no longer a viable proposition. The decision to sell farm and horticulture units situated outside the prison walls, although anticipated, was greeted with disappointment and regret. By the turn of the century, employment in agriculture and horticulture was principally confined to land inside the walls of the prison. In the USA, the Federal penal system experienced a similar asset stripping process before realising that selling land was detrimental to their future development.

I have no doubt that the work-rehabilitation debate will continue. Until now there has been no detailed history of agriculture and horticulture within the prison service in England and Wales. Without Hannah agreeing to help me and her late father Bev, a prison farm manager and close personal friend, to catalogue the contribution made by the group from the pre-war period through to the sale of assets in early 2000s, the extraordinary success and experience of Farms & Gardens might easily have been dismissed or forgotten. *Outside Time* charts the rise, decline and revival of farming and horticulture within the prison service from the establishment of the first prison farm at Dartmoor in 1852 to the present. Managing a large, diverse business requires skill and patience from staff at all levels. Although it is for the reader to judge the success or failure of past achievements I am pleased to see that horticulture continues to be part of the prison regime and in some cases that expansion is once again taking place.

Maurice Codd
Head of HMP Farms & Gardens 1982-1991,
HMP Area Manager 1991-1996

1

Home on the farm

'Tinker, tailor, soldier, sailor, apothecary, ploughboy ... that's me!' she cried, delighted to have it confirmed by the cherry stones that she was a wild child of nature... Tinker, tailor, soldier, sailor, apothecary, ploughboy ... it appears,' said old Bartholomew, laying down his spoon, 'that I am a thief.'
Virginia Woolf, *Between the Acts*

Seven years before my dad, Bev, escaped to prison he moved my mum and I into a dilapidated farmworker's cottage that rocked whenever there was a thunderstorm. In the back garden I dozed in a sturdy, black-hooded pram whilst my mum, Ann, weeded vegetables amongst towering, yellow flowers she dubbed 'Marcham' daisies after the village we lived in. But shortly after the last carrots had been eased from the fine loamy soil, the Scottish farm manager, recently appointed to run the estate by its 21-year-old owner, felt outshone by my industrious father so he dismissed him.

Fortunately, in the late 1960s the number of dairy cows was approaching a peak having tripled in the last one hundred years.[1] Consequently, it took weeks rather than months for my dad to secure another position twenty-five miles further west near the town of Northleach in Gloucestershire, a county famed for its docile, black-spotted, rare-breed pigs.

'Sunnyside', the Cotswold-stone house tied to his new job required refurbishment having been occupied by the former cowman for many years, so we overwintered in a bleak cottage on the edge of Woeful Lake which once brimmed with the blood of warring Roundheads and Cavaliers. Bed sheets and flannelette nappies flapped futilely in merciless rain leading the postman to berate my mum but she didn't have the space or the means to dry them. Inside, an upturned tea chest doubled as a dining table and the back seat of a Triumph Renown, my parents' *going away* car, deputised as a sofa. The absence of luxuries was compounded by the lenders of the removal lorry pilfering a couple of their finer wedding presents.

As my parents wed, eight bells pealed in the squat tower of Clanfield's late twelfth-century church and the photographer caught Bev telling Ann that he couldn't smile because his newly acquired false teeth were still in his pocket. His uncharacteristically tight lips also concealed another secret, one they kept until I reached my mid-twenties and the reason why their wedding photos were never put on display.

My parents, Bev and Ann Wright, on their wedding day, 1967.[2]

Charged with embezzlement, my dad's father, Billie, had been so confident that he wouldn't be sent down that his wife Julie was oblivious of his crime until he called from the court to say he wouldn't be coming home.

Tall and often charming, a twenty-first birthday gift from a well-connected godfather enabled Billie and Julie to fraternise at Masonic dinners and dances until his membership was inexplicably rescinded. A master butcher, he won watches and gold medals at the renowned Smithfield Show and, between his son's errands as a butcher's boy pedalling sausages and steaks, passed on his filleting and carving skills.

Billie kept a string of racing ponies so Bev and his older sister Gilda rode from an early age but my dad never forgave his father for selling his favourite pony 'Mystery' from under him. Articulate and cunning, Billie taught his son to communicate the odds at horse races using tic-tac the bookmakers' secret language, but at home, alcohol exacerbated a short-temper and his ample fists punched holes in the door behind his son's head while my usually reticent aunt Gilda recalled,

Bev at the seaside with his father Billie.[3]

'I don't know how it happened. I broke my arm when I was about 14, then I had the plaster off and it got broken again.'

Nevertheless, when Billie demanded money be sent to him while he was imprisoned, Gilda capitulated despite struggling to feed and clothe five children on the meagre proceeds of a tenanted council farm.

'He never thanked me,' she added.

To escape school and home, aged 14, Bev became 'Peggy', a deck boy on a merchant vessel, *HMS Ivernia*. After setting sail from Southampton he scrubbed cabins, toilets, showers, mess and galley for eight petty officers between five in the morning until ten thirty at night. Between scrubbing he served meals: breakfast, mid-morning tea served with 'cab nabs' or rock buns, lunch, mid-afternoon 'smoko' and high tea at five o'clock. Time permitting Bev 'turned to' on deck to be taught how to splice ropes and steer. He became accustomed to working long hours, a habit all too familiar to two-thirds of British farmers who regularly work over 60 hours a week.[4]

'We worked like mad,' said amiable, former prison Area Manager Howard Morse recalling his agricultural experience prior to joining the prison service in 1973, 'all hours of the day and night.'

After labouring all day for Sunnyside's farmer-owner my dad cultivated a small triangle of land on which we grew all our vegetables and kept various livestock including a couple of doe-eyed Jersey cows, a pony and a handful of turkey poults which were housed in a makeshift, insulated van whilst they plumped up for Christmas. Late into the night he studied for his only formal qualification, a City & Guilds in farm business and accounts. To afford a few weaners for fattening, my mum undertook piecework as a spud picker. When I wasn't skipping behind the stooping women gleaning the potatoes they'd missed, I'd sit on the wall overlooking the fields and let curious black and white Friesians unfurl their rasping tongues along my outstretched hand or tussle with eager, bottle-fed orphaned lambs who'd leave me covered in blood warm milk.

Although I was content with the company of cows my mum missed the hustle and bustle of village life. To cheer her up my dad repainted the walls and skirting boards in vivid Mediterranean colours: jade, topaz and apricot.

'Lovely,' she enthused,

'Bu' no' righ' for a farmworker's cot'age,' muttered Bert, the ageing farm hand who lived next door with his brother Pete, mindful that it was his older brother who'd been ousted from our house as soon as he became too decrepit to look after the cows.

Eviction was familiar to Maurice Codd, who joined the prison service in 1962 and rose through the ranks to head Her Majesty's Prison Service (HMP) Farms & Gardens twenty years later.

'My mum was working at the "big" house, charring really, when my dad became terminally ill. They were in a tied cottage and allowed to stay there until dad couldn't do anything anymore. Once he couldn't contribute to the farm they had to go.'

As there was no prospect of Maurice's parents buying their own home on an agricultural worker's salary,[5] they were rehoused by the council but they spent their last years in a house that was even more remote, dilapidated and unsuitable than the agricultural property from which they'd been evicted.

Likewise, the local council saved affable, former tractor driver and prison Farm Manager Pete Chisholm's family from becoming homeless. When I interviewed him at my mum's house, directly opposite the low-rise Hatfield prison in South Yorkshire where he and my dad had worked, Pete recalled, 'a lovely life and rubbish money' having driven a tractor on his father's tenanted 450-acre farm from the age of twelve.

Pete was still at school when his father died suddenly of lung cancer.

'I came from a small place in the heart of the Scottish Borders. It was a place with two pubs and no shop. My dad rented a farmhouse for himself, my mum and us five kids. My father was a disciplinarian and used to hit us. When I was fifteen or sixteen my dad got lung cancer and within eighteen months he was dead.'

Pete's head teacher told him, 'you might as well leave now' so he left school with no qualifications and went to work on the farm.

'Because I was working the farm we could all stay in the house because it was tied to the farm but I decided that I wanted to get some qualifications but that would mean going to the local college and I knew that if I didn't work full-time on the farm we'd lose the house. It was a difficult decision but I decided to go to college to get some agricultural qualifications. That meant that my mum and my brothers and sister had to move out of the farmhouse. Luckily, they were able to get a council house. So I went to college and got a national certificate in agriculture and then on a two-day a week release from working on a farm I got a City & Guilds in agriculture.'

Living in tied accommodation caused a lot of problems. Aged twenty-one and recently married, former prison service Farm Manager Derek Webber realised he'd lose his home if the landowner employed his own sons instead.

'I could see no matter how loyal I'd be I'd be pushed to one side. It wouldn't 've happened overnight but I could see it coming,' he said.

It was a familiar scenario. A few years before my parents married, my mother's father Joe, who was managing a farm for a man called Colonel Forbes, was told that the farm he worked on had been sold to a neighbouring land owner, Count Munster, a man who a few years before had sacked Joe rather than honour a performance related pay agreement. It was a condition of the sale that Joe, his wife Elsie and their three children would be evicted from the farm manager's house. Aged forty-eight, unable to secure a mortgage and fed up with losing his home and his job, Joe managed to buy a third of an acre with an agricultural tie with the proceeds from selling a portion of a flock of sheep he owned jointly with Colonel Forbes. After securing planning permission to build a home of their own Joe became an early morning dustcart driver so he could buy bricks and have the time to lay them.

My grandparents called their modest bungalow 'Spinner's Way'. Proud to have been taught to spin by a pair of spinster sisters who in

My grandad Joe Shortland teaching visitors how to spin at Cogges Museum, Witney, Oxfordshire.[6]

turn had been tutored by the most revered spinner, Mahatma Gandhi, Joe shared Gandhi's self-sufficient philosophy and his enthusiasm for teaching.

'Feel these hands,' he'd say with a wink, holding out his lanolin softened fingers to the hundreds of people he taught to spin, '*never* done a day's work.' An exceptional yarner, he spun tales as fine as his thread.

When warm-hearted, prison service pig lady Lorraine Coveney was nine, her dad managed to buy his own sixty-acre farm.

'I was always at home and my sister used to do the jobs in the house doing the cooking and cleaning and I used to say, "Can I go and work on the farm?" I used to feed the calves and then I bought a calf and dad said, "I'll feed your calf for you if you look after mine" and that enabled me to buy my first horse.'

Lorraine and I share a love of horses. I was about three-years-old when my first pony 'Peace' arrived foot sore after my dad walked her fifteen miles from Stow Fair to Sunnyside. I'd clamber through the unglazed window of the stone stable, jump aboard and, much to the consternation of my dad sawing logs on the smallholding, ride bare back towards the main road.

Although we had plenty to eat, we could only afford shoes *or* wire to protect the chickens. When my mum patched socks with glue, my dad either got his foot stuck in his sock or the sock stuck inside his mismatched Wellington boots. However, we were notably better off than my dad's great friend, Glaswegian and former prison service cowman Chris McGown. When my mum and I visited Chris at his home on the Isle of Portland off the coast of Dorset, he told us that his father used to carve shoes out of stale bread.

'It's not funny,' he intoned as his wife Sandra giggled.

'You had to do it. I mean they cost. *It's the truth.*'

'What did you do when it was wet?' my mum asked.

'It just came off your feet.'

I wasn't sure if he was joking.

'It's horrible really. We never had electric. I mean we had to watch television in candlelight!'

At that we all laughed.

John Glover, a congenial prison service cowman who worked closely with my dad and Pete Chisholm, was born and brought up on what he described as an 'idyllic' Devon farm where he lived the kind of life that might have featured in an H.E. Bates novel.

'There was no one for miles, we didn't have much. We didn't have a bathroom or nothing. I left, because it was *really* hard work *and* it was rented. There wasn't no future, not with having two kids and that. It was quite a wrench for me. I knew my dad wasn't going to live many more years, he wasn't healthy enough to keep going, but he was a stubborn person and he wouldn't give up the farm. 'Cos it was a small farm we couldn't afford mechanical aids. It was all a lot of physical work and I think that even thou' it was *hard*, it kept me fit. There's nothing like *proper* manual work to keep you fit.'

Every day while we lived at Sunnyside my dad cleaned out the cow stalls, swabbing them down as if he was still on board ship. Yet agricultural work was punishing even for those conditioned to it. One freezing winter, overcome with cold, Bev collapsed in the yard. Luckily, his ever-present Collie dog nudged him awake and he staggered back home.

Farm work makes such constant demands on the body and spirit that agriculture has rates of musculoskeletal injury that are over three times higher than other industries. It isn't uncommon for farmers to be struck by machinery or kicked by animals, to fall from heights, be crushed, poisoned, drowned, electrocuted or suffocated in grain stores. Bev's boss at Sunnyside was a well-respected farmer called Gregory Phillips who'd lost his right arm in an agricultural accident and my dad's broad, freckled back bore the scars of having been whipped by the broken belt of a flailing machine. When my dad fell awkwardly onto his shoulder when lifting a sack of corn that weighed 25% more than his body weight his collarbone was irreparably damaged.[7] Soon after he acquired a characteristic gait after falling on ice, smashing his right kneecap and driving forty miles to get home.

Without a kneecap to support his leg the muscles could give way without warning. But like many my dad never complained. The UK's Health and Safety Executive estimate that UK farmers fail to report approximately 10,000 serious accidents annually and although the industry represents less than 2% of the workforce it accounts for almost 20% of reported fatal injuries each year.[8]

During the sixteen weeks my dad spent in rehab, his sick pay was higher than any wage he was paid as a farmworker. Furthermore, it was while he was wearing a full-length leg plaster that he first made it into the press in a *Countryman* magazine article about a speeding pig.

The pig in question was a monstrous, barbed wire eating sow who had been enticed into the back of my grandad Joe's ex-post office van with a liberal offering of pig nuts. Dissatisfied with her cramped conditions and sniffing leftover nuts under the seats in front of her she surged forward, overpowered my dad in the passenger seat and landed on Joe's lap. As other hapless motorists sped by all they saw was her ferocious snout pressed against the windscreen. Miraculously they made it to the livestock market where they passed her off as a meaty, if somewhat tetchy beasty!

Such encounters may help to explain why so many of the fathers of contributors to this book became debilitated or died prematurely. 'Unfortunately,' said Lorraine, 'my dad had to retire through ill health.' Former prison service Farm Manager Bryan Wakely was only eighteen when he had to leave the family farm after his father suffered, 'about six or eight heart attacks and decided that enough was enough.' John Glover's father eventually retired with bad health aged sixty-five and died a year later and Maurice's father died prematurely of motor neurone disease linked to exposure to agrichemicals.

'My dad was agriculture through and through. He worked in the war as a waggoner who looked after the horses and did all the harvesting and ploughing and all that. Then he got interested in pigs so he was a pigman up until his death. He was always animal oriented: pigs, cows, horses. He lived on a farm all his life, died in 1962 when he was fifty-two, motor neurone disease. I was twenty-six. He died in the May and I joined the service in October. When he was diagnosed he was looking after a dairy herd at Sowton near Exeter airport and how it started was that he was carrying buckets of milk in each hand and walking across the yard to the churn and they dropped out of his hand. That was the first sign of it. Then that happened again about a week later and he went to the doctors and they did all the tests and they told him that he had nine months to live. Shocking.'

Despite plenty of anecdotal evidence, the scientific research community has been slow to establish a link between neurological disorders and exposure to organophosphates such as DDT, a class of chemicals derived from WWII nerve agents and widely used as a pesticide. By the late 1970s over 10 million hectares of British farmland had been sprayed with organophosphates. Although the use of DDT was banned in the UK in 1984, it had already been linked to the premature death of Bid, my aunt Gilda's husband.

Following a post-mortem on Maurice's father, his spine was taken away for research but Maurice never found out the results. So when Maurice told me that his sleep was being disturbed by extremely painful pins and needles in his left arm, symptoms that his two sisters were also experiencing, we were both worried. He became uncharacteristically subdued when he realised that his symptoms might be related to not only childhood exposure to organophosphates but also to a job he'd held between 1958–1960, two years prior to joining the prison service, with a company called May & Brown who ran an experimental testing station for organophosphates. Ruefully he recounted that there was little in the way of protective clothing and some of the chemicals he was exposed to were so toxic that they'd never been licensed for commercial use.

It made me realise that little is known about the consequences of exposure to agrichemicals brought into the home on overalls or boots, especially for young children with immature nervous systems. It is too early to know whether those of us who've grown up on farms will need to rethink our seemingly idyllic childhoods.

'We came to the conclusion that we were killing ourselves so we gave up farming,' said Howard Morse. Likewise, after my dad picked up his City & Guilds certificate he nearly gave up farming when he was offered a job as a panel beater by a previous employer, British Leyland. But like many of those I have spoken to my dad was not the indoor type. Preferring soil under the fingernails on his Atlas-like hands he responded to an ad in the *Farmers Weekly* for a farm manager position on the Isle of Wight.

Interviewed over the phone he was offered the job and in 1974 the four of us, Spot the dog and all our belongings were squashed into a Singer Gazelle and driven to the ferry terminal. Aged five I was on the move for the fourth time. On arrival on the island we looked out for the farm owner, a Mr McDowell, who we'd been told would be carrying a yellow *Farmer's Weekly* under his arm. It lent him a beguiling air of professionalism. A clever man who paid well, he was an early adopter of embryo fertilisation and 'a stickler for everything,' said my mum who was surprised when a neighbour appeared as soon as we'd arrived and asked how long we'd be stopping. Unbeknown to us Ian McDowell no longer advertised locally, he'd had fifty-three farm managers in eleven years!

I've a few memories from then: horror as a farmhand nonchalantly shot but thankfully only wounded Spot (and my dad's bellow as he instantly dismissed him); wonder at bats incorporating my bedroom into their dusky reconnaissance; fascination as a neighbour's model train circled endlessly at eye height, and the disconcerting attention of a predatory farmworker.

After two exceptionally dry seasons my dad realised that McDowell's cattle were starving. Troubled that McDowell showed no interest in buying them feed my dad armed himself with a sharp sickle and set off to cut maize by hand but my mum was concerned that he might harm himself instead. Her fears were well-founded. The rate of suicide amongst farmers is high. Prior to the tightening of gun laws following the 1996 Dunblane massacre, it was easy for a farmer to provide a 'good' reason for owning a firearm: for hunting, controlling vermin or killing injured livestock. Continually dealing with sickness and death, low income, unsociable working patterns and social isolation have all been associated with depression in farmworkers. Following the outbreak of foot and mouth disease in 2001 that led to the slaughter of over 10 million sheep and cattle, the incidence of suicide amongst farmers rose to more than one a week.[9]

One day, only eight months after we'd arrived on the Isle of Wight, McDowell found tools on the floor rather than where he thought they belonged and he dismissed my dad. As the house was tied to the job we had to vacate immediately but because we were taken in by the neighbours with the train-filled room I didn't think it was such a hardship.

My dad frequented the local labour exchange but they were pessimistic about a man with only a City & Guilds finding a job on the island. More widely, agricultural work was beginning to decline. By 2000 over a third of British farms would disappear and only 2% of the UK workforce would be employed in farming.[10] The situation looked bleak until an employee at the labour exchange suggested, 'why don't you do what I'm doing and become a prison officer?'

Consequently, in 1975 my dad escaped inadequate living and working conditions, long working hours, lack of job security, poor prospects, a high risk of injury and ill-health by going to prison. Whilst his father served two years, Bev would serve more than a typical life-sentence but unlike Billie, he'd spend much of his time outside the walls of the prison.

When he signed up my dad thought he'd be drawing upon his stint as 'Peggy' rather than his farming heritage because many English prisons were designed and run according to maritime practices: prison staff carried cutlasses instead of truncheons, wore navy-inspired uniforms and used nautical practices like 'slopping out', which although banned in 1996 persisted in a small number of prisons without in-cell sanitation until 2010. Some prisons still ran 'to the bell' with cells unlocked at seven o'clock, a single chime signifying breakfast at half-past seven and two bells at eight o'clock meaning 'prisoners are going to work'.

Expressing a preference for working with young offenders rather than adult prisoners my dad thought he'd be sent to Hollesley Bay Colony, a borstal on the Suffolk coast but we hopped islands instead, from the Isle of Wight to Dorset's wind-swept, quarried Isle of Portland threaded to the mainland by a treacherous tombola, Chesil beach. Although highly polished black shoes and a pristinely-pressed blue uniform with an HM PRISONS badge replaced mismatched wellies and mud-spattered overalls, out-of-sight prison keys jostled amongst betting slips, extra strong mints and the stub of an occasional, illicit cigar. Appointed as an officer instructor Bev expected to supervise a party or small group of 'borstal boys' in the workshops, kitchen, library or laundry. Totally unaware that the prison service employed 400 farm staff, my dad was very surprised when he was asked to accompany 50-60 'trainees' 'outside the wire' to work on the land.

Finding himself on familiar territory, unlike other officer instructors who might stand idly by and watch the inmates toil, Bev got stuck in. Six weeks later, Peter Stevens, the chief of Farms & Gardens since 1968, made a scheduled visit to Portland borstal and chatted with the party officers. Realising that Bev was atypical of uniformed prison officers, Peter arranged for Bev to transfer from the wings to the fields.

As Maurice noted, 'That was how it all started.'

2

New recruits

'We all have our time machines, don't we. Those that take us back are memories... And those that carry us forward, are dreams.'
HG Wells, *The Time Machine*

'I was determined,' said Maurice. 'My plan before my dad died was that I would get a job that gave me a pension because we weren't rich at all. We had no money. I was working as a pigman then I got a job near Exeter as what they called in those days 'a working farm manager' but you did *everything*. The cowman who was working for me said, "You want to get out of this, go to the health service or the prison service, they've both got farms." But he'd worked in the NHS as a cowman and left because he thought their farms were going to be broken up.'

So in 1962, aged twenty-six, Maurice secured an interview with the prison service.

'I remember the governor at Dartmoor said to me, "Where do you see yourself in twenty years' time?" and without thinking I said, "I'd like your job." It was probably the wrong thing to say!'

A year after joining the service Maurice was promoted firstly to farm foreman then farm manager at HMP Gaynes Hall, an open borstal near Grafham Water in Huntingdonshire. By the end of the following year the cowman was proved right, all the health service farms had disappeared. But farming in the prison service would continue for another fifty years.

When my mum and I visited former cowman and family friend Chris McGown in late 2013, his wife Sandra started to say that before Chris went to prison he was a county examiner for Kingston Maurward agricultural college.

'That sounds good, "before he went to prison",' laughed Chris who applied to become a prison officer ten years after Maurice joined the service.

'I went and sat the exam in Dorchester prison and I was called to Exeter for my interview,' explained Chris. 'I was called to see the governor who said, "I'm sorry to put you to so much trouble, you've scored one of the highest in the exams, 99%, but because of your eyesight Mr McGown, if you got into a fracas, well it's just not done." 'You couldn't get away with that nowadays,' he added. So like Maurice, Chris came in to the service on the agricultural side as a civilian.

Some have suggested that recruitment to the prison service in the 1960s to early 1970s was aimed towards attracting 'people who enjoyed a masculine environment' and whose own industry was in decline: miners, steel workers, fishermen and construction workers.[1] No mention was made of farmers. Civilian staff like Maurice and Chris were typically recruited to the prison service through adverts placed in the local or farming press. Sometimes the adverts simply stated: 'Stockman wanted for prison' and at other times it detailed the type of roles on offer. Pete Chisholm, who joined the service as an agricultural craftsman/tractor driver at Misterton Carr Farm, one of two farms attached to Her Majesty's Young Offender Institution (HMYOI) Hatfield in South Yorkshire, recalled seeing such an advert in the *Farmer's Weekly* in 1979.

'It was a double-sided spread with a long list of all the jobs on offer: gardening, farming, tractor driving etc. To my surprise I got an interview and I thought, "Oh my God!"'

'I never woke up and thought I'm going to join the prison service,' said Jason Errington looking back almost thirty years later but neither did most of the people I spoke to. Having passed the entrance exam for the RAF Jason applied thinking that it would be useful to have work and somewhere to live whilst waiting to join the air force as an aircraft mechanic.

'I left school, I trained to be a mechanic. I went to all the garages and I couldn't get any work, there were no apprenticeships. My dad was a horticulturalist working on the parks along with all his brothers and he said, "They're taking on apprenticeships, the Parks Board."'

'I don't remember ever getting an interview but I started there. I finished my apprenticeship and I did three years at Birmingham horticultural college and I was twenty, twenty-one? Foreman comes in to see me, I was running the nursery at the time, doing all the propagating and he knew I was with this girl and she was expecting and he said, "Jason, there's a job at Norwich prison advertised in the *Eastern Daily Press*, you ought to think about it. They're advertising with a free house.'"

'So I wrote out the application. Graham Norwood interviewed me and at no stage was it *ever* mentioned that it would be working with prisoners. I thought I'd got it to maintain the grounds. I got into the prison and next thing you know *I'm on the wings!*'

Jason was so sure that he'd be working outside that he turned up on the first day wearing jeans. The only way to distinguish him from the inmates was the badge with a crown on it that he was asked to wear. Once inside a familiar voice said, 'Hello Jason,' and turning around he found himself face-to-face with a former school mate, a man who some years later would be murdered.

Sentimentally, and in testament to the strength of attachment that he felt for the Farms & Gardens, 'Big Rob' Haslam who retired in 2015 still has the original job advertisement from when he joined prison service headquarters as an amenity horticulturalist in 1985.

'It's a keepsake.'

Likewise, gentle, well-mannered Howard Morse, retired from the service since 1993, has kept hold of the 1973 advertisement from the *Daily Telegraph* that led him to apply for a post as an assistant regional manager at prison service headquarters. Howard recalled how he was asked to come for an interview but a few weeks later received a 'communication', 'thanks for attending the interview but you've not been successful on this occasion'. With a wry smile he said,

'Well my father-in-law used to talk about "unnecessary letters" and I thought maybe this is an occasion for an "unnecessary letter" so I wrote back and said, "Thank you for interviewing me perhaps there'll be another opportunity." A month or so later another letter came through the post that said, "As a result of promotion there's another vacancy for an assistant regional manager, was I interested?" I said, "Yes please" because it virtually doubled my pay.'

'My time 1973–1993 we saw the best of it,' said Howard who, as a keen amateur photographer and an early-adopter of video technology, amassed an admirable collection of photographs and video footage of people, livestock, machinery and events associated with the prison farms. After sharing home-made quiche with Howard and his delightful wife Isobel at their bungalow in Devon, he very generously digitised and presented them to me along with permission to reproduce them.

Even former Head of Farms & Gardens Bernard Feist, who'd knowingly applied for a job in 1971 as a garden foreman at HMP Coldingley in Surrey, still has the original advert from *The Gardener's Chronicle*. Bernard applied to join because he'd fallen out with a supervisor in Brighton's parks and gardens department where he'd trained in glasshouse management. Recalling with a hearty laugh his interview,

'I remember they said, "What do you think of the wall flowers?" and I said, "I think they're awful, I've seen pencils bigger." But they wrote to me and said, "Would you like to go to Whatton in Nottingham tomorrow?" I thought, "Where's this place?" I'd never been out of Sussex! But I was single and I could just up and go so I went. I was twenty-one, the same age as the lads.'

Few of the new recruits knew the magnitude of agriculture and horticulture within the prison service.

'I had no idea that it had the structure, no idea at all. When I joined you saw these pink notices coming, "What's all this about then?" I wondered. I thought the farm was just one establishment, there was no great thing to tell you this was countrywide or that the opportunities were there,' said Bernard.

Devon-born Derek Webber who'd joined as a cowman in 1964 was awed by the extent of the farms,

'And then blimey, I saw all these papers coming down, 'Farm foreman wanted at so and so' and then I began to realise, bugger me, 'tis all over the country.'

Although integral to the running of the prison service, non-uniformed, non-operational, civilian staff (such as caterers, chaplains and estates personnel) were not generally as highly regarded as uniformed, operational staff whose responsibilities included security and safety. Non-operational activities jostled for recognition and supremacy within a service characterised by hierarchy and control.

Junior positions tended to attract relatively young and inexperienced applicants. John Glover joined the service in 1987 as an agricultural craftsman at Misterton Carr Farm attached to HMYOI Hatfield when the farm was managed by my dad.

'I'd never had a board interview before because I left school at fifteen and went self-employed and worked for my dad. The interview didn't go on very long before I thought they were asking me all about farming and [shaking his head] I thought, "These don't know nothing about this I could tell 'em anything and they're going to believe me." But because I 'ad the knowledge, even though I'd never done an interview, I found it quite easy really.'

'It was necessary,' stated the proceedings from the annual Farm Management Conference in 1969, 'for the farmworker to be recognised as a skilled man,' sentiments that were incorporated into DIS (Department of Industries and Supply) policy a couple of years later.[2] 'It will be accepted that the basis for success will depend upon the quality of the staff. The activities described in this booklet require some 300 staff of various grades, well over 200 of whom are non-uniformed grades. Their tasks demand a high degree of managerial efficiency and technical expertise, in addition to integrity and patience in the instruction of inmates under their charge. They must therefore be very carefully selected not only for their technical skills, but also for their sense of purpose in the training of the inmate. For those who succeed, the work offers a rewarding career.'[3]

Stockmen, according to a representative of the Agricultural Training Board who made a presentation to farm managers at the annual conference in 1978, 'must have skills, practical and perceptual. The stockman must have ability either acquired through training or innate... A stockman must pass on his experience and skill or else when he leaves his skill goes with him.'[4]

When Lorraine Coveney joined the service at Misterton Carr Farm in 1982, she became the Farms & Garden's first 'stockwoman'.

'It was purely by accident. I saw a job that said 'Wanted: General Farmworker with ability to supervise others' and I went for it. It didn't say anything about being a prison! So I didn't apply for the job knowing it was a prison at all. And it didn't say pigs. If I'd known I'd never've applied. The job was to be in charge of 1,800 pigs! At the interview I did say that I'd not worked with pigs and they did ask me questions about pigs. And then they said, "Well, what *do* you know about?" so I said, "Well, dairy and everything else." And then they asked me lots of questions about that.'

Lorraine laughed.

'I came home and said, "Well I won't 've got that job. It's about running pigs and it's in a prison." But I did.'

My dad was very fond of Lorraine and had great admiration for her knowledge and way with both animals and inmates, so he was sad to see her leave HMYOI Hatfield to join her husband Chris when he was promoted to farm manager at HMP Usk in South Wales.

'When I got there,' said Lorraine, 'I was 'general maintenance' party and I had some really rough lads. I *really* had some rough lads. And I thought, "Well, it's another prison this is what it's like." After four months this chap said, "We knew there was this woman coming and we thought we'll stitch her up." So they'd hand picked these lads. "We'll see how she copes!"'

Lorraine coped admirably but she had little time to prove her full worth. Maurice had plans, within a year Chris was promoted to farm manager at all female HMP East Sutton Park, at the other end of the country in Kent. To enable them to live and work together, Lorraine was given four months unpaid leave, then a temporary placement working alongside Ivor Gough at HMP Standford Hill, before moving to East Sutton Park to look after the pigs.

Ivor was a, 'proper farmer,' said Jason who'd worked alongside Ivor for five years, 'a farmer through and through.' 'Lovely' despite a foul temper, Ivor was dedicated to his work, starting each day promptly at 0530.

'Ivor absolutely *loved* the pigs. He always made a point first thing in the morning, go down the dairy and walk around the pigs. *Every day.* Never wore wellies. *Never.* Just little slip on shoes which he used to wear with white socks. They never stayed white, he'd have a tidemark up to his ankle where he'd been under the water. He'd go round and look at the pigs but he'd never have a piece of paper so he'd write on his hand 'R26 due to go the boar'. When we started doing artificial insemination Ivor would 'help the boar in' you know and then he'd say, "Do you want a polo mint Jason?" *No thanks* Ivor!'

Another distinctive member of the Farms & Gardens staff was Brian Budding, who worked at HMP Channings Wood near Newton Abbott.

'He had a very ooh aah 'proper job' Devon accent,' recalled Maurice.

Bryan Wakely remembered Brian Budding being on his interview panel in 1980.

'There in the corner was this guy: brown smock, dirty hobnailed boots on, binder twine tying up his brown smock.'

Although Bryan applied to be a herdsman and was interviewed for the position of pigman, he was asked all sorts of questions about mowing grass and bedding plants.

'I stopped the interview and said, "Sorry I've come for the herdsman job." "Oh," they said, "we filled that internally but we're not turning any candidates down, we'll interview everybody and see what they're like."

At the end of the interview Brian Budding stood up.

"That boy'll do f'r mee, thank you very much."

And then he walked out.

'That was my foreman, everyone knew him as Farmer.'

Unfortunately, the farmer stereotype was pervasive. Lorraine recalled a member of the secretarial staff twenty years later saying to her,

'"Well those farm staff, what do they know? What qualifications have they got?" thinking we must be quite dim. My qualifications were much higher than hers. But that is the perception, you sit on a tractor, chew a bit of straw, you are thick. I don't think people think that you've been to college or that you've travelled. It's not a good perception.' Wearing a lightly checked flat cap, loosely fitted corduroy trousers, taciturn and rarely without a dog, my dad appeared to fit the farmer stereotype. 'Even his Jack Russell Terrier Soi, who went everywhere with him, wore a cap,' quipped Pete Chisholm.

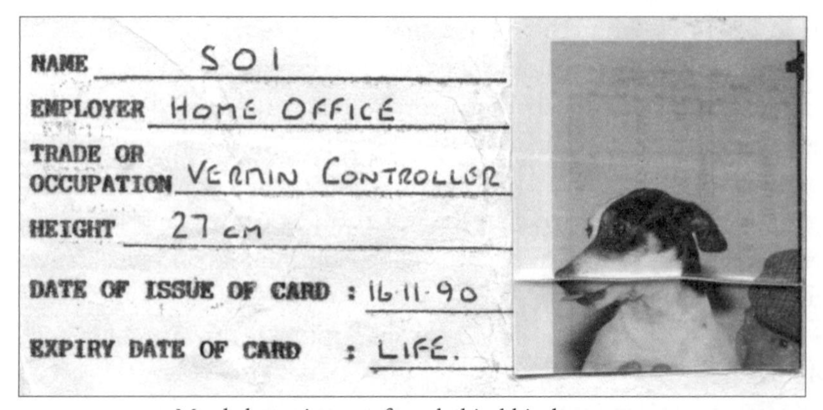
NAME SOI
EMPLOYER HOME OFFICE
TRADE OR OCCUPATION VERMIN CONTROLLER
HEIGHT 27 cm
DATE OF ISSUE OF CARD : 16.11.90
EXPIRY DATE OF CARD : LIFE.

My dad peeping out from behind his dog, on an unofficial Home Office identity pass.[5]

But to those that knew my dad, he was big-hearted, jolly and optimistic and bore an uncanny resemblance to the puddle-jumping character found on a Skegness postcard.

'He was a good laugh Bev was,' said Chris McGown. 'But if he ever got hold of you with his bloody great hands!'

'He dangled Chris over the cliff wall,' recalled Sandra.

'Just a joke that was,' Chris assured her. 'Yeah, we hit it off.'

And it wasn't only because they shared a ribald sense of humour, they both understood how difficult it was to cultivate Portland's marginal soil.

'The trick,' said Chris, 'was to tickle the clay and score it not plough it.'

Without uniforms, farm staff were less distinguishable from inmates and this enabled them to create a better working relationship with anti-authority prisoners.

'I've noticed right throughout that even in the prison if you don't wear a uniform then it makes a big difference,' confirmed John Glover. 'They come across a lot different to you. As soon as you put the uniform on they are a bit anti you. Even now you have to watch it as they will take advantage of you but generally because we are civilian staff they do tend to be a bit better towards you.'

Although there used to be an element of 'us and them' particularly between prison officers and farm staff, in terms of actual power and influence, as head of Farms & Gardens, Peter Stevens, Maurice Codd and Bernard Feist controlled the largest portion of the prison service budget. 'At its height, without being too unkind about myself and my colleagues or ex-colleagues,' said Rob Haslam, 'we were a bunch of folk with straw in our ears who managed to run, organise, manage and deliver a very, very good victualling service, which I think is absolutely fabulous.'

Tall and amiable, Maurice was particularly well able to hold his own with staff, prisoners, governors and politicians alike. Resourceful bordering on wily, his ability to problem-solve was evident when the head office area manager visited Maurice at HMP Usk in the late 1960s. The majority of the 390 acres of marginal land farmed at HMP Usk was situated close to the prison at Cilwrgi farm but the remainder was situated four miles to the west at a hill farm called Prescoed Camp.

Knowing that the area manager would insist on counting the farm's heifers and knowing that he was meant to have fifty heifers but he actually only had thirty Maurice arranged for the area manager to count the cows in the fields closest to the prison and whilst he was inside eating lunch instructed the inmates to move twenty of the heifers to the furthest fields so that his target number could be met.

Colleagues like Bryan Wakely described Maurice as,

'Something of a visionary who could see the bigger picture. He always had a plan even if some of it was tied in to him having to get back to go and do his football training!'

As early as 1971 Maurice was earmarked to replace Peter Stevens as chief of Farms & Gardens. Four years later a spoof football programme distributed at the Farm Management Conference shows

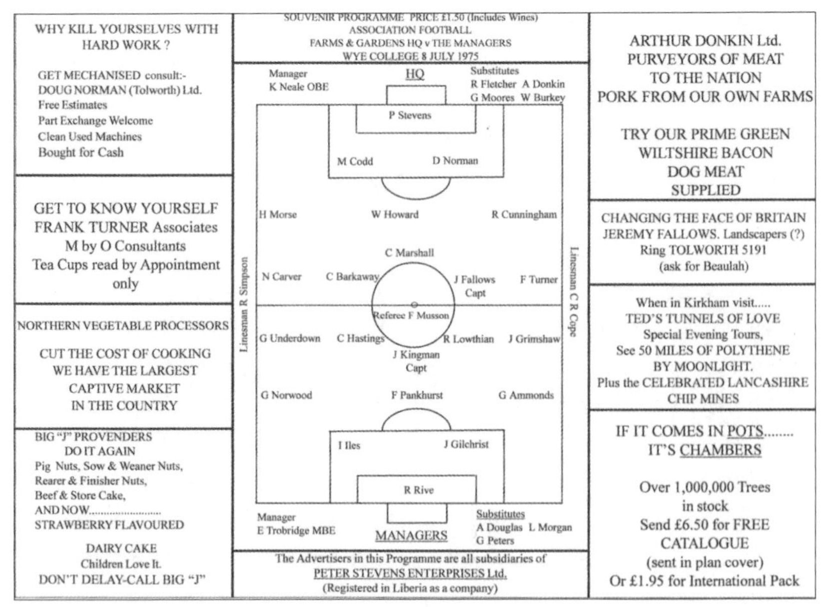

Farms & Gardens HQ vs. Managers souvenir programme distributed to attendees at the 1975 Farm management conference.[6]

Maurice moving into position as a defender representing 'Farms & Gardens HQ' in a match against 'The Managers'.

Hard-working, loyal and humble, Maurice expected those around him to be the same.

'You always used to say that you wouldn't ask anyone to do anything that you wouldn't do yourself,' said his wife Mo.

'That's true.'

'If you cut Maurice in half,' said Chris Coveney, 'he'd have Farms & Gardens written across his core.'

According to Bernard, when Maurice became chief, he 'took Farms & Gardens in a different direction and a sensible direction.'

When I met former Director General Phil Wheatley over a cup of tea in the foyer of the Barbican he agreed, 'Maurice didn't do anything that wasn't sensible.'

Phil was only twenty-one when he joined the prison service as an officer at HMYOI Hatfield in 1969,

'It was fairly challenging trying to get the balance of being in charge right when they weren't used to having bosses and I was as young as them.'

Phil claimed that his 'best job' wasn't in the prison service at all, but in the town gardens in central Leeds where he'd worked during school and university vacations in the mid–late 1960s, although he stressed that it was never going to be his career because it was poorly paid.

'Garden labour. I really enjoyed it. I worked with gardeners who were absolutely fascinated by what they did. It didn't pay very much though.'

He thought it was inequitable that dustbin men, like my grandad Joe, were paid supplementary 'dirty' money unlike those who toiled in the soil. As he rose through the ranks becoming a governor at HMP Hull, then regional manager, director of dispersals and deputy director general from 1998 until heading the prison service from 2003 until 2010, Phil maintained his interest in horticulture,

'I knew the people involved in gardening and rather liked what they were doing. It suited me. It was probably one of the reasons why I got on with Bernard.'

Horticulture was also popular amongst inmates but there were some governors who reported that 'during the summer inmates had relatives who were gardeners too, but once winter had come developed bad colds and chests!'[7]

Expected to be practical and resourceful civilian farm staff were typically inducted in a single day, 'shown the ropes' and left to get on with the job. On Maurice's first day at high security HMP Dartmoor he was told to turn up at the farm at half past seven.

'I turned up and went into the piggery and this bloke was feeding the pigs and I was asking him all about the job. He asked me where I was from and I said, "Exeter." He *assumed* that I'd come from Exeter prison! The farm manager turned up and said, "You *idiot*, that was one of the high security prisoners."'

Maurice found himself face-to-face with a large number of prisoners without knowing what was expected of him,

'It was amazing. I never had any real training at all. We were harvesting potatoes and had about 100 prisoners in a line. The farm manager said to me, "Go over there and look after them." I thought to myself, "Blimey, what do I do?"'

Bryan Wakely was similarly ill-prepared. Laughing, he said of his first day,

'I remember it as if it was yesterday. Tommy Watson said, "I'll show you round and then take you to Nottingham to show you where we buy the spare parts and where we buy the petrol." That was it. Lunchtime he said, "I won't be here." I had 45 prisoners, 1 officer and me!' Still laughing he added, 'I remember the night. I walked out the gate at 6 o'clock and the gatekeeper said to me, "Have you got any spanners?" and I said, "Well there's quite a set round there on the farm, what size do you want?" and he meant the prison keys (of course)!'

After two days in Exeter prison, Derek Webber was allowed out on the farm.

'There was an officer that I had to shadow, we went to see all the units in the prison, we went to the hospital for quarter of a day, because when you were out on the farm a lot of the time you were relying on one of those units, if a bloke was sick whatever. Just had two days in the prison and then went out with Bill Symonds, farm manager at Witheridge, the farm attached to Exeter prison. I was thrown in the deep end and given six prisoners to look after.'

Chris McGown reported to the farm at 6 o'clock on his first day.

'I met the relief cowman and jumped on the back of a little trailer. *Off we went* holding the churns that had hot and cold water in them for doin' the milking. And the Borstal boys had to hold them on. Didn't have seats. Just stood there. We used to rattle out there and of course the milking machine was petrol so we'd crank it up by hand with the starting handle. And then we'd hang the churns in the middle bit and the milk used to go into the churns. But that was my first day. The relief cowman said, "There you are, that's all you do." That was it. Training over.'

Without formal officer training or time spent on the landings, civilian farm staff had to acquire implicit prison knowledge such as prison jargon from those around them. Much of the time they picked up what they needed to know from inmates.

'You've got to speak in a language prisoners know: abrupt and scream and shout more!'

All quite different from modern 'best' management practice that includes: close supervision, regular debriefings and reward by career planning.[8]

When I asked Bernard whether he'd had any training he just laughed.

'I had half a day with Walter Selby who said, "This is a *farm 1 form* don't ever fill one of them in. This is a *farm 27 form*, use this if you want to get some money." He threw all the paperwork in the bin and said, "I think I've covered everything"'

Ever resourceful, the new Farms & Gardens recruits had to rely on their wit and wits. None of the staff that I talked to recalled feeling especially threatened by inmates but between cups of tea and cake at his home near HMP Kirkham in Lancashire, dry humoured Steve Horrocks recalled his first couple of days as a dairyman at HMYOI Gaynes Hall in 1980.

'On the first day you're walking round with a prison officer and you're shown round everything and everybody and then on the second day they just leave you. Six o'clock in the morning I'm left on my own with these six to eight prisoners, hard men from London and I'm thinking, Glasgow boy, you'll be alright here just don't worry you'll be fine. Quarter past six I'm thinking, *I want my mummy! I'm going home!*'

The character and knowledge of those recruited to Farms & Gardens shaped how it operated and in return Farms & Gardens shaped them, their 'farmilies' and their experience of home.

Steve and others, including my dad, remained in the prison service until they retired, albeit that Steve retired at a relatively early age.

Shortly after my dad retired in 2003, he met up with Maurice and Mo, or 'M&M' as they are affectionately known. While they reminisced about the people, places and events that had defined Farms & Gardens, Mo took notes that barely filled a single sheet of A4 paper. They thought these notes might one day form the basis for a book about farming in the prison service. But neither Bev nor Maurice could expand upon Mo's notes. Although my dad's expansive hands were adept at signing odds and singling out winners, Mr Wright was no writer and Maurice was too busy volunteering. A decade later, I encountered 'M&M' for the first time when they paid an unscheduled visit to see my ailing dad.

Over a cup of tea Maurice and Bev recruited me to their stalled project.

'When shall we start?' I asked.

'Later, later,' my ever-optimistic father said.

3

Hooves and shoots

'Bulb-stealing has never had the same atmosphere or produced the same literature as cattle-raiding. Man the gardener is kept very busy and behaves himself. At the only cost – a high cost but a fair one – that he makes less history.' Butts, *The Bookman*[1]

It was almost too late. By early 2013 when I first encountered Maurice Codd, the former Head of Farms & Gardens, 95% of the farmland that was once attached to prisons in England and Wales had disappeared. As a consequence, my dad's colleagues and their stories were becoming as rare as the heritage livestock they once championed.

'How often do you get the chance to talk like this?' I asked Chris McGown.

'I don't think I ever have.'

'A lot of people don't even know the prison farms exist,' said the current Head of Land Based Activities, Jason Errington when we met for a chat in a pub near HMP Dartmoor. I nodded. Although I'd grown up on a prison farm, I knew little about the background to farming in the prison service.

Farming has been at the heart of the penal system in England and Wales for more than 160 years. The first and, at nearly 650 hectares (1,600 acres), one of the largest prison farms was established at Dartmoor prison in 1852. Now the farmyard and dairy accommodate a prison museum curated by the farm's former shepherd, Brian Dingle.

Originally built to hold Napoleonic prisoners of war, as an early photograph (overleaf) from the National Justice Museum shows, Dartmoor's austere granite exterior was hacked from a nearby quarry by convicts watched over by armed officers.

Following the Prison Acts of 1865 and 1877 which established the Prison Commission and a national Prison Service, the Prison

Act of 1898 asserted that the main role of imprisonment was to reform miscreants rather than punish or simply contain them. One popular and enduring way to achieve this was to classify prisoners' skills, aptitudes and experience as: '...the good hands, the capable hands, the promising hands, and the drones.'[3] Consequently, purposeful work such as farming which was 'both constructive and fairly heavy'[4] became a key feature of imprisonment. Farms were an integral feature of borstals, the first of which was built in 1905 at Rochester in Kent, specifically designed to hold juvenile offenders.

Without the unscalable perimeter walls or barred windows characteristic of high security prisons like Dartmoor, borstals encouraged greater permeability between incarceration and outside society. In the early years, the borstal regime mimicked that of boarding schools; birching was permissible, dormitories were overseen by housemasters, inmates rose early and undertook domestic chores. A two-mile run before breakfast was not unusual and meals were basic but filling.

By the onset of the Second World War, Dartmoor and Rochester were two of six prison farms, with others situated mainly in the south-east of England: Eastchurch on the Isle of Sheppey, now known as Standford Hill, Feltham in West London, Hollesley Bay Colony on the Suffolk coast and North Sea Camp near Boston on the Lincolnshire coast. Between 1938 and 1947 the number of prisoners employed daily in agriculture doubled to 1,000 partly due to the WWII *Dig for Victory* campaign that addressed food rationing by replanting ornamental gardens, including those in prisons, with edible produce. Post-WWII expansion was accompanied by an associated increase in expenditure and total annual budget. 'By 1947 the farming industry within the Service had expanded to 13 holdings [the land a farmer manages and uses for agricultural purposes] totalling 5,000 acres, realising an annual return from the sales and transfers of £80,000.'[6] By 1959 the amount of land farmed by prisoners in England and Wales reached 4,040 hectares (10,000 acres) spread across 28 holdings and by 1971 there were 35 prison farms, two of which were in Wales and the rest spread throughout England.

Armed officers guarding convicts from Dartmoor prison as they quarry stone at 'The Herne Hole', circa 1886.[2]

'Borstal boys' building hayricks on the farm attached to the first borstal at Rochester in Kent.[5]

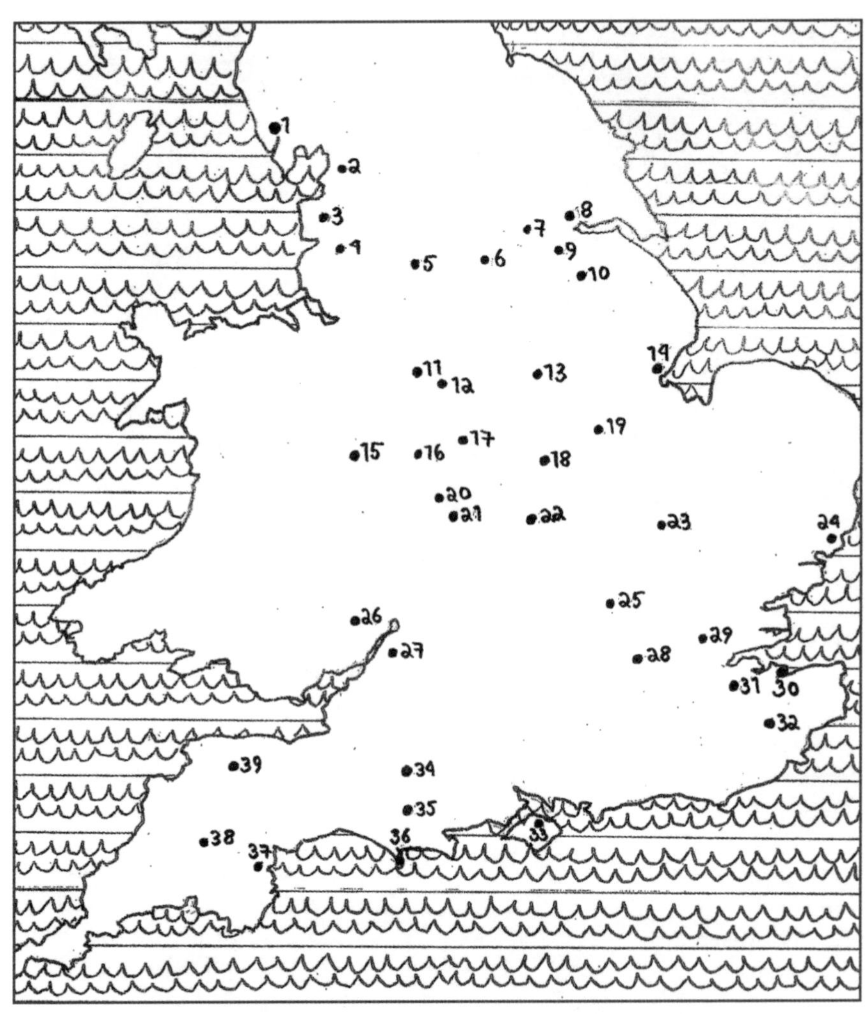

Map showing prisons that had a large farm attached pre-modernisation.[7]

Legend: Prison (previous name), County (livestock, crops, activities)
CAPITAL = farm operating prior to WWII
Bold = farm with vegetable preparation and distribution facility
Italic = major farm operating in 1982

1 – Haverigg, Cumbria (pigs, vegetables)
2 – Lancaster, Lancashire (dairy, beef, pigs, cereals, potatoes, vegetables, forestry)
3 – ***Kirkham***, Lancashire (poly tunnels, glasshouses, veg prep, machinery repairs)
4 – *Wymott*, Lancashire (beef, potatoes, vegetables, polytunnels, glasshouses)
5 – *Buckley Hall*, Lancashire (dairy, polytunnels)
6 – *New Hall*, West Yorkshire (dairy, pigs, vegetables, polytunnels, glasshouses, forestry)
7 – Pollington, Yorkshire (beef, pigs, arable)

8 – *Everthorpe*, South Yorkshire (dairy, pigs, potatoes, vegetables, forestry, machinery repairs)
9 – *Hatfield*, South Yorkshire (dairy, beef, pigs, cereals, potatoes, vegetables, polytunnels, glasshouses, veg prep, provender milling, forestry)
10 – **Lindholme**, South Yorkshire (arable, veg prep)
11 – *Werrington*, Staffordshire (dairy, vegetables, polytunnels, glasshouses)
12 – *Moor Court*, Staffordshire (dairy, pigs, polytunnels, glasshouses, forestry)
13 – *Lowdham Grange*, Nottinghamshire (dairy, pigs, cereals, potatoes, vegetables, polytunnels, glasshouses, forestry)
14 – *NORTH SEA CAMP*, Lincolnshire (beef, sheep, pigs, cereals, potatoes, vegetables, polytunnels)
15 – Shrewsbury, Shropshire (dairy, beef) (sold 1980s)
16 – *Featherstone*, Staffordshire (pigs, cereals, potatoes, vegetables, forestry, machinery repairs)
17 – *Swinfen Hall*, Staffordshire (beef, potatoes, vegetables, polytunnels, glasshouses, forestry)
18 – Gartree, Leicestershire (beef)
19 – *Ashwell* (Stocken), Rutland (dairy, pigs, cereals, potatoes, vegetables, glasshouses, provender milling, forestry, machinery repairs)
20 – Frankley, Worcestershire (beef, animal feed mill)
21 – *Hewell Grange*, Worcestershire (dairy, pigs, potatoes, vegetables, glasshouses, forestry)
22 – Onley, Warwickshire (beef)
23 – Littlehay (*Gaynes Hall*), Cambridgeshire (dairying, pigs, vegetables, polytunnels, glasshouses, forestry)
24 – ***HOLLESLEY BAY COLONY***, Suffolk (dairying, sheep, pigs, horses, potatoes, vegetables, polytunnels, glasshouses, veg prep, provender milling, grass drying, forestry, machinery repairs)
25 – Aylesbury, Buckinghamshire (dairy, poultry) (milked by hand in 1960s)
26 – *Usk*, Monmouthshire, Wales (dairying, pigs, potatoes, vegetables, polytunnels, glasshouses, forestry)
27 – ***Leyhill*** (Falfield), Gloucestershire (pigs, vegetables, polytunnels, glasshouses, veg prep, forestry, machinery repairs)
28 – FELTHAM, London (small dairy herd, pigs, market gardening)
29 – Theydon Bois (Pentonville), London (beef, arable)
30 – ***Standford Hill*** (EASTCHURCH), Kent (dairy, pigs, potatoes, vegetables, polytunnels, glasshouses, veg prep, provender milling, machinery repairs)
31 – *ROCHESTER*, Kent (dairy, pigs, vegetables, glasshouses, forestry)
32 – *East Sutton Park*, Kent (dairy, pigs, vegetables, polytunnels, glasshouses, forestry)
33 – Albany (*Camp Hill*), Isle of Wight (dairy, pigs, vegetables, polytunnels, glasshouses, forestry, machinery repairs)
34 – *Guys Marsh*, Dorset (small dairy herd, market gardening)
35 – *Tadnoll Mill Farm* attached to The Verne, Dorset (dairy, pigs, potatoes, vegetables, glasshouses, forestry, machinery repairs)
36 – *Portland*, Dorset (dairy, pigs, potatoes, vegetables, polytunnels, glasshouses)
37 – Channings Wood, Devon (woodland – produced bean sticks, small market garden, large sports field used by outside teams)
38 – *DARTMOOR*, Devon (dairy, beef, sheep, pigs, vegetables, polytunnels, glasshouses, provender milling, grass drying, forestry, machinery repairs)
39 – *Irishcombe Farm* attached to Exeter prison, Devon (dairy, forestry, machinery repairs)

Working with the local soil and climatic conditions, the service was able to grow, harvest, pack and prepare a wide range of produce.

'Sudbury in Derbyshire pasteurised milk. Haverigg in North West England grew carrots. Lovely soil,' noted Steve.

'Hollesley Bay grew onions, North Sea Camp grew potatoes and Kirkham grew cabbages. We were the *cabbage people*,' he claimed, 'Misterton, where your dad was, grew beetroot amongst other crops.'

Misterton's foreman John Glover was equally proud.

'We grew some lovely stuff down here. Carrots. I've never known the like. You can't buy 'em as nice as 'em. No, they were brilliant. We used to grow more than we needed. And potatoes. We used to grow *beautiful* potatoes down there. And cabbages. *Massive* great cabbages,' he said holding his hands out wide to demonstrate their size.

Often prisons like North Sea Camp that had a large farm were built on cheap reclaimed or marginal land that was turned into productive farmland using inmate labour. North Sea Camp was established on 31st May 1935 when Major WW Llewellin, five members of staff and twenty 'lads', arrived on the Lincolnshire coast having marched 110 miles in eight days eastwards from Stafford prison. Although it's hard to imagine now, the prisoners and staff overnighted in village halls other than a mid-way stop at HMP Lowdham Grange in Nottinghamshire. On arrival the 'lads' worked hard to reclaim land from the North sea.

Inmates building sea defences and drainage ditches to create farmland at North Sea Camp, Lincolnshire.[8]

Eastchurch Prison on the Isle of Sheppey was built on a pre-WWI airfield.

'When you went into the fitting shop they had the bits where they used to put the aircraft together,' explained Jason. The 263 hectares (650 acres) cultivated around what became HMP Standford Hill was such poor quality that whilst Grade 3 was considered the lowest for farming purposes, it was rated Grade 3 minus. Until the late 1960s, the heavy clay soil which was littered with roughly filled bomb craters was ploughed by Suffolk Punch horses.

Inmates loading manure by hand onto a cart drawn by a Suffolk Punch horse at Eastchurch (Standford Hill) Prison on the Isle of Sheppey, Kent.[9]

Originally requisitioned in 1939 by the Ministry of Agriculture, Fisheries and Food (MAFF), Misterton Carr Farm in South Yorkshire was acquired by the prison service in 1951. A holding of approximately 200 hectares (500 acres), the name of the farm reflected the prevalence of derelict areas of bog known locally as 'Carrs'. The soil which was well below the level of the water table and the River Idle had to be continually drained and so much bog wood was unearthed that it could take 10 to 12 days to plough a 4-hectare (10-acre) field. Sodden and remote, my mum refused to live there when my dad became the farm manager in 1987.

Despite the challenging conditions, the predominantly light sand and peat soil at Misterton was well suited to growing potatoes alongside barley, sugar beet, carrots and kale. But every year, inmates who were typically 'average 18 years of age of fairly tough robust physique, with a normal background of labouring and therefore suited to the arduous nature of the work undertaken on the farm,'[10] toiled for weeks clearing twitch grass by hand as the bog-oak filled fields were too wet to plough. In the 1960s, when Misterton was attached to the borstal at Gringley-on-the-Hill rather than HMYOI Hatfield, inmates cycled the 8 kilometers (5 miles) to and from the farm unsupervised, a not uncommon sight throughout the service at the time.

'Borstal boys' cycling to work on the farm at Hollesley Bay, Suffolk.[11]

Unlike Misterton, the soil at Hollesley Bay Colony, known locally as 'The Colony', was well-drained and sandy. This enabled it to become one of the most productive and profitable prison farms. It was 'widely regarded as one of the most important in the Service, both in size – 1,400 acres – and in output, with a gross margin of some £35,000 per annum [in 1968].'[12] Like other large prison farms, it was run along the lines of a country estate with farm managers overseeing farm bailiffs, estate workers and prisoners who fulfilled the role of temporary or seasonal workers.

Consequently, throughout the 1970s and 80s prison farm managers were, '*Immensely* powerful, immensely powerful,' reiterated 'Big Rob' Haslam. 'Alan Douglas, who was at Hollesley Bay got paid as much as the governor. In board meetings the farm manager would *always* be present and have a view on anything and everything. So they were *immensely* powerful at some places. Because Hollesley Bay was nothing if there wasn't a farm. The whole thing was *the farm* and very, very important it was too.'

Founded in 1887 as a Colonial College offering a two-year course to fee paying students to develop 'an inbuilt stiff upper lip' and 'a thoroughly sound and practical training before their departure to the colonies', Hollesley Bay Colony was taken over in 1905 by the 'grim yet enlightened' London Central Unemployed Body who recruited batches of two to three hundred unemployed men from London to spend a month at a time at the college. If they proved themselves 'industrious and adapted to the work', they were provided with permanent employment either within the estate or nearby villages and expected to bring their families to join them.[13] The college was acquired by the Prison Commission in 1938.

The Colony land was divided into two sections: a 485 hectare (1,200 acre) farm and a 93 hectare (230 acre) garden. The highlight of the farm section was a Pedigree Suffolk horse stud but there were also Pedigree Suffolk ewes and prize-winning rams which roamed alongside a mixed herd of mainly Shorthorn cows and a flock of 200 'semi range' hens. Like North Sea camp, Hollesley Bay kept Pedigree Essex sows and gilts (young female pigs), 'entirely out of doors and folded on heathland for reclamation.'[14]

The Colony garden section cultivated brassicas (spring and winter cabbage, kohl rabi and kale) carrots, onions and swedes for use in the prison kitchen and enough oats, barley and sugar beet to feed all their livestock. More than 100 acres (47 hectares) were dedicated to the production of fruit. The soil conditions were perfect for growing plums, blackcurrants and gooseberries, specially certified varieties of strawberries and pears grafted onto quince stock.

A wide variety of cooking, eating and dessert apples were grown and staff conducted trials of different rootstock for Malling Research Station based in Maidstone, Kent. Old orchards were continually restocked with fruit trees and shrubs, roses and standard trees were propagated in a two-acre nursery. From greenhouses covering three-quarters of an acre came annual flower plants, cucumbers, tomatoes and cut flowers. Late chrysanthemums were grown in pots in the walled garden for retail sale and willows planted in Carr Marsh in February 1957 were coppiced for use in the basket industry.[15]

In 1956 sixteen institutions sent delegates to the first 'Farm Walk' held at HMP Lowdham Grange. The programme, even then, reflected a desire for farming within the prison service to operate in accordance with the demands of the wider agricultural industry as well as fit with specific prison objectives such as occupying prisoners and providing food to supply the prison kitchens. Presentations at the Farm Walk included: 'Records: Are they necessary for efficient management?', 'Prisoner labour: Problems of organisation and management' and 'Vegetable production: Planning and cropping to meet dietary requirements throughout the year'.[16]

The Farm Walk three years later was attended by staff from eighteen institutions including Dartmoor's short but notorious 'Chilly' Charles Frampton who delighted in making work needlessly hard for prisoners.

'In '62 '63 at Dartmoor we used to get prisoners in a line with a spade each and we'd put a string across the garden and they'd all get in a line and dig. And when they had all dug their little bit you'd move the string and they'd dig again. It was soul destroying! I remember seeing that and thinking, "Oh My God!"' The memory stuck in Maurice's mind. 'Nothing worse. When you've got a tractor and plough that could just do that but the farm manager, who was Frampton at the time, would say, "Don't worry boys, we've got to give them *work*."'

'Chilly' was the prison service's last 'official birch', authorised to administer corporal punishment and until his retirement in 1978 the last person allowed to carry a loaded rifle within the Firearm Activity Service. With few roads across Dartmoor, the most efficient way to pursue escapees was on horseback so Chilly would ride out with the Dartmoor Pony Patrol armed with a gun and permission to fire at the prisoner's legs.

The last armed officer, 'Chilly' Charles Frampton, riding out with the Dartmoor Pony Patrol.[17]

As Maurice knew, 'Chilly could be cruel. He was someone you wanted on your side. Chilly by name and chilly by nature. He put the fear of God in inmates. He was a bit like the character Mackay in the 1970s TV series *Porridge* only not as jovial. I was with him one day and he says to me, "Come on let's go and look at the dairy." This was about half seven one morning and I thought, "What's up?" We went into the dairy and under this cooler, where they were cooling the milk where the churns come out, there's this prisoner drinking cream out of the churn. So Chilly said to me, "Watch" and he went up behind him and grabbed him by his legs and held him there and counted to ten. Absolutely drowned! Well he wasn't going to steal any more milk!'

By 1966 there were twelve borstals accommodating approximately 2,000 'lads'. Most of them were 'in the country and have land enough for farming and the like to be learnt.'[18] Gaynes Hall (rebuilt as Littlehey) was typical, with gardens supplying food for its own kitchens, excess salad crops sold locally, a pig-breeding unit and a herd of beef cattle.

The opening address at the Farm Walk in 1967 was jointly delivered by the governor of nearby Gringley-on-the-Hill, the director of industries and stores and the governor of Hatfield Borstal, Mr LWF Steinhausen.

According to Maurice, Steinhausen was one of three 'eccentric' ex-servicemen prison governors. The other two were Manchester's 'Scarface Brown', a very thin, wiry man who was probably disfigured whilst serving as a bomber pilot in WWII and 'Fisher Finch' from Eastchurch whose stutter led inmates to mercilessly tease him by addressing him as 'F- F- F- Fisher Finch.' Steinhausen, a former German prisoner-of-war, generally disliked by prisoners, nevertheless showed great appreciation for the farms.

'I guess because he'd been cooped up at other times of his life he just wanted to get out,' observed Maurice.

As the number of prison farms and prisoners employed increased, the Prison Commission decided that there should be more coordination between them so they asked three farm managers and an officer instructor, A. MacArthur from Feltham, to apply for a supervisor of Farms & Gardens position. Chilly wasn't at all interested in an administrative post and E.J. 'Tro' Trobridge from North Sea Camp, although well-known having been appointed the first secretary of the farm section of the Institution of Professional Civil Servants (IPCS) union, was passed over in favour of A.A. Wylie from Hollesley Bay Colony, who used to write in green ink. According to Maurice, Wylie became 'the original boss'.

'Everyone was afraid of him,' said Maurice, 'because as it was a new enterprise he ruled it with a firm hand.'

When 'Tro' retired as union secretary in 1966, Maurice took over his position. Initially, the Head of Farms & Gardens Peter Stevens fulfilled the role of chair before passing it to Maurice who held it until 1982. When he became senior Farms & Gardens manager, he gave up the role of chair as he felt there was a conflict of interest between chairing the union and being in charge of staff pay. The committee also had a vice-chair but there was no need for a treasurer as all the money for the farms was allocated centrally from the Treasury.

Over time, amongst others, my dad, Bernard Feist, Derek Webber and Pete Chisholm served alongside Maurice in the IPCS/IPMS (Institute of Professionals, Managers and Specialists) union. Quite uniquely they had what was called, 'The BEC, the Branch Executive Committee, but most people thought it stood for "Bev, Eddie [Chambers], Chris [Hastings],"' laughed Bryan Wakely. Collectively they petitioned the Prison Commission and thereafter the Prison Department within the Home Office for change in the pay and conditions of farm staff with one of the most hotly debated issues within the committee being the requirement for agricultural staff to live in tied accommodation.

When farm staff were recruited into the Service, their joining letters made it clear that occupation of a prison quarter on or near the farm was a condition of their employment. Farm staff had to pay a percentage of their salary plus a small stipend to live in tied accommodation until the union successfully argued that housing should be rent free as staff had no choice about where to live. Maurice was adamant that farm staff, unlike prison chaplains or prison governors who had the right to live in their own house, should live on site so that they would be on hand at any time of day or night to tend the livestock. This was a contentious issue. Many of the senior farm staff felt that the prerequisite to live in tied accommodation was archaic and deeply offensive as it condoned servitude.

Some union members began to argue that farm staff should be able to buy their homes at a discount when the Right to Buy housing act was passed in 1980. However, Maurice, according to Derek, 'was like a dog with a bone' in his opposition to farm staff exercising their right to buy. 'It was the first decision that I made,' said Bernard when he took over from Maurice as head of Farms and Gardens, 'Apart from half a dozen places that you couldn't sell, they could all buy their quarter.' Many, including Derek, saw this as, 'a major step forward for working conditions and a turning point because then you were put on a level with a lot of the prison officer grades working in the same place.'

A Cabinet directive in 1968 had stipulated that prison farms had to become more professional and cost effective. They adapted quickly. A deliberate and symbolic shift in 1969 saw the annual Farm Walk replaced by a 'Farm Management Conference'. For the first time farm managers and senior prison staff met at Wye College, part of the University of London, rather than on a particular prison farm. There was no longer a hand-drawn illustration to accompany the Farm Walk for example, a cartoon of a stricken farmer trapped in a tree by hungry pigs at Leyhill or a bow-tie wearing pig carrying a rake and 'spanners' for the Farm Walk at Misterton Carr in 1957.

The opening address was delivered by Mr Quirk, the deputy director of industries and stores who welcomed the delegates to the first of the Farm Management Conferences. He referred to the previous practice of "Farm Walks" and the benefits these had given in previous years. 'However,' said Mr Quirk, 'it was necessary to move on to a new conception of of how we should make the best use of the annual meeting since the requirement of the service was for improved management techniques. Changing the title of the Annual Conference implied no criticism of what had gone on before; in fact the form in which previous meetings were held was a necessary part of our development, but now it was time to move on to the more difficult field of real management. Delegates would see from the content of the programme and the variety of people attending (whose knowledge of farming was not necessarily great) that an attempt was being made to break new ground.'[19]

'At conferences they used to have a bank of flowers and people used to gasp,' said Howard.

There was a significant increase in the number of attendees at the revamped conference, fifty-six compared to forty in 1968. Amongst the speakers was Mr AD Jackson, head of work study, the first non-farming external 'expert' to be brought in to advise Farms & Gardens. 'Although his roots lay in the country, Mr Jackson confessed that he was not an expert on farming, neither was he an expert on work study in an agricultural context but work study was theoretically the same anywhere, whether in shipyard, workshop or farmyard.'[21]

When Mr Quirk addressed delegates the following year he stressed that work was no longer required for its own sake, it had to be

Former Head of Farms & Gardens, Maurice Codd, surrounded by prison service grown flowers at a Farm Management Conference.[20]

purposeful and satisfying: 'The work carried out both on the farms and the gardens met in full measure the first responsibility of DIS [Department of Industries and Supply] to provide for prisoners useful work occupying a full working day and of a nature to inculcate a habit of hard work coupled with satisfaction.'[22] Accordingly it was decreed that: 'The purpose of both the industrial work in prison and the farming programme is less to train a man to do the job he may get in the outside world than to help him to cultivate the habit of regular work and the self-respect that comes from doing useful work.'[23]

Throughout the country, the rehabilitation of prisoners was tied to the rehabilitation of marginal land into viable agricultural holdings. The 91 hectare (224 acre) site at Featherstone in Staffordshire was a former ordnance depot, a wartime munitions dump: 'What had once been farmland bore all the hallmarks of industrial occupation, buildings of various descriptions including a railway station complete with signal boxes, goods yard sidings, broken down wagons, concrete pads, sewage works and acres of rubble.'[24]

A firm of contractors was brought in to clear the rubble and prepare the land for planting but a proportion of their work was deemed such poor quality that in February 1975, inmates from Stafford prison were given the job of clearing, cleaning and reclaiming the site. By October the first seedlings were planted and the following year three good hay harvests were achieved.

'Roads were built, miles of post and wire fencing erected, landscaping carried out and old bunkers converted to workshops and a milking parlour installed (in Bunker 5). Three and a half hectares which required 30,000 cubic metres of subsoil and 2,000 square metres of top soil was reclaimed, levelled, landscaped and seeded down to become the 'Governor's Bank' a focal point of the staff quarters, and young trees and shrubs are being planted to form new coppices for the future. The target date for completion was March 1981.'[25]

In 1978 Maurice, as head of finance and admin, interviewed Bev for his first Farms & Gardens position.

'We converted a hangar at Featherstone into a mill for animal feed and Bev was the first operator of it.

Inmates milling animal feed at Provender Mill, Dartmoor, one of three prison service feed mills.[26]

Consequently, Featherstone along with two other feed mills, one based in the Midlands at Ashwell prison and another in the south-west at Dartmoor prison, were able to fulfil the orders for animal feed from prison farms throughout England and Wales.

The Governor's Bank was installed on the orders of the new and compassionate governor at Featherstone, John Sandy, who joined the service in 1956 as a housemaster at Portland and was quickly promoted. John Sandy was credited with introducing 'social work in prisons before social work in prisons was thought of'.[27] Consequently, HMP Featherstone sponsored events at the UK's premier indoor athletics arena at nearby RAF Cosford, where No. 4 Workshop (now Hangar 146) housed an athletics track. On his order my dad supplied and arranged the trackside floral displays. To show his appreciation, John Sandy ensured my dad received complimentary tickets to watch what turned out to be the heyday of English athletics. My sister and I eagerly collected autographs as world indoor records tumbled with athletes including Sebastian Coe, Daley Thomson and shot putter Geoff Capes collecting their gold medals from a podium barely visible behind a multitude of prison flowers.

My dad applied for the position at Featherstone having already undertaken a period of lucrative 'detached duty' whilst a prison officer on Portland. Such stints to address staff shortages or other operational issues were commonplace and although staff were paid a premium, detached duty could be quite disruptive for staff and their families. Having been assigned a three-bedroom, semi-detached house in a Black Country mining village five miles away from Featherstone prison, my dad ensured it was sparkling clean on our arrival. As we wandered around, awaiting the arrival of our furniture I remember my dad shouting, '*Get out*!' so forcibly that our collie dog Spot, who wasn't allowed in the house let alone the best front room, jumped straight through the front room window. Fortunately, her minor cuts healed within days but it took weeks for the prison's 'Works' department to replace the glass.

To celebrate his new appointment my dad purchased a bargain-priced second-hand Jaguar XJ6 in his favourite colour, bright yellow. Too wide for my mum to park with ease, it wasn't long before a faulty petrol tank left us standing dripping in the car park of a municipal swimming pool while the local fire brigade extinguished my dad's dream.

I started at yet another new school and found it challenging; for the first month I couldn't understand a word that anybody other than one teacher, Mr Cartwright, said to me and everyone else thought I spoke 'posh'.

'Do you live in a *council* house Susan?' asked another teacher of one of the cleverest girls and a newly acquired best friend.

'Yes.'

'Then you're *working class*.'

The rest of us shifted around uneasily.

It was the early 1980s and most of my friends' fathers were coal miners. I kept my head down. What was I if I lived in a tied house *and* my dad was a farmer *and* he worked for the Home Office?

Within a couple of years some striking coal miners found themselves sentenced to prison and working alongside my dad and his staff.

'I stood alongside a man kind of keeping himself to himself and we started chatting,' recalled cowman John Glover.

'He said, "I've been a really stupid person. I did a silly thing. I had a good job, a wife and everything."'

John shrugged his shoulders.

'Some of the inmates that we've had over the years, you know, I just think they made a mistake which perhaps some people just can.'

In 1979, following a general election in which law and order was a significant issue, Margaret Thatcher appointed 'Willie' Whitelaw as home secretary. His popular but ineffectual 'short sharp shock' programme that instilled military rather than boarding school discipline in young offenders, did little to reduce crime. But even if he didn't reduce recidivism he inadvertently saved other kinds of captives. Many of the prison farms kept pigs, as they were well-suited to small areas of land, with breeding and fattening stock supplied from two herds, one based at HMYOI Hatfield's closest holding, Tudworth Farm and another at Hollesley Bay Colony. Knowing that Whitelaw's father had been a pig farmer, Maurice ensured that the new home secretary's first prison tour included a farm with a substantial piggery.

'Of course Maurice is a canny fella and he knows what's what,' said Chris McGown, 'they had a conversation about rare breeds in the prison service and it went straight to the top.'

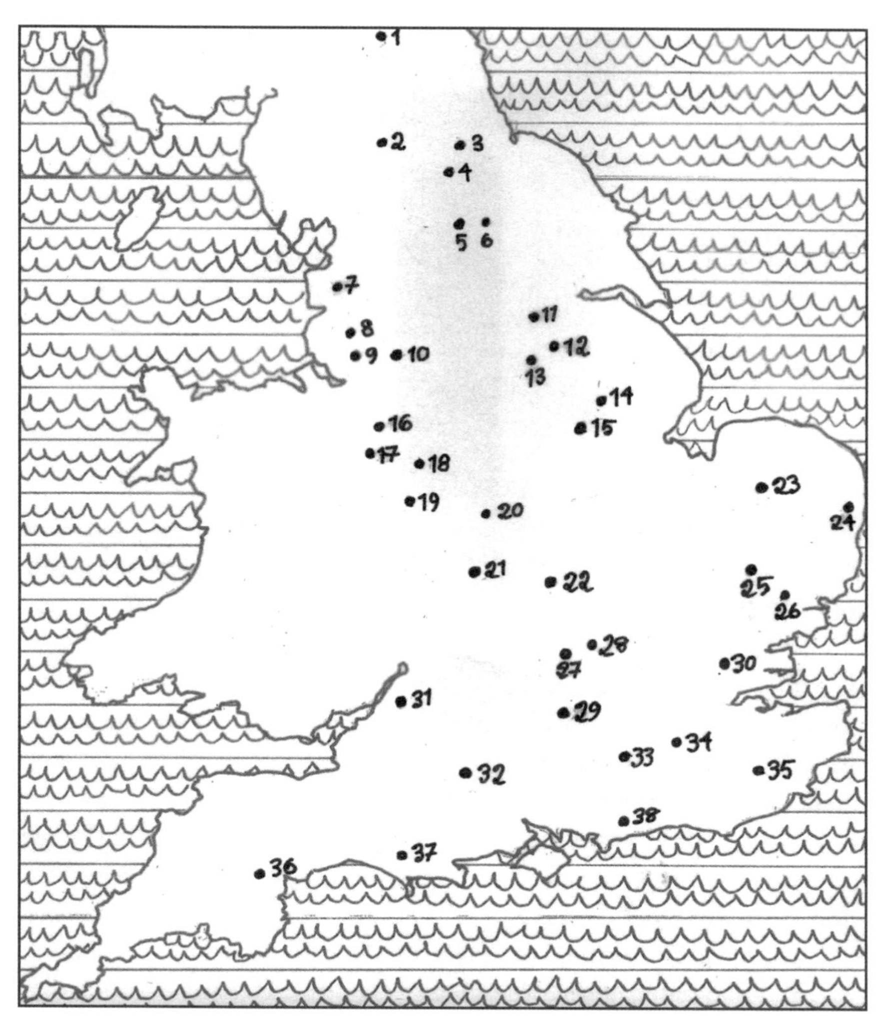

Map of prison farms with large market gardens pre-modernisation.[28]

Legend: Prisons with large market gardens pre-modernisation

1 – Acklington, Northumberland
2 – Deerbolt, County Durham
3 – Kirklevington Grange, North Yorkshire
4 – Northallerton, North Yorkshire (closed 2013)
5 – Wetherby, West Yorkshire
6 – Askham Grange, North Yorkshire
7 – Kirkham, Lancashire
8 – Hindley, Wigan
9 – Thorn Cross, Cheshire
10 – Styal, Cheshire
11 – Lindholme, South Yorkshire
12 – Gringley-on-the-Hill, Nottinghamshire (closed 1988)
13 – Ranby, Nottinghamshire
14 – Morton Hall, Lincolnshire
15 – Whatton, Nottinghamshire

16 – Werrington, Staffordshire
17 – Drake Hall, Staffordshire
18 – Foston Hall and Sudbury, Derbyshire
19 – Sudbury, Derbyshire
20 – Swinfen Hall, Staffordshire
21 – Glen Parva, Leicestershire
22 – Onley, Warwickshire
23 – Wellingborough, Northamptonshire (closed 2012)
24 – Wayland, Norfolk
25 – Blundeston, Suffolk (closed 2013)
26 – Highpoint, Suffolk
27 – Bullingdon, Oxfordshire
28 – Grendon, Buckinghamshire
29 – Huntercombe, Oxfordshire
30 – Chelmsford, Essex
31 – Leyhill (Falfield), Gloucestershire
32 – Erlestoke, Wiltshire
33 – Send, Surrey
34 – Downview, Surrey
35 – Blantyre House, Kent (closed 2016)
36 – Channings Wood, Devon
37 – Dorchester, Dorset
38 – Ford, West Sussex

By the mid-1980s Farms & Gardens were ubiquitous across the prison service with staff attached to all but three of the 147 establishments in England and Wales.

The status of Farms & Gardens within the prison service was reflected not only practically in high levels of funding and staffing but also in the siting of the farm manager's office. Especially in open prisons, it could usually be found in the building closest to the main gate, not just in the same corridor but immediately adjacent to the governor's office. This enabled farm managers to exert a significant influence on prison life within the walls as well as outside them. By contrast, at secure sites with grounds maintenance but no farm, the gardens department's office was usually situated at the other end of the site, as far as way as possible from the main gate.

'There were some reasons, for example, security wouldn't want it right by the main gate but equally it said something,' said Big Rob, a horticulturalist through and through.

'Generally, gardens whether you are in local government or on a private estate, are the least important thing. But curiously it's the bit that everyone notices. As a result, you can't afford to ignore it completely, the gardens department is something of a necessary evil.'
Throughout the 1980s the average daily prison population hovered around 43,000. In 1985 Douglas Hurd took over as home secretary and to address concerns about the effectiveness of prison for rehabilitating offenders and reducing the incidence of crime he

proposed alternative forms of sentencing. Critically, these measures did little to reduce a prison population that was gradually rising.

Farming in the prison service reached a peak in the mid-1990s when the prison service farmed 5,500 hectares (13,590 acres) of marginal land much of it situated on 17 large farms. Consequently, the prison service in England and Wales became the third largest farming operation in the UK, only marginally smaller than the Co-operative Food Group.

'But the big problem,' stated Bernard, 'was that once the population went over 50,000. The land we had couldn't support it.'

'That,' agreed Maurice, 'was the critical point.'

4

Escape to the country

'How did I escape? With difficulty. How did I plan the moment? With pleasure.' Alexandre Dumas, *The Count of Monte Cristo*[1]

'For those working on the gardens it was better being outside than being in the confines of the prison,' said Maurice. Glasshouses, polytunnels and cultivated fields provided legitimate places for staff and inmates to escape the physical and psychological boundaries imposed by prison cells, walls and routines.

'The beauty of farm work of course was that you were outside of what were very smelly places, especially in the 1970s. Prisons stunk. They were ghastly places. Horrible,' exhorted Bernard.

'They might not like it when it was adverse weather conditions but then you had to look after them a bit,' Maurice conceded. 'For the

Officer Instructor Neville and Officer Instructor Boon in the geranium greenhouse with inmates, Eastchurch (Standford Hill), Kent.[2]

prisoners it was freedom. Nine hours a day. They didn't want to lose that.'

Compared to other prison departments, Farms & Gardens was unusually outward-facing. When North Sea Camp changed from a YOI to an adult male prison in the late 1980s, a number of community projects were introduced but 'due to the insular outlook of people in the Boston area, these were slow to develop and it was decided to invite the public to visit the prison, using the farm as a focal point.'[3] Between February and March 1990, 800 school children visited the farm, primarily to see the lambing. Building on this, an open day organised for 7 July 1990 attracted 1,500 visitors. 'The inmates had proved to be ambassadors for the positive side of the Prison Service. The integration of inmates into the community was a delicate and sensitive task and tribute was paid particularly to the farm staff for their positive contribution to the success of these ventures. It was believed that farm staff underestimated the value of instruction they gave to inmates.'[4]

Farms & Gardens enabled inmates, the majority of whom, even at open prisons, spent much of their time 'behind the scenes' hidden from public view, to engage with the wider community. Jason remembered a forward thinking governor at Blantyre House instigating a 'family day',

'This prisoner had his private helicopter and he was using it to give pleasure flights on and off the sports field!'

Farms & Gardens placed a lot of emphasis on creating attractive places. Visitors, particularly at lower category establishments, could find themselves walking along paths lined with colourful annual or herbaceous borders; lobelia, geraniums, begonias and petunias cascading from overstuffed hanging baskets. Waiting rooms sported potted plants grown in prison service greenhouses and the feeling was that such displays: 'Contribute greatly towards the atmosphere of any establishment and in many of the older prisons the flowers and lawns are the only relieving factors to the general drabness.'[5]

According to Mr Neale, director of the Department of Industries and Supply in the early 1970s: 'Gardens were the shop window of the Department and the impact these made on people visiting prisons as well as the people in custody was considerable; attractive and well cared for gardens gave the impression of a well-run establishment.'[6]

Steve Horrocks' mentor when he became a farm manager, in charge of 50 acres and 50 cows, at Werrington in 1990 was Reg Simpson who advised him: 'When the Board of Visitors come round or the Governors come up to the farm don't rattle on about how this cow is giving 7500 litres at 3.42% butterfat and all that. They don't know what you're talking about and they're not interested. If you make the farm look beautiful and get first impressions right then you're already brilliant before they even get out the car.'

'Werrington,' Steve explained, 'was a lovely place. Cracking farmers.'

The farm, perched on a hill, was visited twice daily by cows ambling along the driveway that swept between the farm and the prison. Steve set about creating a good impression; he tidied the trees, installed a black chain fence slung between white concrete posts and planted the lawns with thousands of snowdrops and daffodil bulbs.

'It looked an absolute picture. If you drove down people went, "Wow, what a beautiful place this is," and then they thought, "This guy's a great farm manager," and that was before they'd even seen me!' he laughed.

Farms & Gardens staff took a great deal of care over their environs. Most amenity areas like gardens and playing fields were as well-groomed, neat and orderly as officers' shoes. Occasionally however, a prison governor expressed a preference for prison lawns to have a more natural, unkempt look which didn't impress either Maurice or my dad who thought that unmown wild meadows looked dishevelled and, importantly, removed a significant source of revenue.

Where there was support from the prison governor, Farms & Gardens provided transitional places that could aid the reintegration of prisoners into society.

'We used to feed them on the farm. Eventually we used to shower them on the farm so that when they went back to the prison they went straight back to their cell as if it was their normal home. In some prisons, where the governors were co-operative, they had their own wings for people working out on the farm and that became their accommodation but that depended on the whims and rules of the governor. Like in any community, you would always get the odd one who would mess it up but then you had the group looking after themselves, they were their own security, but not all governors agreed with that,' concluded Maurice.

Some governors confined their interest in Farms & Gardens to expressing a preference for ornamental features. Like many of their charges, governors often hailed from urban areas and this made it difficult at times for them to relate to agricultural practices. Bryan Wakely found that governors struggled with processes that occurred across more than one year, for example, barley is sown annually but harvested the following year so it requires two-year accounting.

'"Why have we got cows? Why have we got animals? What's the benefit?" they'd ask.'

Bryan described an encounter with the governor at Northeye prison in Sussex where he was the temporary herdsman.

'I was trying to educate him about what was out there and what the benefits of the farms were. I asked him, "Do you want to come and look at the dairy?" "What's a dairy?" "Where we milk the cows." "Cows, they're smelly," "No they're not. Can you smell them now?" "Not really. I can smell some other stuff." I told him it was silage. "What's silage?" I showed him the silage pit. It could be a hopeless task,' he lamented.

The regime and consequently the importance and responsibility attributed to the farm manager at any one establishment could change quickly and drastically with the arrival of a new governor.

'I supplied the budgets so I had to get to know what they were doing otherwise I couldn't sign it off,' declared Phil Wheatley, 'so I began to know more about farming than I knew before. I learnt about what they actually did, apart from sitting on the back of a potato picking lorry to sort potatoes in the days when we worked alongside borstal boys, rather than just stood back and watched them.' But it wasn't always apparent whether a particular governor would be supportive of farms.

'A lot of the governors weren't pro farms,' said Lorraine. 'When East Sutton Park was on *Countryfile* [a weekly television programme about rural and environmental issues aired on BBC One] the governor came and took an interview but that was the only time he'd been round the farm! He took the interview and walked straight off. He didn't wait and he didn't talk to us.'

'Other governors,' said Big Rob, 'understood about farms: they make milk and money, they are very interesting and a good employer.'

Farms & Gardens were particularly useful to governors as they could accommodate fluctuations in the inmate population. On a typical day at HMYOI Portland, Chris McGown took 80 borstal boys to work on the farm,

'I had 4 up the piggery and 6 on the milking parlour. They were mine. About 30 went down the gardens and the other 40 or 50 used to go out the Bill.'

'What did they do on Portland Bill?' I asked.

'Well, hoeing, cleaning out ditches, weeding, fencing, picking up stones in the field. You name it, they did it. You know it didn't matter what they were doing, *no* trouble finding them work to do.'

At some prisons, governors used the farms and gardens for their own rest and recuperation.

'All the time, till I got to head office, I was working on the gardens and the governors would come out for their escape,' noted Bryan.

Maurice agreed, 'some would come round to the farm on a fine day if they wanted to get away, they came just for a chat sometimes. Mainly they'd come because they wanted to have a cup of tea in the farm manager's office so they'd come round at 11am! And then they'd talk to the officer instructor and ask how it was going. It was all very informal. Sometimes it was a nice trip out in the car, a way for the chief to get out of the prison. When I was at Dartmoor, the governor would say that he had come for half an hour *just to escape*. You are outside the walls. Inside is where the pressure is.'

'The governor at Northeye would come out on a bad day, stressed out as hell and he'd say, "I need to inspect your football pitches." It was winter and it was dark. We'd look up at the night sky, see all the stars and talk about a load of nothing,' said Bryan.

Of course it wasn't just the governors who enjoyed escaping even if it was only temporary. The triple white lines on the back of the thick, black 'Dartmoor' coats worn by inmates returning from the dairy meant that they were allowed to work outside. By contrast, patches sewn on to their prison issue clothes indicated that they were not allowed to pass through the prison gates.

Unaccompanied prisoners carrying milk pails as they return to Dartmoor prison 'DP'.[7]

A couple of the most notorious escapes occurred from the farm attached to austere and remote Dartmoor prison. In 1964 three prisoners were recaptured five miles away after hijacking an oil tanker that had been making deliveries to the farm. Two years later, in 1966, Frank 'Mad Axeman' Mitchell, a very strong, 'gentle giant with the mind of a child' who was prone to acts of aggression, slipped away from farm staff and never returned.[8] Maurice recalled meeting Frank for the first time when he took the prisoners' dairy clothes to the laundry. 'This instructor said to me, "If anything happens don't worry, you haven't got to worry about it." Well Mitchell was stark naked and he came over and picked me up under his arm and was parading around the laundry! I was *absolutely terrified*.'

Mitchell had committed a series of violent offences including attacks on prison 'warders' and had spent a short time imprisoned at Wandsworth where he was befriended by Ronnie Kray, one of the infamous Kray brothers. After attempting a burglary armed with an axe he earned his nickname and life imprisonment. Trusted to work outside, Frank spent most of his time feeding wild ponies rather than alongside other prisoners who, supervised by a single officer, worked out-of-sight along a two-mile fence. On one occasion he managed to get away from the farm work party, commandeered a taxi to nearby Tavistock and bought a budgerigar before returning to Dartmoor. The governor allowed Frank the privilege of keeping the bird.[9]

Following the relaxation of the incentives and earned privileges scheme introduced in 2013, prisoners can no longer purchase birds but those long-term inmates, at a small number of facilities, who already keep a caged bird, can continue until it dies.

As the early December weather on exposed Dartmoor deteriorated so the guard and all the prisoners bar Mitchell took shelter in a hut. When Mitchell failed to return from feeding the ponies, a search party made up of soldiers as well as police and officers including Chilly Frampton and other members of the Pony Patrol scoured the moor but to no avail. Unbeknownst to them Mitchell was on his way to a London flat having been seized and driven away by members of the Kray gang. Sensational media coverage ensued along with extensive debate within the House of Commons about the appropriateness of allowing a prisoner like Frank, who had previously been incarcerated in Broadmoor psychiatric prison and had a history of disruptive and aggressive behaviour, to be working, effectively without supervision, outside the walls of the prison.

The consequences of his escape were dire for Frank. It is presumed that his anger and frustration intensified as the Kray gang kept him locked up in the flat while the media storm raged. Although his body was never found, another member of the Kray gang called Freddie Foreman, who along with Ronnie and Reggie Kray was acquitted of Mitchell's murder and knew that he could not be charged twice, appeared on television in 1999 and admitted that he'd shot Mitchell.[10]

In March 1969 the Kray twins were sentenced to life imprisonment for murdering two men: George Cornell and Jack 'the hat' McVitie. Shortly after they were sentenced Maurice Codd visited high security Category A Parkhurst on the Isle of Wight where Reggie Kray was being held.

'Kray was on the gardens rather than the farms. When they first got sentenced I went to Parkhurst to meet them. They were segregated in their own area; it was a glass cage almost and Farms & Gardens were asked to provide them with some work. The manager and I worked out where they could work and they weeded and planted from within portable six-foot cages. Actually they were quite good. You wouldn't think they were 'villains', they did a lot of vegetable and flower growing for use in other areas of the prison. We made it that they had productive work that they would see a benefit from which was all very 'rehabilitative'. But whether they saw it like that remains to be seen!'

A series of high profile escapes in the late-1960s, including in 1966 notorious spy George Blake breaking out from high security Wormwood Scrubs and Great Train Robber Ronnie Biggs escaping from Wandsworth, led to the commissioning of an official enquiry into prison security. Published in 1967, the *Mountbatten Report* recommended that prisoners should be divided into four categories according to the degree of security necessary for their containment (Cat. A, B, C and D, with A the highest level of security). The *Mountbatten Report* also recommended that a fortress be built on the Isle of Wight to hold Category A prisoners but this was rejected the following year by the Advisory Council on the Penal System whose report *The Regime for Long-term Prisoners in Conditions of Maximum Security* (1968) recommended that rather than concentrating high security prisoners in one place, they should be dispersed amongst three or four specially fortified establishments. Consequently, six Category A dispersal prisons were established: Albany on the Isle of Wight, Whitemoor in Cambridgeshire, Long Lartin in Worcestershire, Full Sutton near Pocklington in the East Riding of Yorkshire, Wakefield in West Yorkshire and Frankland in County Durham.

Punch cartoon depicting an inmate and officer instructor in a prison garden.[11]

To reduce tension and the desire to escape from mainstream prisons, the *Mountbatten Report* recommended that attention be paid to the physical environs of prisons and, in accordance with its liberal and constructive view, the report suggested that prisons be places of containment rather than places of labour and hard work. At the peak of agriculture within the prison service, all Cat. D 'open' prisons, most Cat C. 'training' prisons and some Cat. B 'local' prisons had farms. Only two Cat. B prisons didn't have gardens (Leicester and Exeter) but they still had a gardens officer appointed to take care of the flowerbeds and potted plants. Even the highest security prisons, used to incarcerate murderers and other lifers, had spaces in which to grow plants within the walls.

However, although the report supported the enlivening of public and private spaces within the establishment with floral displays and the like, the renewed emphasis on security led to a significant reduction in the 16,100 prisoners employed daily in prison industries at that time. Governors became increasingly reluctant to provide temporary licenses for prisoners to carry out activities beyond the confines of the prison and escapes still occurred.

'At Hatfield in 1969,' recalled Phil, 'we had more prisoners escaped in a year than we had on our total roll. There were 180 on roll and we had 200 absconds a year. For the surrounding people they'd turn up and thieve from the houses, they stole cars. Very few of them really escaped. But for the surrounding people they caused a degree of angst.'

Typically, if an inmate failed to be present at roll call it was because they'd tried to reach home or a loved one in which case they were usually recaptured within a few hours.

Chris McGown laughed about a resourceful attempt to escape from Portland.

'One of mine got out at night. He got out from inside and he climbed down into the farmyard where you can open the gates from the inside even though they are padlocked from the outside. He drove a Ford 3000 tractor over beach road till they caught him.'

Steve remembered an unusual episode when he was a dairyman at Gaynes Hall.

'There was an inmate who was one of a twin. It took the authorities a long time to realise that they'd swop places during visiting time so that the one on the inside could spend the weekend out! He got every other weekend off. It only stopped when one got caught sneaking back in!'

Steve also told me his favourite almost-lost-them story.

'The Bishop of Liverpool invited a group of lifers from Kirkham to visit his garden. I took nine inmates in a minibus. One lad was very clever and he'd been in a long time. While we there the bishop and his wife served afternoon tea! I kept counting them because I was terrified that one of them would do a runner and even more terrified when the bishop said, "I've got to go now so I will leave you with my wife." Me, his wife and nine male inmates! I thought right, let's get out of here and I said to the lads, "Let's get going." I wasn't surprised when one of them said, "Can we use the bathroom?" I knew they were trying it on but the bishop's wife piped up, "Of course. There's one just here, another down the corridor and others not far away." Off they scarpered. I held my breath till they started to come back one by one. I'd counted eight when I heard *Morning* from Grieg's *Peer Gynt* being played on a piano. It was absolutely beautiful. Alarmed, I said to the bishop's wife, "Is that your daughter playing the piano?" whilst at the same time thinking, I'm still one inmate short. "No," she said. And then I knew that the ninth inmate, the clever lad, had found a fine piano and was finding a great deal of enjoyment in playing such an exquisite instrument. It wasn't long till he finished and sauntered back into the room to the applause of the bishop's wife and the smirks of the other lads.'

Throughout the 1970s, 80s and early 90s, escapes were commonplace and generally accepted as inevitable.

'We thought that was OK,' said Phil before adding, 'we don't any longer.'

Security was one of three elements identified within the *Woolf Report* compiled in 1991 following a series of prison riots, most notably Strangeways in Manchester on April Fool's Day 1990.[12] The other two elements focused on by Lord Chief Justice Woolf were control (preventing disturbances) and justice (treating prisoners with humanity and fairness). Unfortunately, according to Lord Woolf political parties are still competing about who, according to the media and the voting public, is 'toughest on crime', that is, best at security and control within the walls of the prison rather than justice which permeates boundaries.[13]

On 9 September 1994, six inmates including five members of the IRA tried to escape from Whitemoor, a dispersal prison which had been built in 1991 and included 'a prison within a prison', a Special Security Unit (SSU) designed to securely hold Cat. A male prisoners.[14] By contrast to the 'prison within a prison' design of the SSU, the original plans for Whitemoor also included a specially constructed conservation area outside the walls that was accessible to the public as well as staff. 'The "green" plan for Whitemoor grew out of the need to avoid costly removal and dumping of large amounts of contaminated surface material while at the same time making sure that rainwater coming off the prison's huge covered areas did not cause problems to the carefully balanced fenland drainage system. Now the amenity area – the first of its kind on Home Office prison land – has won praise from the local community.'[15]

The escapees, armed with two pistols, ammunition and 'a willingness to use them', made ropes from bed sheets with which to scale the walls. However, they didn't get very far across the fen because their exit coincided with a change of shift with officers arriving at the prison well-placed outside to help those finishing work inside. The *Woodcock Enquiry* also uncovered Semtex explosive, short fuses and three detonators hidden in an inmate's artist paint box. Weaknesses in the tendering process for the construction of the SSU included the distribution of so many detailed plans that several were found at the side of a road by a local farmer. Another plan was used for painting on by a nursery school pupil. The report suggested that during construction, potential escape equipment and weaponry had been built into the fabric of the building.[16]

'Lots of things that I've done have been interesting like trying to tighten up on dispersals after the escapes from Whitemoor and other high security escapes,' said Phil. 'There used to be one or two a year but they don't happen now. It's an amazing trick. It was a real achievement. We steadily chipped away at it.'

Between 1980–1995, 27 Cat. A prisoners escaped but after 3 escapes in 1995/96 there were none until 2011, a year after Phil left the prison service. All prisons had nil escapes as a key performance target. Technically, escapes occurred when a physical security restraint like a wall or fence or handcuffs were overcome or an inmate managed to get away while under the direct supervision of staff. Although escapes reduced, absconds continued with approximately three quarters of absconds being from male open prisons or YOIs like Thorn Cross in Cheshire which for two years prior to 2014 experienced one escape every two weeks according to the local press.[17]

Pete Chisholm remembered two 'lasses' escaping from the farm attached to New Hall, a Cat. C prison near Wakefield, in the mid-1990s during a visit by the then Minister of State for Prisons, Ann Widdecombe. Every day twenty inmates were given a temporary licence to leave the prison early to work 'outside the wire'. In preparation for Ann Widdecombe's visit, those who'd arrived early at the farm were tasked with cleaning and tidying. But instead of vacuuming the empty office, one of the inmates rummaged through the drawers and found three cash-filled envelopes containing the weekly wage (£200) of a civilian member of staff. She kept two, gave one to another inmate and, whilst attention was focused on the impending visit, they ran into the local village and boarded a bus.

As they were out on license, the inmates technically absconded rather than escaped, nevertheless the farm manager at the time 'couldn't sleep,' said Pete as he was terrified that he'd be held responsible.

'At the meeting the next morning with the governor, a 'terrier-like' Scotsman, the farm manager was told to, "sit here and have a coffee and don't effing worry so long as the paperwork is okay."'

Ann Widdecombe was informed and no further action was taken. A couple of months later the 'lasses' were found in London, working in a bar and pretending to be Australian. Pete revealed that within a few years of being returned to prison they were both 'dead with drugs.'

In the early 1960s and 70s it wasn't uncommon for inmates to brew hooch but widescale importation of drugs into prisons didn't occur until the mid-1970s.

'It became what the criminal classes do,' professed Phil, 'I remember saying to a repeat offender I'd met in the early 1980s and again at Parkhurst in 2008, "Doesn't anybody do robbery anymore?" "Nah," he said, "All the money is in drugs, only mugs do robbery." And that showed how things moved, my old armed robbers all moved into drug importing. I mean the train robbers all went in eventually for drug importation on a major scale.'

Consequently, from time-to-time Farms & Gardens staff assisted in searches for 'clandestine items which are suspected of being secreted on farm premises, and in searches for missing tools which in the wrong hands may be used as weapons or for the furtherance of escape attempts.'[18] Most of the time Maurice and his staff only found counterfeit money and cigarettes, 'not drugs in those days, only latterly,' said Maurice.

'The favourite place to hide money or anything that you wanted to keep dry was in the yards where the cows used to sleep, where the walls came down and joined the floor, there was always some dry straw right in the corners and that is where they used to put it. So we used to walk around with a fork and just lift up the straw and you found all sorts of things there,' he laughed.

'You could never find who did it! If something was out-of-place then you'd have a look. I've still got that habit now! If I'm walking round town and I see something in the hedge I'll go and have a look and see what it is.'

According to Steve there was a big problem with drugs at Kirkham.

'Drugs used to be dropped off at the edge of the farm and the lads who were going to fetch the cows or the lad who was driving the tractor would go and pick the drugs up and bring them back to the dairy. The lads who were pasteurising the milk would pack the milk into bags and then seal the bags *and* the drugs in the cardboard boxes that would be sent into the prison. The veg prep lads would receive the cardboard boxes and take out the drugs and then the drugs would be sent into the prison.'

But when I asked Maurice he was adamant that the farms were not especially bad for drugs. Phil disagreed and cited a visit, when he was deputy director general, to Featherstone prison.

'I was sitting down with the then area manager and going through the performance figures and Featherstone was off the scale for drug use and the major source in was through the farm. And I remember saying, "It looks like they are growing more opium than anything else." There was tons of the stuff coming in.'

Maurice didn't contest that drugs could come in through farms but he stressed that they could come in through lots of avenues at any time when inmates were allowed outside, for example, on visits, attending appointments or on work experience. According to Maurice these situations provided more opportunities for meeting up with 'friends' (and exchanging illicit goods) than work on isolated farms. As this was an era before unmanned aircraft or drones could pass goods over the wall, everything and everyone passed through the prison gate. Maurice felt it was the responsibility of the governor to ensure that searches at the gate were sufficiently robust to prevent drugs entering or leaving the prison.

After Steve mentioned that his spare bedroom was wallpapered with maps of all the prison farms he had worked on, he described with glee how he regularly helped the governor prevent contraband from entering Werrington prison by recruiting his children to help with the search for illegal goods. Visiting times were 1–3pm on Saturday and Sunday and as no inmates were allowed outside until all the visitors had gone, the dairyman would have to wait until 3pm to pick up the lads who were going to help him with the milking.

'The lads out on the farm were always being pressurised to pick up as much as they could and sneak it back into the prison. The officers would search the farm lads and nine times out of ten they'd have something on them because they were being told if they didn't bring it in then they'd get a kicking from the other inmates. On Saturday and Sunday at quarter to three one of the other staff would call at the house and ask if my daughters were in, "I just need them for a bit.'"

Being under ten they went willingly with their 'uncle' to play a *special* game of hide-and-seek come treasure hunt.

'"You hide in that bush and you hide behind that wall. There'll be cars coming up here and they'll stop and someone will jump out. Watch where they hide stuff."

After the last visitor's car had gone he'd shout, "All clear, go!"

"Look what we got this week Daddy, two bottles of whiskey, a load of plastic packets with white stuff and 200 cigarettes."

They they'd walk down to the main gate of the prison and hand it all in.'

Early one memorable Monday morning, after a particularly successful Sunday, the governor looked at the pile of 'treasure' on his desk before addressing senior staff including Steve and a new female head of education,

'"Morning everybody and well done Stephen, make sure to thank those girls."

"What girls?" asked the head of education.

When the Governor explained she was horrified, "They shouldn't be doing that. How old? *Six*! *Six*!'"

I smiled. I knew what it was like to feel secure growing up amongst prisoners.

Of course,' said Steve, 'the girls were always wanting to go out. And they were safe.'

His certainty reminded me of my dad.

'I was watching them like a hawk!'

5

Growing our own

'Interdependence is and ought to be as much the ideal of man as self-sufficiency.' Mahatma Gandhi

Amongst the National Justice Museum archive in Nottingham I happened upon an unstamped postcard of a photograph of Birmingham prison dated 23 December 1932. Addressed to F.C. Shackel Esq from 'W.J.E.' the inscription on the reverse read, 'Your kind greetings are heartily reciprocated by self and family. This is an excellent Hotel, but the menu is a bit plain, tho: the quarters are free.'

Such simple fare was an eighteenth-century legacy, a belief that prison food should replicate 'the diet of the poorest elements of society lest it was thought they be tempted into crime to improve their dietary

A postcard of Birmingham prison dated 1932.[1]

condition.'[2] A century later, food supplied to the prison kitchens by the Farms & Gardens was such high quality that 'the average householder in nutritive and quantitative terms would be better off in custody!'[3] By the time Farms & Gardens' staff gathered at the Farm Conference in 1969 it was noted that: 'Cooks and Bakers were on trial every time they produce a meal. The meal must be good otherwise there was trouble.'[4]

For some who found themselves confined to cells or classrooms, meals punctuated the boredom and monotony of an otherwise routine existence. But if the meal contained a substantial amount of sugar it could have a deleterious effect on behaviour. Amongst young offenders, a double-blind controlled study conducted in the USA found that, over a two-year period, antisocial behaviour almost halved amongst those on a low sugar diet and the effect was particularly marked amongst those arrested for assault. 'Horseplay' reduced by two-thirds and refusal to obey dropped by more than half.[5] A similar study in 2002 about the effect of nutritional supplements on disciplinary offences[6] looked so promising that the Natural Justice research team (with the support of Lord Ramsbotham, a trustee of Natural Justice) secured £1 million to fund a larger study. But in 2006 it was announced that the research would not proceed as the Home Office did not accept the earlier research findings.

Amongst a melee of school children eagerly awaiting a performance in the Barbican Centre I strained to hear former Director General Phil Wheatley as he said, 'If you look through analyses of incidences in early 90s and mid-90s the main cause of "concerted and disciplines" [riots, sit downs and protests] was complaints about food.'

'Food,' according to prison governors was, 'one of the four things, along with mail, hot water and prison visits, you must get right if you like having a roof on your prison.'[7]

'One thing that hasn't changed is prison food is the most important thing. If they're not fed, they will riot,' said Chris Coveney when we met in a café adjacent to prison service headquarters in London.

But during Maurice's time in the prison service there was only one protest over food that he was called to account for. In this case twenty inmates gathered in the dining hall allegedly protesting about the quality of the food but on further enquiry it turned out that their real grievance was that their right to receive visitors the next day had been withdrawn. Other commentators have also downplayed a diet-crime connection, suggesting that it is an example of how 'food faddism' has been incorporated into public policy.[8] Even a series of official prison reports published in the early 1990s by Lord Justice Woolf, Judge Stephen Tumim and Sir Raymond Lygo cautioned against seeing food as the sole or main cause of disturbances.[9]

Bernard recalled inadvertently causing a strike at Birmingham prison.

'There was a farm manager who became a prison officer and he was serving at Birmingham. I was regional manager of Midlands and I got Tom Houston to go over and cut the grass in Birmingham prison and the POA (Prison Officers Association) didn't like the fact that I'd sent someone over there to cut the grass and they closed Birmingham prison! I'd only been a regional manager for a couple of weeks and I had to go to Maurice and say I'd made a mistake!'

However, the Woolf, Tumim and Lygo reports acknowledged that prison meals had to be produced within a specified budget and contain an adequate amount of varied, high quality, nutritionally-balanced ingredients. Even though less than two percent of prisoners complain about prison food[10] 'Cooks & Bakers', as prison caterers were colloquially known, could be vociferous critics of Farms & Gardens produce. At the 1969 Farm Management Conference the catering advisor, Mr Belcham, addressed prison farm managers directly, reminding them that Cooks & Bakers were their major customers.

'He thought the ideas of the Managers and himself might differ on what were acceptable standards of produce, but he thought we must have one thing in common and that was to provide only produce that was acceptable in the stalls of the markets so that he, as a caterer, could provide meals in establishments that would be comparable with outside canteens and restaurants. He was pleased to note that vegetables, which had so often in the past suffered rapid deterioration because of the length of time in transit, now reached the customer within twenty-four hours. This had been achieved by the organisation of supply on a district basis and on the use of our own transport. It was a big step forward.'[11] Until the early 1970s vegetables had usually been transported by rail but, 'It could get kicked about. There were huge cabbage nets. Stuff that would eventually arrive at prisons would be hideous,' said Big Rob.

Relations between Farms & Gardens and Cooks & Bakers were hampered by poor channels of communication with farm staff feeling that caterers had unrealistic expectations.[12]

'There was a lot of pressure at the time from the catering department, they didn't think the vegetables were as good but they forgot that they weren't paying for it, they kept on saying, "This isn't great, the cucumbers are bent,"' recalled Chris Coveney.

One of the major suppliers of cucumbers was HMP Kirkham which opened in 1962 on the site of a former RAF camp. At the forefront of horticultural enterprise, Kirkham installed polythene structures in 1965 to extend the growing season for salad crops. In the winter of 1974, prisoners supervised by garden staff built enormous greenhouses that enabled Kirkham to become the largest horticultural unit in the service. The heated greenhouses and polytunnels not only extended the seasonal supply of fresh produce, they provided an all-weather place for 180 prisoners to work under commercial conditions and encouraged a fork-to-fork perspective.

'This was also a motivating factor, in that inmates were building the greenhouse, in which they would work to produce the food which they would eventually eat…the fact that they were dealing with growing crops enabled them to see the work completed. Many in fact volunteered for overtime without pay and when questioned stated that it helped their "bird" to go more quickly.'[13]

By 1977 Kirkham's annual production amounted to approximately 140,000 cucumbers, 140,000 heads of celery, 120,000 lettuces and 100 tons of tomatoes.

The seeds of my family's self-sufficiency were, like those of the prison service, sown during the WWII *Dig for Victory* campaign when ornamental gardens, including those in penal institutions, were devoted to the growing of vegetables to meet the demand for fresh produce during a time of food rationing. Prison gardens were replanted using plants propagated within the service and by 1953 the Farm Section, as the department was then known, provided almost £49,000 worth of produce to the prison kitchens.[14]

The extent of self-sufficiency within the prison service in England and Wales was staggering. By 1970 prison farms were meeting over half the demand from prison kitchens for vegetables. They supplied two-thirds of green and root vegetables, half the potatoes and a third of the onions consumed within prisons. Herbs, particularly parsley, which caterers demanded because of its high vitamin C content, were plentiful.

Peas and broad beans were not widely grown as they required specialist and therefore costly machinery to sow and harvest. Otherwise the prison farms supplied to order and surplus produce, including short shelf-life produce such as eggs and tomatoes, if it couldn't be preserved, was sold externally at wholesale markets. To cope with the annual glut of tomatoes Maurice considered canning them.

The service grew all its own livestock feed (for example, sugar beet) and cultivated cash crops such as soft fruit. As strawberries, raspberries and other soft fruits were highly perishable, part of the crop was preserved as jam at a factory installed at Hollesley Bay prison. This enabled prison farms to meet one hundred percent of the prison service demand for jam.

'I got more satisfaction out of the jam machine than anything else I did,' said softly spoken, former Area Manager Howard Morse as we discussed food waste on a day that the national press reported that the typical household throws out the equivalent of four meals a week.

Trainees making jam at Hollesley Bay Colony, Suffolk in the 1980s.[15]

'I had to find pumps and a canning machine. In the end, I found a reconditioned canning machine.' Pointing at the photograph of the jam making facility at Hollesley Bay he added, 'I had those trolleys made too. When they were setting up the jam factory they wanted to do a trial run but none of the all male staff knew what the setting point of jam was! I had to ring Isobel and ask her. After the success of the jam factory at Hollesley Bay we decided to set up another one at High Point in Suffolk.'

'The jam was never sold,' asserted Maurice, 'we used to use all sorts of things to make jam not just fruit. Marrows. Fruit essence. Jam and fruit pies. Apples, strawberries and we also used to get common market stuff. That was free. If a place had grown too much then it had to be taken out of the system and got rid of and they used to destroy it but we got to the situation where we could take it for nil cost and use it so long as it was used internally. The only benefit we got out of it as Farms & Gardens was the processing cost. We didn't even get the sales price because it went straight into the kitchens, so it was nil in and nil out with a value-added bit in the middle. Stuff like jam, we could process it and store it.'

At Hollesley Bay late variety potatoes were harvested and passed through a grading machine to remove small or damaged potatoes and dirt. In the 'Farms Review' video from 1992, kindly given to me by Howard, he can be heard narrating the process by which potatoes were peeled and dipped in sodium metabisulphate to prevent them from turning black, while carrots, mixed diced vegetables and lettuces were placed in cold storage, packed and boxed ready to be dispatched to the prison kitchens. A similar potato processing plant at Stanford Hill occupied twenty prisoners; between them they peeled 60 tonnes a week.

But when the potatoes reached the caterers they tended to steam rather than boil them. Sometimes the heavily preserved potatoes would develop a 'shell' or crust on them.

'The caterers would go bananas and the prisoners wouldn't eat them,' explained Jason. 'When the head of catering at Parkhurst called he said, "I just want to clarify, we are *caterers* on the island. We are not *magicians. What* are we supposed to do with these spuds you've sent me? It was partially our fault,' Jason conceded, 'and partially the caterers fault because they'd steam them to hell.'

Trainees sorting potatoes on a vegetable processing line, Hollesley Bay Colony, Suffolk.[16]

All the produce supplied to the prison kitchens had to be grade A quality. For example, it had to meet animal welfare standards set by the EU, dairy standards set by the Milk Marketing Board, and the Lion standard for eggs. But there was an absence of equivalent standards for cooking the produce. Clearly not a fan of cabbage Phil said, 'If all you were producing was cabbage, which was what we did produce, all those big, globe, wishy-washy, tasteless cabbage then you always got wet, wishy-washy, tasteless cabbage. Not that many people like cabbage today, certainly not when it's overcooked. And if it's that sort of cabbage, overcooked, *yuk*!'

Although environmental health officers visited farms frequently to ensure they complied with all the legislation laid down by the Health and Safety Executive, prior to 1 April 1992 Crown property was immune from compliance with all food safety legislation. It wasn't until 1998 following a Committee of Public Account report that key catering standards, including food safety, were introduced into prisons.

Under the Common Agricultural Policy individual farms were given a quota for milk production that they were not allowed to exceed. However, the prison service was 'lucky,' said Maurice, because it was given a national quota covering all fifty dairy farms rather than individual quotas for each prison farm. This gave the prison service a degree of flexibility in milk production that was not available to private

The inscription on the reverse of this early photograph of the farmyard at Dartmoor prison distinguished between milk producing dairy cattle and meat producing beef cattle: 'These are not the animals that supply the milk for the prisoner's porridge.'[17]

dairy farmers and contributed to the service becoming largely self-sufficient in the production and supply of milk. To meet demand for semi-skimmed rather than full fat milk a skimmer was installed at HMP Rochester. In the late 1980s Farms & Gardens met the milk requirements for ninety prisons plus some Crown Courts.[18]

Cows milked within a state-of-the-art automated dairy at Dartmoor attracted a lot of visitors[19] but Bryan, who was responsible for livestock enterprises, insisted that, 'Our problem was that our dairy herd might have been the third largest milk producer in the country but our way of milking was nineteenth century not twenty-first century.'

At the instigation of the area manager, a new dairy, 'a proper milking parlour,' according to Chris McGown, was built on spare land adjoining the football and cricket fields used by inmates at HMYOI Portland in the mid-1980s.

'I built it myself,' he said. 'I built all the surrounds and everything, I put all the irons in the ground, they had all this money, somehow they got all this money. *Up* they went to the Burma, an area on Portland, chose a site behind where the old piggery had been knocked down. They asked me to go up and clear which I did with a JCB. They had a private company to come and install it. Got it all in. Spanking new. Beautiful it was. You know, proper. I think it was a 12 12 herringbone.'

'We had all the electrics put in. We had all the fences up, the yards were all concreted up with the help of prisoners. The works did the yards up there. And then all of a sudden they don't want it. *Never used.* Not one cow. I don't know why they shelved it but governors were not signing forms to allow inmates to come out. It was a 'health and safety' issue. *Everything was there.* It must have cost £150,000 or more. I heard a private farmer on the Isle of Wight bought it for 20 grand.'

My mum, who was with me when I visited Chris piped up, 'I wonder if it was Ian McDowell, Bev's former boss? Because he did Friesians.'

Many agreed that by producing their own food the service enjoyed 'a higher quality product than had been obtainable in the past.'[20] In response to a request in the early 1970s from the chief catering manager, when animals were slaughtered the farms started to get back the offal as well as the carcasses. Liver is a particularly valuable source of vitamin D for prisoners with limited access to sunlight but over the last forty years offal has 'fallen out of favour among younger, more squeamish Britons,' with consumption falling by more than ninety percent.[21] Rather than consume bloody liver the UK government is currently advocating that everyone, not only prisoners, should take vitamin D supplements.[22]

With 1,400 breeding sows, pigs were so plentiful that by the mid-1970s the prison service was wholly self-sufficient in pork and bacon. Prison kitchens were traditionally run by prison officer kitchen managers supported by inmate catering assistants whilst the chefs were prison officers who had chosen to specialise in catering. Up to 2,300 inmates were employed in prison kitchens, each paid between £7–£34 per week depending on their responsibilities and hours, which cost the service £1.7 million in inmate wages.

Curing was undertaken through contracts with various bacon factories and the carcasses were butchered by staff and inmates trained to use knives. Inmates volunteered for kitchen duties and only those considered trustworthy and healthy were accepted: 'Kitchen knives in the hands of an unbalanced prisoner would be highly dangerous.'[23]

To ensure that there was an adequate quantity of produce for use in the prison, administrative staff recorded and managed the supply and delivery of food. When my dad's former farm clerk Sarah Croft started working in Hatfield borstal she was victualing, that is, ordering quantities of food for the kitchens.

'We used to have huge sheets of paper and we'd work out our average population for the week. They were allowed x amount of cheese or x amount of whatever every week. They get a budget now. Then it was quantities of food and we had a big store and the caterer would go to it and take what food they needed. The food for that store, some of it was supplied by Farms & Gardens.'

Between 1970 and the mid-1980s it was relatively easy for regional managers to work out how much food was required to serve the prison population. The amount of food was calculated using a dietary scale that listed what every prisoner was entitled to, for example, 12oz potatoes for adult male prisoners, 15oz for young offenders and 10oz 'if they were ladies,' explained Bernard. Each prisoner was allowed two eggs per week.

In November 1985 dietary scales were revised. Dripping was withdrawn, a move that 'significantly reduced the level of saturated fatty acids' in prisoners' diet and a monetary system was introduced that allocated a daily amount for food per prisoner. [24]

'Straightaway, when it was a cash basis, it was very difficult to work out the figures because each catering officer was going to order different stuff; their expectations went up,' said Bernard.

Initially, the monetary system required prison caterers to purchase staple goods such as milk, bacon, eggs and salad crops direct from the prison farms. All the prison farm produce had to be equivalent to the food the kitchen catering officers, whose budget in 1992 for feeding a grown man varied varied from 88 pence to £1.20 per day, could buy from outside suppliers.

Every month HMYOI Hatfield supplied the prison service with fifty tons of pork and bacon but the demand was such that at times my dad had to purchase extra pigs at livestock auctions. Sometimes he was accompanied by Steve Horrocks, the farm foreman.

'So we're at this pig auction and Bev said to me, "Go and get a couple of coffees." So, I'm walking back into where the ring is with these coffees and there's this girl standing in the ring with a basque on and a pair of knickers on and you know what hanging out. It was the auctioneers 60th birthday and I'm walking down the steps with two coffees but I was just so surprised that I fell down the step and threw the coffee all over myself. I got a bigger laugh than the girl did!'

Prior to moving to Hatfield to oversee its two farms: Misterton Carr, an arable farm situated about fifteen miles from Lindholme prison and Tudworth, a mixed farm close to Hatfield prison, my dad managed Tadnoll Mill Farm in Dorset. Situated in the middle of Hardy's Egdon Heath yet within view of an experimental nuclear facility poorly camouflaged by an abstract dragon mural, the farm was worked by prisoners who travelled 16 miles daily from The Verne on Portland. Tadnoll Mill Farm extended to 83 hectares (205 acres) and included a greenhouse unit that produced tomatoes and salad crops to meet the dietary needs of prisons in the Southwest Region but the main enterprises were a 95 cow dairy herd and a 60 sow Camborough hybrid pig-breeding unit that charmingly, according to the Farm Walk held there in 1979 produced "gifts" rather than gilts for commercial breeding within the Service.

Superficially, to the few who passed by, Tadnoll Mill Farm looked much like any other dairy farm with its concrete yard flanked by bitumen blackened sheds and an onsite farmhouse. But on closer inspection they might have noticed the yellow, tax-exempt, Home Office-issue Landrover, the 'Do not enter or get 90 days' sign above the calf shed door and an unusual number of brown-overall-clad farmhands. To minimise contact with the 'cons' I'd cross the yard to collect unpasteurised, 'top-of-the-milk' directly from the parlour before their day started but during the long, hot school holidays it was difficult to avoid catcalls, whistles and eyes that pried through the fir trees that barely separated our garden from the farmyard.

From Tadnoll my dad travelled to the Farm Management Conference held at Riseholme Agricultural College in Lincolnshire. There the catering manager noted that the financial value of produce supplied by the Farms & Gardens Group to the prison kitchens in 1986 amounted to nearly £5 million.[25]

After welcoming the guests and delegates Maurice told them that the past year had been a traumatic one for the Farms & Gardens but he anticipated that they'd be able to increase production to meet the needs of a rising prison population and this would be aided by supplying the prison dietary with cheese. However, the main theme of the conference was an internal report compiled by Chris Bolt of the Finance Accountancy and Procurement Unit that dealt with the *Economics of the Farms and Gardens Contribution to the Victualling System*. The 'Bolt Report' confirmed that the Farms & Gardens operated on a sound economic basis regarding supplies to the prison dietary but noted that supply could be increased by introducing cold storage facilities that could also act as distribution centres.

Following up this recommendation, Maurice duly created a national distribution network centred around five vegetable preparation units that strove to meet international standards in efficiency and quality-management (ISO 9002). The five 'veg prep' units as they were known were based at Kirkham, Hollesley Bay, Leyhill, Standford Hill and Lindholme prison in South Yorkshire. Each veg prep acted as a collection point for farm produce including eggs, meat, potatoes and vegetables.

'They brought in the cold chain distribution and set up the five veg preps and Lindholme was one of the five. It was then for the next ten years that we were really going for it. It was all being planned-out with cropping rotas and it was working really well, with the cartoning machines and that sort of stuff. If one veg prep was a bit low, say Leyhill was short of potatoes, we could send them some and they could send us brussel sprouts in return. It was good,' said Chris Coveney.

'Vegetables would be picked up from prison farms in one area and then distributed to other prisons en route to pick up other vegetables from farms on the other side of the country. The Farms & Gardens were not just growers, they were part of a distribution and processing network,' said Steve proudly.

'Whatever happened the caterers always had the food. And we managed it in-house, 365 days a year,' said Chris.

The dedication of farm staff was obvious to HQ staff like Rob Haslam who commended them for being prepared to go the extra mile to ensure that prison caterers received the food they required for the prison dietary.

'If for instance someone overlooked something or they forgot something then when we had a national distribution network they'd ring up and then they'd just chuck it on the lorry and they'd have it whereas now you ring 3663 who is the latter day counterpart and it'll certainly be at an additional cost because it's a late order.'

Both Chris and Jason recalled making special deliveries to supply prisons with produce at the weekend or during bad weather.

'It didn't matter about the weather. I mean I've done it before. We've loaded the Landrover up with milk and driven a delivery to the next prison because the lorry couldn't get through. But we got there,' said Chris.

'I delivered a machine from Standford Hill to the veg prep at Leyhill,' said Jason.

'When I got there they said they'd missed some mixed veg off the order for Usk. "Could you drop it over for us?"' Usk was 40 miles away to the west, over the Severn Bridge while Standford Hill was in the opposite direction on the east coast. 'I said, "I don't mind," and carried on. It was a bit of a journey but I did it.'

The veg preps graded, cleaned and chopped raw vegetables and arranged for them to be delivered alongside eggs, meat and other food items to the prison kitchens. Home-grown produce was stamped with a blue Farms & Gardens logo so that the service could be identified as the manufacturer. Prisons throughout the country received deliveries of quality farm produce three times a week via a host of private contractors.

With large cold storage facilities goods could be bought in bulk at favourable rates from outside suppliers, stockpiled and distributed as required. But Bryan noticed that buying in bulk at a national level didn't always fit well with local distribution networks.

'If you were going to buy twenty tons of Maris Piper potatoes it didn't matter which agent you got them from, you still got the same potatoes. And that gave us all sorts of problems. Head Office might have done a national tender for the five veg preps but the reality was that the vegetables were supplied at a regional level because the chap who was supplying potatoes in Lancaster wasn't going to go to Bristol but might be happy to do Doncaster. So sometimes Lindholme and Kirkham were tied in but Hollesley Bay, Stafford Hill and Leyhill would have no option.'

In 1992 prison farms reached a pinnacle of productivity with Her Majesty's prison service producing enough food to feed 47,000 inmates three times a day. The prison service became self-sufficient in bacon and pork as well as jam and salad crops. A staggering 12,000 tonnes of potatoes, 6,000 tonnes of cabbage and 3,000 tonnes of carrots were grown each year. 2,400 cows across 19 dairy units produced 11 million litres of milk which was enough to supply the whole service and sell a surplus 6.5 million litres to the Milk Marketing Board.

An example menu from HMP Gloucester dated 2nd April 1992 exemplified the field to plate philosophy. Breakfast consisted of porridge, toast, bacon, tea, bread, margarine. Dinner was a choice between curry, fried liver, fried fish, gammon, chicken and ham pie, vegetable stew and dumplings, all served with creamed potatoes, carrots, cabbage and gravy. For pudding inmates were offered jam tart with custard. In the afternoon, 'tea' was either Nasi Goreng (a Malaysian dish of mixed meats and rice), faggots, meat or vegetable quiche served with creamed potatoes and peas and followed by tea, bread and margarine. Supper was simply bread pudding and a cup of tea.[26]

Of this, the prison farms supplied meat in the form of bacon, gammon, liver, ham, chicken and offal for the faggots; vegetables (potatoes, carrots, cabbage, peas), eggs for the quiche and the Nasi Goreng, jam for the tart, milk for use in the custard and tea as well as bread for the pudding and oats for the porridge.

The ethos of self-sufficiency extended well beyond growing their own food for the prison dietary. The prison farms also manufactured and supplied essential commodities such as fencing poles, gates, greenhouses and polytunnels, the latter manufactured at Wymott in Lancashire. Wooden stables were made at Kirkham and at Lowdham Grange, a borstal situated a few miles northeast of Nottingham. Poles and rails for use within the prison estate were created from a small afforestation scheme that was introduced to improve a 68-acre wood. Stretching to 470 acres (190 hectares) Lowdham Grange also supplied the service with peas, carrots, onions, potatoes and cabbage, Aberdeen Angus beef, Essex pig meat and high fat content milk from a pedigree herd of Ayrshire cows until they were dispersed.

'We had all prison-made gates. Usk used to do the fencing posts. I had to buy them at the going rate,' confirmed Chris McGown. Usk's fence posts were made from larch harvested from its own forest. Farms & Gardens collaborated closely with the Forestry Commission to introduce a scheme that included a nursery for forest tree plants and the rehabilitation of a large area of scrub woodland. 'They didn't make barbed wire but the piggery was all made in the prison service, the fabricated roofs, the slabs, that type of thing, was all made in the prison service at Usk.'

On the whole staff were satisfied with the prison-made products but occasionally there were complaints, for example a delegate at the 1973 Farm Management Conference expressed concern about 'the price and quality of prison-made articles, particularly relating to seed trays, which were found to be too light, not to size and often badly made.'[27]

In 1996, prisons spent a quarter of their catering budget on purchases from the veg prep units, equivalent to 36 pence per prisoner per day.[28] The majority of prisons fully used this 'non-cash' value and some exceeded it but because this was a virtual market place in which no actual money changed hands the veg prep units didn't receive any usable revenue for any overspend or excess goods that they provided. This meant that they could find themselves incurring costs that couldn't be offset.

To help the Farms & Gardens' bottom-line the veg preps had been established as independent entities outside of individual institutions. This enabled money to be 'manipulated from the budget quicker and easier as they only had 5 contracts (one for each veg prep) rather than 125 contracts (one for each prison). There was one boss and five entities,' explained Bryan. But others thought that situating the veg prep units outside the walls was Farms & Gardens' biggest mistake. Firstly, it distanced catering staff and inmates employed in the kitchens from the process of vegetable and meat preparation and, importantly, it went against what the head of catering had requested at the Farm Management Conference in 1986, to take control of food preparation and install grading equipment in every prison kitchen.[29]

Caterers began to demand produce that was easier to deal with, for example, meat joints rather than whole carcasses. Catering officers lost interest in training inmates in butchery skills. Rather than using all parts of a carcass, they preferred to be supplied with joints or ready sliced meat, which had a negative effect on the economics of producing pigs for the service. 'You had to find a market for all the scrag ends,' said Bernard.

Sausages were an option as they could be made from non-jointed parts of the carcass but in the mid-1980s caterers wanted sausages to be produced for, 'a ridiculous price, 10 pence a pound,' said Bernard, to which Derek added, 'to have sawdust in 'em.' This, combined with the advent of cheap supermarket produce, led caterers to turn increasingly to supermarkets to supply their produce. Phil Wheatley empathised,

'Caterers wanted to buy things that were easier and cheaper to produce and things that didn't need lots of preparation. You actually built in costs of preparation.'

For caterers, it was simpler and easier to instruct inmates to fetch vegetables from the freezer, cut open a packet and follow the instructions than supervise the use of peelers and knives. Kitchens were cleaner with pre-prepared, pre-packaged, frozen vegetables, there was less decomposing fresh matter, less malodour, less clearing up required but the use of pre-prepared meals eroded essential food preparation skills.

Derek recalled a visit to HMP Cardiff when he'd visited the kitchen and found four inmates sitting on a bench taking the labels off yoghurts, 'the out-of-date stuff.' The catering officer had picked them up from one of the supermarkets, 'they were only a day out.'

'Caterers knew they could get food cheaper from the supermarkets but as everyone said, "You'll get it cheaper until you dismantle the distribution system and in four years' time, when the supermarkets renegotiate the contract, it'll be a lot more expensive." That's what happened. The caterers stabbed us in the back and got rid of the veg preps. But when they dismantled the distribution system the supermarkets renegotiated the contract and it became a lot more expensive,' said Chris Coveney.

In 1998 nine prisons decided to contract out catering services but within a couple of years five of these prisons realised that there were greater costs savings and an improved service with in-house rather than external catering. Contracted out services were more expensive partly because the external caterers didn't use prison labour. In 1999 following a review of procurement methods the prison service, in an attempt to promote consistency in quality standards and save money, reduced 43 national and numerous local purchasing supply contracts to a few central and regional contracts. In April 2003 the National Audit Office reported that using centrally let food contracts had produced cost savings in the region of £2.6 million.[30] In the main this was achieved by buying frozen rather than fresh produce and bringing in more civilian staff to work in the kitchens.

Nevertheless, these cost savings were dwarfed by the value of produce that Farms & Gardens provided to the dietary in 1996 when the value of their produce amounted to £9.7m. In 2003 prison caterers in public sector prisons were still spending the equivalent of £130 per year per prisoner on Farms & Gardens produce (principally vegetables). However, despite the vegetables being processed at four of the five distribution centres, the National Audit Office advised: 'The quality of food could be further improved by dispensing with Land Based Activities.' Twelve of sixteen catering managers interviewed reported that they were not satisfied with the quality of vegetables, that they were dirty or not fit for purpose, for example, some of the varieties of potatoes supplied were not suitable for chipping. They reported that they'd thrown away produce and in doing so incurred additional replacement costs.

Caterers interviewed by the National Audit Office requested a better range of vegetables and salads and for these to be available for more than six months per year, that is, out-of-season. Unfortunately, nobody from the Farms & Gardens or veg prep units were interviewed by the National Audit Office so the views of the producers were not represented. Farm staff I spoke to thought that the reason why caterers disposed of produce was less to do with quality and variety and more to do with a lack of motivation.

'We grew quite a few cabbages and French beans and that but I think the problem is that you grow it and you take it to the kitchen and they say, "I ain't bothered preparing that" and they throw it out,' shrugged John Glover.

As the prison population increased dramatically and land was requisitioned to build private prisons it became increasingly difficult to supply enough home-grown farm produce to feed the burgeoning inmate population.

'The only thing we were self-sufficient in in the end was milk and eggs,' said Bernard, 'but even eggs were a problem because chickens don't just lay one size of egg and the kitchens only wanted one size of egg. So we were selling large eggs and buying in medium eggs.'

He shook his head in disbelief.

'It all gets very,' he paused before saying, 'people start thinking you are on'

'The fiddle?' said Derek.

'Yeah,' said Bernard, 'it gets very difficult to write the contracts.'

Despite incurring additional replacement costs prison caterers managed to reduce costs and improve standards, however, they cautioned that government recommendations on healthy diets were still only being 'partially' met. Two years after the farms were disbanded a Food Standards Agency (FSA) study of prison service meals in eight establishments found that prison food was not following government guidelines on nutrition and healthy eating. Food in all the prisons was found to contain excessive levels of sodium, vegetables were usually tinned or frozen, and only one prison provided fresh produce, in this case, courgettes and aubergines.[31]

In 2006 as part of a cost-saving measure, the prison service in England and Wales moved away from serving prisoners with a hot breakfast or porridge, ubiquitous with 'doing time', and replaced it with a 'breakfast pack' (costed at 27 pence) and designed to be consumed in the inmate's cell. The cold breakfast pack contained cereal, two slices of bread, teabags, instant coffee, 10g of jam or marmalade, 10g of margarine and a small UHT carton of semi-skimmed milk. It was typically delivered to the inmate the night before and if an inmate consumed their pack in the evening then it could be 14 hours before they ate again.

In 2007 two companies were awarded four-year contracts for the supply of all food purchased for UK prisons: 3663 First for Foodservice and Premier Food. 3663 (the numbers in the name correspond to the letters 'FOOD' on a telephone number pad) was contracted to distribute frozen, fresh and chilled foods to the Ministry of Justice. There was a notable difference between the cold breakfast pack eaten alone in a cell and the hot breakfast typically served and consumed in a canteen in 1992 that consisted of porridge, toast, bacon, tea, bread and margarine. The Food Standards Agency found levels of sodium in the breakfast pack were more than six percent higher than recommended by the government.[32] Inmates and catering staff disliked the breakfast packs with their 'perceived frugal content and nutritional value.'[33]

For their main meal inmates were offered a variety of pre-prepared 'meals' suitable for non-meat and religious diets, for example: a spicy chicken with fruit meal, a fish pie meal, vegetable lasagne meal or an egg and tomato sandwich.[34] Only women's prison menus included chocolate chip muffins. But prisoners noticed the move away from own-grown produce towards pre-prepared meals and began to express their dissatisfaction. 'This is bought in isn't it? It's not fresh,' and the number of prisoners' complaints about the price of goods and the quality of food increased.[35]

In 2010 the standards that needed to be met to be awarded a prison food supply contract included: 'compliance with Prison Service technical specifications and quality standards... Thereafter the deciding factor in the award of the contract is price.'[36] At HMYOI Northallerton in North Yorkshire central contracts were found to be inefficient and costly but nevertheless defended by government ministers who insisted that the contract with 3663 met all the required legal, quality and service standards for providing food to the prison dietary and reiterated that food had a crucial role to play in enabling the smooth operation of the prison.[37]

In February 2013 the FSA considered taking legal action against the Ministry of Justice when meat pies and pasties supplied to prisons in England and Wales were labelled and served as halal but they contained traces of pork DNA.[38] The Ministry of Justice suspended 3663 from supplying meat to prisons after it was traced to one of their suppliers based in Northern Ireland.

Recently, it has been the Prison Service Food Buyers and Catering Service Team who has been responsible for visiting the farmers and growers who supply food to prisons. Their aim is to improve standards and identify where efficiencies can be improved upon as supplying food to prisons is a lucrative business. In the year ending March 2012 the average daily cost for food (including beverages) per prisoner in public sector prisons in England and Wales was £2.26 and the total cost spent on food was more than £62 million.[39] In October 2012, the prison service signed a new food contract with the aim of reducing the cost of prison food and the overall cost of imprisonment. 'The actual average national daily meal cost across all public sector prisons (including young offender institutions and Immigration Referral Centres) for fiscal year ending March 2013 was £2.20. Based on the new food contract agreed in October 2012 which is set to achieve significant food spend savings of 11% over the term of the contract, NOMS has been able to reduce food budgets in prisons to £1.96 per prisoner per day for 2013–14.'[40]

Whilst external suppliers seem to be cost effective, the reduction in food budgets masks the additional value that home-grown produce provides to the prison service, not only in terms of training, rehabilitation, education and therapeutic contribution, but also in terms of self-sufficiency and sustainability in the form of low food miles, low carbon emissions and importantly, full traceability from 'farm to plate'. For an institution that has security at its very heart, growing and supplying their own produce is a way to enhance the reliability of supply, ensure full traceability and increase food security.

Ten years ago, seasonal, locally-grown food was seen as a way to not only provide essential nutritional qualities but, through encouraging inmates to participate in the production and preparation of food, address poor food habits. For example, food being used as a form of currency, a way of bullying, a type of bonus or a means of asserting independence.[41] Big Rob said, 'What we were putting in place was very much better and whilst the catering managers as they are now known, Cooks & Bakers as was, were forever saying we can do better than this and go down the road and get it from someone else. Having achieved that aim, I suspect that given the opportunity they'd turn it on its head and for the farms to still be supplying them now.' When Jason Errington looked set to fill the Head of Land Based Activities position recently vacated by Big Rob to my surprise he said, somewhat cautiously, 'There's a will from the caterers to have us back.'

6

Animals don't ask anything of you

'He moved among the animals, touching one here and there, went to the top of the slope and sat, walked across to the far side, and sat again. One or two of the sheep ambled nearer so that he could feel the warmth of their breath on the air around him.' Susan Hill, *Black Sheep*[1]

Growing enough food to sustain around 50,000 prisoners was not the Farms & Gardens only objective; as department policy in the early 1970s stated: 'the justification for commercial farming and horticultural activities within the Prison Service lies with the contribution it can make towards the wellbeing and rehabilitation of the inmates.'[2]

In contrast to industrial work, land-based activities were lauded because they were based outside the confines of the prison, they were arduous, they required and developed practical and basic skills and their very nature imposed similar conditions and disciplines on both staff and inmates alike. Participation in rural activities was seen as a transformative antidote for urban ills: 'Farms and Gardens had a settled place in many regimes. Most inmates were from towns and work on farms presented a complete change to them, which was both therapeutic and instructional.'[3]

'None of them had a farming background at all. All city people,' said former cowman John Glover, 'some *loved* working down here on the pigs and on the cattle and different things.'

Amy Cullen typified the self-confessed rural convert. With no previous agricultural experience she started working on the farm at East Sutton Park part-way through a two year sentence for fraud. I met Amy when she was released on temporary license (ROTL) to accompany Lorraine and I on a trip to the local abattoir with rare breed Saddleback pigs.

'I have always been an animal lover but, other than a brief stint of horse riding when I became pony-mad around the age of 12 or so, I have never been anywhere near a working farm. I am an accountant by trade and have spent the past 20 years working in an office, cosily tucked up behind my computer, so this really was like entering a completely different world and I absolutely love it.'

With little prior experience of agriculture or horticulture it was not surprising that some inmates made the odd mistake. Steve Horrocks recalled an episode when inmates were asked to plant out annual bedding plants.

'I was walking round with John the gardener and this lad had planted French marigolds upside down. He'd put the flower head in the soil. John had gone, "Bloody idiot," and I'd said, "Wait a minute, maybe he genuinely doesn't know, he's a 14-year-old kid from the city centre who probably hasn't seen a plant before. He isn't clever enough to take the piss." It was genuine. He simply didn't know how to plant a flower.'

Whilst it was inconvenient to lose the odd bedding plant, it was paramount to ensure that staff and inmates maintained standards of animal welfare.

'Bedding up the calves with straw was always a popular job. I'd say to the lads, "If you won't lie down there then don't expect a calf to."' Then Steve added,

'One lad who'd got out of prison came back because he said he just wanted to be with the calves.'

'The fact that the animals are small and dependent mattered,' said former member of the support staff Christine Wakely, 'You see inmates with little pigs and they just melt.'

'If they thought that the animals were not being looked after they'd give them extra straw and extra food if they could,' said Maurice. 'And if they thought you were being "cruel" in that sort of way then they'd stitch you up because they started to like the animals, they were *their* charges, *their* responsibility. In some cases, in the worst scenario, they'd overfeed them. They'd nick the food to give to them and then the animals would get ill and the inmates wouldn't appreciate that.'

'Being a dairyman and a farmer's son you learn very young that there are *hatches, matches and dispatches*,' said Christine's husband Bryan.

'I learnt very quickly that it hurts just as much when an animal dies as when one of your relations die but you always have happy

The inscription on the reverse of this photograph taken at Eastchurch (Standford Hill) prison in March 1970 read: 'Rearing chicks – these fortnight old chicks are looked after by an inmate.'[4]

memories. If your prize cow got mastitis and you've got the vet out and you've done all you can, you've dosed her up and now she dies and is hauled up the knacker's wagon, as a man you're trying to hold back those tears.'

'The only time I saw my dad cry was when his dog Spot died.' I said, 'He probably let her go on a bit too long. But growing up with animals, you get more used to death.'

'So what I'm trying to say is when a family friend or family pass away there's a vacuum and I fill that vacuum with all good memories,' said Bryan.

He paused, we were both thinking about my dad. 'It's always there. Market day it's there. Crude way of putting it.'

At the Farm Management Conference in 1977 Mr Nash, Governor of Wymott prison summed up the benefits of land-based work, 'It not only taught about living things, but about life itself, and in so doing broadened horizons, extended capabilities, increased self-respect and gave pleasure and sustenance to many.'[5]

Farm managers the following year went so far as to conclude that: 'Commercial farming could be abandoned and a policy of therapeutic farming adopted'[6] but nobody at that time called it 'care farming'. By 2003 it was reported that more than one hundred care farming or therapeutic gardening projects were located in UK prisons or secure psychiatric units,[7] and this was acknowledged to be an underestimate as only a third of prisons completed the survey.[8]

A recent Annual Independent Monitoring Board Report on East Sutton Park found 'The therapeutic effect of working in the gardens or on the farm clearly benefits the women in a number of ways. Self-esteem and self confidence are gained as the women work in the fresh air with plants, animals and staff gaining transferable skills. Women eligible for ROTL are able to work at the farmers markets that are held regularly in surrounding villages. By working with members of the public, whilst in a safe atmosphere, the women gain the confidence that will help them to re integrate when they are released.'[9]

Few within Farms & Gardens would be surprised that research, conducted since the demise of the majority of prison farms, has found that people benefit from the relationship they have with the people who look after the livestock as much as the animals themselves. 'Farm staff had the opportunity to work alongside inmates, sharing common tasks and thereby creating chances to develop mutual self-confidence. No-one could be certain what made a man go straight on leaving prison, but it was felt that there was a good chance that this was the result of his gaining a better understanding of himself, which could have been helped by the guidance and assistance given by a member of staff.'[10]

John Glover was one who liked to work alongside rather than preside over inmates,

'In the vegetable preparation area all day long you just stood with a peeler with the inmates taking eyes out and peeling the green off. I do like to do a little bit to show willing and how I want it done. I've said to them, "I wouldn't ask you to do something", and they've said, "Well this is bloody hard work" and I've said, "Well I wouldn't ask you to do something that I wouldn't do myself."'

I asked John if he'd been commended for his work with inmates. 'I think it will be lost now but I actually had a letter from an inmate thanking me. Yeah, 'cos your dad put it in my records. But you know over the years it will be lost.'

'What did it say?'

'He thanked me for looking after him whilst he was down there. He was one of the showing ones.'

One of the ways in which outstanding practice amongst those working with offenders has been recognised and celebrated is through the annual Butler Trust Award. David Carr, an agricultural craftsman at Lowdham Grange was an early recipient of the award in 1986.

'His love of and respect for land and animals does not make David Carr a "country hick", by any stretch of the imagination. It is, perhaps, his unusual ability to slip easily from a baffling explanation of the complex technology employed in his dairy to a universal and timeless appreciation of the natural order of life which makes him a kindly yet firm, gentle yet intelligent character. He possesses a talent which can't be learned from textbooks, and which some would never gain in a million years: a natural feel for the right way of going about things. His eyes and ears are attuned to the subtle warning signs of things that could go wrong – and perhaps they're not so different in animals or young lads ... to many observers he's very different to the traditional figure of authority... He expects hard and willing work from the lads. But he's also fair – something young lads respect and appreciate. The authority is there – he's a big man, and while he might find it easy to smile, he doesn't mince his words when it comes to giving a ticking-off. You get the feeling that while he might tolerate fools, the one thing he will not tolerate is deliberate laziness or behaviour which could harm his beloved animals... Watching the lads at work with him, one can see straight away that they look up to and respect him, and yet can enjoy the odd joke. There was a hard-working yet light-hearted atmosphere among them. No-one looked resentful or bored.'[11] His award noted that most young offenders were hostile to authority and to older people but David received more thank you letters and cards than any other member of staff.

'Sometimes,' David Carr was quoted as saying, 'the lads will come and help in my garden at weekends (his house adjoined the farm) and we'll have a cup of coffee.'

'We get letters from people after they have left saying that they are doing well and to me that speaks volumes,' said Lorraine, 'I love working with the animals too but it just speaks volumes when people manage to turn their lives around. Even if it's just a few. Even the people who maybe do go back to a life of crime, for a time they've felt better.'

In 2016, the Butler Trust Award was given to Bob Leckie, Land Based Activities Manager at HMYOI Thorn Cross, a Category D male prison in Cheshire. Bob was given the award for having taken 'traditional expectations of his work and transformed them in ways that have brought significant benefits to staff and prisoners alike.' His lead nominator, Michael Polyall, the deputy governor at Thorn Cross, stated, 'Bob lives and breathes his vocation. His extreme passion and love of his work is shared with whomever shows an interest.'[12]

Bob was commended for enhancing the reputation of the prison in the local community, raising prisoners' self-esteem and using his land based knowledge and practices to revolutionise the teaching of essential functional skills like numeracy and literacy. 'Football pitches became his stage. The penny dropped with many prisoners who now understand previously boring mathematics such as diameters, radius, right angles and parallel lines... Flower pots, water butts and compost heaps were used to understand weights and measures. Bob's resilience, selflessness and diligence came to the fore and he has inspired many prisoners to gain qualifications in Horticulture that they never thought possible.'[13]

'I've always maintained that whatever we did on the Farms & Gardens there was always something that the inmates got out of it, even simple arithmetic and that,' said Maurice.

However, the central importance and long history of rehabilitation, education and training within Farms & Gardens seems to have been forgotten. Pia Sinha, the governor at Thorn Cross since 2014 stated that Bob's approach 'has never been used within horticultural departments in the service. When Governors of other open prisons heard about this, they were very keen to introduce similar schemes in their prisons.'[14]

One reason for the forgetting may be that despite encouragement from Maurice to publicise their achievements, Farms & Gardens staff were modest and their contribution could be easily overlooked. At the 1991

Farm Management Conference, the director of Prison Service Industries & Farms (PSIF) Joan MacNaughton said 'their strengths were great, but hidden, and that staff did not receive sufficient recognition. She felt that Farms staff were in the "people business" but that other departments did not always recognise this.'[15]

In the mid-1990s, the *Pollett Review* of prison service agricultural and horticultural activities concluded: 'The values exemplified by agricultural and horticultural staff wherever they may be stationed, are very closely aligned to those set out for the Service as a whole. To be able to display this approach to inmates, through examples set by plain dealing people, provides the very best opportunity to engender these valuable attributes in their charges.'[16]

Land based activities were regarded as particularly suitable for certain types of inmates, notably those deemed wanting in some way.

'Prisoners constitute a broad cross section of the community amongst whom are individuals such as youths who have proved to be difficult, uncooperative or emotionally disturbed, men who have found themselves to be out of phase with the pace of modern life and those who in many ways are inadequate. Opinion is that work on the land helps to change the outlook and attitudes of such persons with character defects or emotional problems' with care of livestock 'considered to have special merit in character training.'[17,18]

It wasn't unusual for 'difficult' prisoners to be given to the farm manager to deal with.

'All the good boys, all the sensible ones, the ones who had any brain cells went into the workshops and all the "nutters", we had them,' observed Bryan wryly.

There was an understanding at the level of the institution and beyond, that farm managers possessed the skills to manage these difficult prisoners.

'When the board discussed a lad they'd say, "We know where he should be, he should be on the farm" and education would come second to that. Once he got stabilised then he could go into the classroom and that was the way that the prisoners' rehabilitation programme was mapped out. When I was the farm manager at Usk,' said Maurice, 'we used to have some right little tearaways and the governor used to say to me, "Take him even if it's only for a month." I had a worker called Jack Bevan, he is dead now bless him but he could deal with those sort of people. He was a "Dutch uncle" to them. He was harsh and fair. The kids got to know that and they'd trust him. And once they were stabilised then the governor would take the lad off and he'd go onto education or whatever was needed.'

The wider prison community benefited from the calming effect of farm work on the most difficult inmates. 'Farms occupied inmates who would otherwise be locked up, they became more mellow and therefore less aggressive and were probably accountable for easing tension in some prisons.'[19]

Looking after animals helped develop a whole range of social and life skills such as patience and planning. Many of the daily activities associated with caring for an animal, such as grooming, enhanced dexterity, whilst effective verbal and non-verbal communication skills were required to move or reassure the animals.

Maurice thought, 'If prisoners can relate to animals and control them then they can see and learn about how you are treating them. You have to treat animals almost like humans and some humans you have to treat like animals.'

In 2001 at HMP Prescoed near Usk, South Wales, two prisoners were granted early release after saving the life of the farm manager, Roger Murray, after he was hurled into the air and gored by a giant, 32-stone Royal Berkshire boar. 'Mark Collerton, 32 and Andrew Good, 33 who were serving unrelated sentences for wounding and theft respectively, dragged Roger clear of the boar, squeezed his Wellington boot against the wound and lifted his leg in the air to prevent further blood loss. They then radioed for help, paramedics were called and the farm manager was taken to hospital... Roger returned to work nine months later. He has since left the Service. The boar was later destroyed. As a reward for their courage and quick thinking, Good and Collerton were granted their freedom 28 days early under a Royal Prerogative of Mercy by the then Home Secretary Jack Straw.'[20]

At any one time about a third of prisons have animals or caged birds on-site (fish are rarely kept because of concerns about drugs being hidden in the tanks).[21] I found an account of an inmate in Scotland, who'd experienced years of solitary confinement and adopted an orphaned kitten humorously named 'Cat A' after the type of prison said, 'The cat has brought me through some very difficult times. If you have lost that concern for other people and you get a pet to care for, I think that's where caring begins in a place like this.'[22]

In his review of a biodiversity scheme at Foston Hall, a female prison in Derby, former farm manager Dr Phil Thomas wrote: 'It was amazing to see prisoners who had often themselves been abused... adopting these parrots and other small animals and birds, taking care of them and looking after them. And you could see what they were learning was what we all need to learn – when you invest time and care and effort into another being that being flourishes and you get back a great deal for all the effort you've put in. That's enormously important in these people's lives, because they've often had chaotic backgrounds and have missed out on learning about the importance of caring and of making connections, which is partly why they've got into the problems they've got into. So this is a fundamental lesson to teach, and it's one animal projects do incredibly well.'[23]

As animals require regular and frequent attention, sometimes at unsocial hours, attending to them was seen as way to motivate action and instill a sense of routine and responsibility in inmates. 'Looking after livestock has a good effect, especially at borstals. You're giving a fellow responsibility for living creatures, perhaps the first real responsibility in his life.'[24]

On the reverse of an early photograph of the farmyard at Dartmoor prison in Devon the inscription read: 'The bull in this picture is a dangerous customer, and respects nobody but the prisoner beside him.'[25]

'Pigs are cute and cuddly, cows are big and ugly and they can hurt you,' said Bryan. 'If you don't treat them with any sort of respect you are going to get hurt and if you don't do the right things to the animal, if you don't feed and water them, you see the response straight away. And it could be the first time that a prisoner had come across something bigger and uglier than what he is. The biggest, ugliest prisoners you can think of were the biggest cry babies with animals, not with anyone else, just amazing.'

But livestock, just like prison inmates, require care every day of the week, sometimes 24-hours a day and this inevitably impacts on staff. In 1978 it was recognised that 'unnecessary strain' could be placed on the institution and the local community by cattle straying or causing damage to local property especially if it occurred at night as staff would have to be called in to round them up.[26] Twenty years later the 365-days a year operation of farms and the requirement for early morning starts was seen to 'place a considerable burden on the establishment regime' as staff were required to oversee the milking of the cows and feeding of the animals at unsocial hours and caterers had to provide snacks for the 'early milkers'.[27]

The needs of livestock, however, were not always fully appreciated by those in charge of staffing as Lorraine found, 'At one point they said farm staff could work Monday to Friday, that they didn't need to work weekends! What about the stock? That's difficult.'

An independent monitoring board report on Blantyre House, when it was a female prison in 2011, stated: 'The farm manager, Chris Coveney, is now responsible for both East Sutton Park and Blantyre House. Prisoners report that working with the animals has proved challenging in practical terms but that it has been very rewarding in their responsibility.'[28] Practical challenges included dealing with the smell and effluent produced by the animals.[29]

'Interestingly, women who have been the victims of physical abuse find the tactile nature of the work has a calming therapeutic effect.'[30]

'Prisoners, especially female prisoners, get to love and cherish the animals and make fantastic stock people,' agreed former farm manager Pete Chisholm.

Recalling her experience at East Sutton Park Amy wrote: 'When we say it is the farm, there is a lot that makes it what it is. As everybody knows there is undeniably a therapeutic benefit to working with animals. For many of us, we are mothers and care givers and one of the things that is the most difficult to come to terms with when being in prison is the separation from your children and loved ones. Being in a position where we actually have something to care for, whether it is a pig, lamb, horse, whatever it may be and seeing that creature thrive can be one of the most satisfying and fulfilling feelings that we can get.'[31]

Some have suggested that inmates find it easier to confide in and bond with an animal rather than another person because status, social skills or material possessions are simply not important for animals.[32] Everyone, not just inmates, can describe experiences or feelings to animals without confrontation, judgement or fear of retribution. Christine remembered a similar experience to my own at Sunnyside.

'We used to have the cows at the end of the garden and I'd put my arms round them and tell them all my secrets – having a quiet moment. They just let you touch them and talk to them.'

Lorraine summed up the therapeutic benefit of working with farm animals, 'I see people turn their lives around. People who haven't had much hope, felt any self-worth suddenly get a little bit more of a spark about them. We have so many people with depression of different types and they've been ground down, told they are useless and they're no good and suddenly they can start to feel better about themselves. Animals don't ask anything of you. The whole persona improves.'

A recent Annual Independent Monitoring Board Report on East Sutton Park stated: 'The therapeutic effect of working in the gardens or on the farm clearly benefits the women in a number of ways. Self-esteem and self-confidence are gained as the women work in the fresh air with plants, animals and staff gaining transferable skills. Women eligible for ROTL are able to work at the farmers markets that are held regularly in surrounding villages. By working with members of the public, whilst in a safe atmosphere, the women gain the confidence that will help them to reintegrate when they are released... The therapeutic value of working with animals is beyond price, particularly for women who come from violent and abusive backgrounds.'[33]

Amy meanwhile was sanguine about the fate of the Saddleback pigs, 'The pigs and lambs are reared for the meat industry, but knowing that they have been raised and cared for with love and with their best interests at heart, even though they are destined for the abattoir eventually, makes it all feel so worthwhile.'

At Lorraine's bidding Amy entered the abattoir's on-site office and submitted the animal passports and necessary forms while Lorraine and I chatted outside. She emerged smiling; they'd asked her to sign the forms. What seemed to me like a simple administrative task was for Amy an acknowledgement of responsibility, rehabilitation and a sign of transitioning to a life outside the walls. As Amy and Lorraine steered the pigs inside using plywood boards Lorraine mentioned that some inmates, particularly lifers, think it's so evident to outsiders that they've served time, that like the pigs, they might as well wear ear tags or be branded with tattoos.

For inmates with limited knowledge or experience of farming and sentimental rather than practical sensitivities, realising the true destiny of the animals that they cared for could be devastating. When Steve Horrocks was a Cluster Head Manager he used to make monthly visits to the prisons within his area which included HMP Drake Hall, a closed woman's prison, near Eccleshall in Staffordshire.

'Miss Montieff was the Governor at the time. At Drake Hall they kept Manx Loaghtan sheep, they have beautiful horns. The sheep were being looked after by the gardener and had been interbreeding as they'd never sold any. I said they should keep half a dozen females and get another ram in for a new bloodline. Well, I get home at 6 o'clock and the phone rings. It was Werrington, my boss, saying Miss Montieff was screaming at him. The prisoners at Drake Hall had barracked themselves into the dining hall and they were refusing to come out because they'd heard that the lambs were going to market. The women were more animal lovers than the lads and they'd looked after the lambs and petted them. It looked like they were going to take the roof off! The governor didn't want a riot so I was called back immediately to assure the inmates that they wouldn't be sent to market. Riot averted. But come next spring I went back to Drake Hall and told the inmates that the sheep needed to be moved to new pastures. They didn't object to them being transferred to another prison farm. But from there they were swiftly sent to market!'

Evidence indeed that prison farm management required empathy, understanding, strategy and tact!

Spending time outside in natural environments rich in wildlife is considered particularly beneficial for wellbeing.[34] According to Maurice's predecessor, Peter Stevens, inmates felt that by looking after animals or plants they were 'doing' rather than 'wasting' time.

'Their day lasts from 8.30 am till 5 pm (earlier when it gets dark and later in the summer) and there is a break for lunch midday in a hut with a rudimentary stove in it. One of the prisoners stays in the hut to cook the food for the others. Working in the open, away from the claustrophobic atmosphere of the 150-year old prison one of the most cramped in the country – means a great deal to the prisoners... 'most of us would willingly work on Sunday as well if we could.'[35]

But time outside could be challenging. With prisoners allocated only one clean shirt per week, 'this week's best shirt was next week's working shirt,' explained Derek. 'If inmates were outside working on the pig unit imagine going back into the wing with all the rest of the inmates smelling of pigs!'

'Whatever the weather, they had to work. Sometimes you had to give them jobs that weren't really suitable just to occupy them. And there was no way they'd be allowed to be inside just because it was raining,' said Bernard.

However, the conditions imposed by nature applied to both staff and inmates alike.[36] When I spoke with John Glover he said, 'We used to have to go out and cut the cabbages and it was always in the winter when it was cold and frosty and you'd have inmates out and they'd be, "I ain't doin' this." The cabbages were put into half ton boxes. If they refused you'd make them stand in there all day. Just standing there. They'd soon get sick of it. It was colder standing in there than it was doing something.'

'Although those working in the prison denied it they always treated the gardens party as the punishment party. If there was somebody who was really awkward who was a pain for the officers then they would stick him on farms or gardens because it was *out there*,' claimed Chris Coveney whilst Maurice vehemently denied that time served outside was ever a form of punishment.

In fact, many inmates relished the opportunity of being part of a Farms & Gardens working party although there was one criminal that Maurice wouldn't ever let on the farm.

'No matter what, *no arsonists*. We were lucky. We had a fire at Gaynes Hall once in the barn opposite the farm manager's office. What they did was they got an old cigarette tin, put a candle in it and left it in a bale of straw. It took a long time, about three hours according to the fire brigade, for it to get hot enough to ignite the straw, so it happened at 10 o'clock at night when there was nobody about. They never found out who did it.'

And there were other notable acts of rebellion such as one recounted by Steve whilst he was based at Kirkham.

'The "lads" had planted daffodils in the grass near the entrance of the prison. Spring came and all of a sudden the daffodils came out in flower. The governor looked out of his window and he's fuming, he's going ballistic, because in daffodils, right across the front entrance of the prison it said "Fuck Off" in giant letters! Of course they'd been planted nine months ago. All of sudden they all came out and you could read it. That was something else!'

'My argument with the governors was always, one day they are in prison, the next day you turf them out on the street, so better to let them out on the farms before you let them out on the street. It took a lot of convincing, to help them to de-institutionalise, to make that transition,' said Maurice, who from1985 onwards made seventeen trips to the United States to learn about how they operated their prison farms. He felt that they, rightly, placed more emphasis on rehabilitation than punishment.

'I went to a top security prison in California where they used to get these inmates out of prison at 6am and they'd stay out till night. The staff lived on the farm, slaughtered and butchered their own animals and delivered the meat to the penitentiaries but they didn't use civilians they used prisoners to drive the lorries. The ones who worked in the abattoir were paid the going rate and when I mentioned it over here there was a *horrific* response, *prisoners killing animals!* But they were qualified, they went through all the training and then they went out and got jobs. I did a paper on it and the Prisons Board said, "Thank you, thank you," and put it in the bin. When I came back I spoke to the Home Secretary and he had a *fit*. They just didn't have the courage to do it in the UK, in case something went wrong. Michael Howard said it was more than his job was worth.'

For policy makers who, like the majority of inmates hailed from urban areas, clean, regular office work might seem more palatable than dirty field work but it overlooked how important 'traditional masculine' employment was, especially for working-class men, as a way to express their identity.[37]

'The prisoners who used to go out and work on the farms they were very *proud* of it. The prisoners who were more likely to move on and learn were those who were actually doing what they classed as "manual work", on the works department, on the gardens department. They felt they were doing "manly" work. Prisoners used to come in from the farm and they used to be covered in mud and you'd say, "You've had a right day," and they'd say, "It's been a good day today boss, a good day." They felt like they were *doing* something,' said Steve. Being tired and muddy contributed to what some commenters have described as a healthy form of masculine pride.[38]

'Manly' aggressive behaviours were less commonplace but when they did occur staff found a range of ways to address them.

'I fought with a prisoner me,' admitted one of the interviewees, 'We just smacked each other. I was on my own in the piggery. I learnt my lesson.'

From time to time, Chris McGown witnessed aggressive behaviour.

'I used to have eight inmates out in the morning and this time they were all Hell's Angels,' he laughed. 'And one of the farm managers nearly got killed with those Hell's Angels. Every day I went out with a little Ford 3000 tractor to move the milking bale. I picked the milking bale up with the tractor and then all these Hell's Angels had to push it, sometimes they had to push it up hills. Every day the prisoners had to move the milking bale to a new patch but of course there are only so many times that you can move round and on this day we'd had very wet weather and one of the managers accused me of not moving the milking bale. He came out to the field with a rolled-up newspaper in his hand that he used to threaten you with. He used to shake it at ya and poke it at ya to make his point. He said, "You've never moved this milking bale for a week" and of course the Hell's Angels were all there and the second-in-command was as wild as you can get. He picked up a bloody shovel and was waving it about in the bloody air. I said, "Quit that." He might have finished that manager off. Well he's dead now but he never knew how close he was. They were already in for murder.'

Land based work requires persistence, resilience, reliability, responsibility, respect and team working. Whilst Farms & Gardens work was typically labour intensive and well-suited to physically strong inmates, less physical administrative roles were also available.

'Leyhill was very good for gardening,' said Phil. 'There was an arboretum. People in those days had quite a set-up. I remember if you rang up the Farms and Gardens you got, "Hanruker here." It was a very posh place! He was in for fraud, surprise surprise. He'd been in the paid corps of the army but he behaved as if he was one of the guards!'

Fifty years after Maurice decided to join the prison service because the national health service farms were being disbanded, land based activities are being prescribed by health professionals as a cost-effective treatment for mental ill-health.[39] A longitudinal study in the late 1990s into the impact of horticultural therapy on inmates in the USA, most of whom were serving sentences for drug or drug-related offences, found a greater reduction in the number of substances abused, less depression and a sustained desire to seek help amongst inmates undertaking gardening compared to a non-gardening therapy group.[40] Gardening relieves boredom, provides physical exercise and reduces sleep problems such as insomnia.[41] As such it suits inmates with less interest in vigorous exercise. Given that the proportion of older inmates is rising and rates of illness in elderly male prisoners are higher than in the general population, light exercise initiatives like gardening are accessible, meaningful and cost-effective.[42] For every one pound invested in nature-based therapy the social return on investment is £6.75.[43] However, a National Audit Office report in 2006 on prisoner diet and exercise showed little support for Land Based Activities to supply vegetables for the prison dietary and failed to recognise gardening as exercise.[44] This seems like an oversight.

When I'd visited Howard and Isobel at their bungalow on the outskirts of Crediton in Devon I'd noticed a 'top dog' rosette in a rose bowl on the sideboard. On the wall above was a painting of their pet collie which Isobel described as a 'therapeutic dog'. Isobel regularly took the dog to visit patients in the local hospital and the portrait was painted by a talented hospital cleaner.

Research has shown that having animals in prisons reduces feelings of isolation and frustration,[45] violence, levels of medication, suicide attempts and the rate of recidivism[46] yet, until very recently, there have been few programmes in the UK. One initiative at Garth Prison in Lancashire encouraged inmates to breed budgies and give them to older residents in the local community but it ended in 2001 with the arrival of a new governor who subscribed to the 'get tough' regime established by the former Conservative Home Secretary Michael Howard. Ten years later a dog training programme, modelled on an American scheme called Paws for Progress was introduced to YOI Palmont near Falkirk. By September 2013 forty-eight young male offenders had trained abandoned dogs so that they could be rehomed. Groups made up of new students and former participants who acted as peer mentors spent eight weeks on a mix of practical training sessions with the rescue dogs and classroom based sessions covering dog training theory and animal care. Those that wanted to could gain academic qualifications through the local college. Of eighteen participants who returned to the community, ten found jobs, one joined a training scheme, another enrolled at college, four were seeking work and two secured work experience placements.

In 2010, the 'Horse Course', a form of equine-assisted therapy was piloted at HMP/YOI Portland. Twenty-five prisoners participated in the scheme which was evaluated by Professor Rosie Meek of Royal Holloway, University of London. Twelve months post-release the re-offending rate for those who had taken part in the Horse Course was 36%, considerably lower than the typical re-offending rate for young adult men (58%) or the predicted rate for this particular cohort (63%). Attendance on the course cost £750 per inmate. As it costs the Ministry of Justice £47,137 per annum to incarcerate a young offender under the age of twenty-one, if only one out of every sixty Horse Course participants didn't re-offend it could be considered cost-effective. When I talked to Bernard about the Horse Course he said,

'That's the same as nursing homes and petting farms. Yes, you can give a big horse to someone whose been a rogue and they've something to depend on them but you will never see the likes of Farms & Gardens again.'

In October 2015 a BBC *Panorama* programme followed the Justice Secretary at the time, Michael Gove, on a visit to a pet project in the USA called Patriot Paws. Inmates were allowed to share their cell with the dog that they were training to help wounded veterans. A female inmate reported how participation in the Patriot Paws project kept her busy and gave her a sense of responsibility whilst also allowing her to give back to society. She also appreciated the unconditional positive regard afforded by the dog. Over a two-year period the rate of recidivism was three percent, significantly less than the comparable fifty percent rate in England and Wales.[47] However, no dog training projects have been established within prisons in England and Wales. Apparently the dog section has refused to have other dogs on site; they regard it as a health and safety issue.

'It was killed by security!' quipped Chris Coveney.

For many inmates, including Amy, the positive impact that Farms & Gardens made on their personal development and well-being was down to the staff she encountered.

'The farm is managed on a daily basis by two managers who share shifts and is then overseen by a further individual whose remit includes gardens, meats/butchery and various other aspects too. Our two hands-on managers are amazing. Totally different to each other in almost every way, affectionately known as Mrs C and Mr B. Despite their different approaches to daily tasks, they do have a number of things in common – they both care, not just about the animals and their work, but I do genuinely believe that they really care about us too, *The Farm Girls*. They make us feel that they rely on us, they trust us and they appreciate what we do and the feeling of self-worth that results from this is something very unique in a prison environment and it is this that I fear will never truly be appreciated by anyone not directly involved in the farm. In a place where we are regularly expected to shut up and do what we are told, on the farm not only do we get to have an opinion, we also get to express it and have someone really listen to it. We are trusted to administer medication to the animals, we are trusted to work with and handle heavy machinery, we are given an opportunity to study and learn about what we are doing and why we do it. What we get from working on the farm can't be measured by stats, can't be judged by financial viability, can't be monitored through Boards and Reviews, because what it gives us is a sense of being.'[48]

In 2016 I learnt that in recognition of her outstanding commitment and exceptional rehabilitative impact on prisoners,

Lorraine became the first civilian *ever* to be nominated for a regional Prison Officer award.

'We all face restrictions, frustrations, segregation and hardships,' wrote Amy, 'but the *Farm Girls* are able to cope because they've been allowed to discover who they are: passionate, hardworking, empathic, organised, reliable, trustworthy people who care about the animals they look after and the staff who care about them. They can work towards formal qualifications but the real gains are in experiencing compassion and trust. Each in their own way both Mrs C and Mr B have touched my heart and lifted me up and I have never had so must trust instilled, as I have from Mrs C, and that will stay with me forever. East Sutton Park Farm has changed my life for the better forever.'[49]

Nevertheless, despite official reports, anecdotal and growing research evidence about the therapeutic benefit of land based activities, 'They didn't really understand what we were doing and what it was about – the value of what we were doing as in life skills, soft skills whatever you want to call it, it was just not recognised,' lamented Lorraine's husband Chris, 'So they dismantled it all.'

7

A rare breed

'The lost cannot be recovered; but let us save what remains.'
Thomas Jefferson, *Letter to Ebenezer Hazard*[1]

Many rare breed livestock owe their ongoing existence to the prison service in England and Wales, including the stocky, mild-mannered, 'chesnut'[2], Suffolk Punch heavy horse that became emblematic of the rare breeds within the service. When the Prison Commissioners took over Hollesley Bay Colony's flat, marshy fields from London City Council in 1938 they adopted the resident Suffolk Punch horse stud.

'The horses were very nice and it would've been wrong for the prison service to have taken over Hollesley Bay and not take on the horses,' explained Bernard.

Former Area Manager Howard Morse standing beside a Suffolk Punch drawn cart. An inmate holds the horse whilst the driver, 'probably an estate hand at North Sea Camp', according to Maurice, is accompanied by prison farm managers including bearded Mick Bingham and Tom Houston facing the front.'[3]

The largest herd of Suffolk Punch horses in the world, the stud supplied Farms & Gardens with 'a large number of willing workers and although their role has largely been taken over by tractors, they still have a place within the service and find a ready sale elsewhere.'[4]

Suffolk Punches became a kind of farmers' currency, exchanged between institutions and used to boost staff morale. When, after being loss making for years, Stocken Hall and Usk returned a profit in 1971, the Stocken Hall farm manager requested, 'A couple of Suffolk Punch mares for mating with local stallions to produce hunters for the neighbourhood gentry.'[5]

'We all had a Suffolk Punch,' said Steve, 'I think the area manager thought, "Oh, the managers are a bit down, what can we do? Oh, I know let's give them all a Suffolk Punch!" It was like a bonus that year.'

Affection for the horses was widespread; when Chris Train retired in 1991 after heading the prison service for eight years he was presented with a photograph, taken by Howard Morse, of Chris holding two award-winning Suffolk Punch horses at the London Parks open day held at Crystal Palace in the late 1980s.

Former HMP Director General Chris Train photographed holding two Suffolk Punch horses at the London Parks open day held at Crystal Palace in the late 1980s.[6]

'One of those horses was Mo's favourite,' said Maurice, 'the one called Zina.'

At Kirkham there was a legendary Suffolk Punch called 'Valentine'.

'I always wondered why they kept a Suffolk Punch horse on the farm until the farm manager, Alec Bundred said, "I'll show you why." One night he invited me out to the pub and he tacked up the horse and put it in a small trap and off we went to the pub. Well, we got hammered and that horse, well, we got back into that trap, and nobody was going to breath test a horse so it was OK. The horse knew its way back to the farm. It did mean though that we had to go to the same pub each week!' laughed Steve.

'Valentine was famous. It was the only Suffolk Punch in the village. We used to keep it up in the top field and all the villagers would see it as they passed along the road to the village. It was quite a talking point.'

He added, 'My daughter and I stayed up all night with that horse when it ate sugar beet by mistake.'

Another infamous Suffolk Punch was allocated to Hatfield,

'At Peterborough show this horse spooked at what it thought was the exit,' explained John Glover. Young, and new to showing, it jumped out the ring and accidentally clipped an onlooker in the head, killing her.

'Unicorn as it was called, was going to be put down before it got rescued by your dad. At Misterton Carr farm they 'ad an inmate looking after the horse and one day one of the lads rode bareback over to the river'.

'I knew Bev was keen on that horse. One day he got 'im in the cart and started coming out down the road but the horse took off and even though Bev was well-built and very strong he couldn't stop it. When he came back the horse was steaming!'

Crucially, the service's interest in rare breeds was not limited to the Suffolk Punch horses. From the mid-1950s, pedigree Jersey, Ayrshire and Friesian dairy herds as well as long established beef breeds such as the South Devon and Galloway were commonplace throughout the service. However, in the 1970s big-boned cattle breeds were widely introduced to the UK to boost milk production, which led to a decline in the popularity of indigenous British breeds. Chris McGown described what happened to the 110-head herd of pedigree Ayrshires on Portland in Dorset,

'We still had the Ayrshires in 1976 when Bev came to Portland. It took years to breed it out. The first black Holstein cross was born and that was 'Begonia'. They wanted milk quantity so they thought if you crossed them you'd get better butter content. A bit like the Jerseys. We had all sorts of problems because Holsteins are huge.'

Most commercial dairy herds in the USA and Europe are now Holstein–Friesian since the relatively compact, usually black on white British Friesian has been crossed with larger, black and white Holsteins imported from the USA. To accommodate them, stalls and equipment such as milking parlours have to be upgraded and their large frame makes them susceptible to lameness. Their over-sized udders are prone to infection and as this makes them unsuitable for automatic milking they are more likely to be culled at a young age.

Whilst certain characteristics could be emphasised or eliminated through selective breeding across generations it was a slow process. To speed it up the prison service farmers were early adopters of embryo fertilisation and transplantation, techniques that my dad was introduced to by McDowell on the Isle of Wight.

'We got embryo transplant at Usk, after me and the herdsman went to Spain,' said Bryan, 'There's an article in a genetics magazine, a report on what we were doing, embryo implanting being the way forward as it was cheaper and guaranteed.' Then he added, somewhat enigmatically, 'I got my knuckles rapped on that.'

Farm staff like Maurice and my dad regarded rare breeds as an insurance policy, a living genetic database that could be called upon to reintroduce characteristics such as ease of reproducing, docility or even flavour into commercial livestock. Maurice worked very closely with MAFF, the Ministry of Agriculture, Fisheries and Food, who unofficially provided a lot of support for prison farms to preserve genetic stock and effectively build and maintain a national genetic base for rare breed livestock. MAFF was dissolved in March 2002 following criticism of its handling of the 2001 outbreak of foot and mouth disease and Bovine Spongiform Encephalopathy (BSE or 'Mad Cow Disease'). Its responsibilities, including overseeing genetic resources were passed to the Department for Environment, Food and Rural Affairs (DEFRA) in which agriculture became subsumed within 'rural affairs'. Whilst DEFRA invested £545,000 in plant collections to preserve plant genetics, only a negligible amount was dedicated to the preservation of farm livestock genetics. This was despite a review in 1992 recommending that: 'DEFRA should consider the desirability of supporting indigenous breeds at risk where they have a positive contribution to make to the environment and heritage value of the countryside.'[7]

Maurice argued that any additional costs associated with keeping native and rare breeds could be offset by the premium price commanded when they were sold. But Director General Phil Wheatley's view was, 'If the Ministry of Agriculture wants to keep the genetic stock then they should pay for it.'

In Finland the state pays prison farms a financial subsidy to protect genetic resources of native breeds. For example, Pelso prison in Vaala holds the gene bank for Northern Finncattle; a white, naturally hornless breed that can be used for meat and milk, and Finnsheep; a small variety renowned for giving birth to multiple lambs. Established in 1984, the Finnish Nordic Gene Bank for Farm Animals (renamed NordGen in 2008), coordinates information across institutions like prisons and breeding organisations to conserve livestock genetic diversity and address diseases that might befall less robust commercial livestock.

Unlike Finland, there is no official, national genetic database for food and agriculture in the UK and little in the way of strategic government policy on Genetic Resource for Food and Agriculture (GRFA) beyond a DEFRA rare breed database, compiled with the help of the Rare Breed Survival Trust (RBST). Since 1900 twenty-six breeds of large, native livestock have become extinct, for example, the Lincolnshire Curly Coat pig, the last of which disappeared in the late 1970s. The RBST database lists over eighty rare breeds of sheep, over seventy cattle, fifteen pig and eight goat breeds but doesn't acknowledge the historic or future potential of the prison service in England and Wales as a livestock conservation partner despite rare breeds being at the heart of the service for over seventy years.

Maurice and his colleagues' livestock conservation efforts were unfunded and largely unrecognised. An obituary for Joe Henson, founder of the RBST, who died in 2015 aged 82, stated 'In 1973 Joe and a small group of farmers and animal geneticists founded the Rare Breed Survival Trust, to preserve animals' but no mention was made of the prison service.[8]

'Without the Farms & Gardens the rare breed society would never have taken off. We actually increased their whole knowledge,' said Bernard.

Maurice met with Joe Henson whenever a heritage breed was under serious threat of extinction. As there were prison farms dotted across the country it was often possible to house the animals on a farm in their county of origin.

'The Rare Breeds Survival Trust came to the prison service with a plea saying, "We are losing rare breeds faster than ever would the prison service consider helping us out," so every farm was allocated a rare breed,' said Steve.

Each establishment with rare breeds became a member of the RBST and a member of the applicable breed society. Often the RBST would donate animals so the rare breeds were added at nil cost to the service. Derek recalled meeting Joe Henson's son at a city farm in Leeds,

'Adam Henson was in charge of it. He kept saying, "I wouldn't be where I was if it wasn't for my dad."' After listening to Derek, Bernard added, somewhat surprisingly, 'we didn't buy any cattle from Joe because we didn't really like him.'

Phil Wheatley conceded, 'We started the rare breeds because we were interested in it, people like Maurice were interested in it.'

Rare breeds provided the prison service with a much needed, positive public profile.

'If you have a rare breed and attach it to a prison it's good for the prison and it's good for the prison population, the inmates,' said Chris McGown.

'We'd never have had the rare breeds in the service, never have had the same sort of publicity, if it hadn't been for Maurice,' acknowledged Bernard. 'We were never going to have cows that were producing 10,000 litres of milk. With rare breeds we could compete, we could show, we could sell.'

The prison service made the most of its land, labour and facilities to stock over forty species of native and rare breed animals alongside their commercial livestock.

'The Prison Service has a keen interest in conservation and its work with rare breeds forms a part of that' stated Bernard Feist in 1994 by which time prison farms hosted all seven RBST listed rare breed pigs, eleven RBST listed sheep and seven RBST cattle together with the Suffolk Punch horses and various pedigree poultry.[9] In addition to Indian Runner ducks, Maurice recalled,

'We had all the chickens: the Silkies and the White Wine Dots and the Black Leghorns, the Morans, Plymouth Rock was the black speckled one and these were generally at Leyhill and then we had an array of banties (bantams) that appeared at most prisons and they were all rare breeds. The ducks we had Aylesbury's and Khaki Cambles the brown ones that look like Mallards.'

Most of the rare breeds were kept outside although some, including birds of prey, resided within the confines of the institution. Occasionally, animals that should have been outside found themselves inside.

'Christmas Eve was the worst,' laughed Maurice, 'they used to get the animals and take them down the dorms. This was a borstal and there'd be a cow or a sheep ambling down the dorms and it would frighten the life out of some of them. That used to happen regularly. It was all light-hearted.'

The farm staff loved a joke.

'At Dartmoor they had the Whitbread herd of shorthorns and the Galloways and they named all the pedigree bulls after people at Head Office: Bernard, Maurice, Nick Carver. They did this for years before they realised and the penny dropped!' smiled Chris Coveney.

In the late 1980s Derek and Bernard went down to Alton in Hampshire to buy a herd of Belted Galloways or 'Belties' as they are known on account of their distinctive white band. Galloway cattle and Wales' only native cattle breed the Welsh Black are well suited to the UK's cold and wet climate so much so that Galloway, who are happy to eat weeds and moorland grasses, are increasingly being used to improve the ecology of uplands. A hardy breed they have a double coat with longer hair on the outside and a soft, mossy layer on the inside which means that they don't need to grow a thick layer of fat under their skin to keep warm which, according to the Rare Breed Survival Trust, makes the beef taste better.

'We went down this night as the bloke's wife had died and he was selling it all off for death duties,' explained Bernard. 'After a few pints we agreed we'd buy the herd.'

'About thirty animals,' said Derek.

'We were paying for these cows with a cheque from HQ,' noted Bernard. 'We'd just bought this farm at Onley, over 100 miles away near Rugby, Worcestershire. I went to load them on at five thirty but the Head of Activities at Onley was not happy, "I'm not having them," she said. So we had these three lorry loads of cows that had left Alton and were on their way to Onley. In the end they went to Gartree in Leicestershire because we had to find somewhere to unload them. It was a bit nerve wracking. They didn't stay at Gartree, we moved them around somewhere else. They were lovely animals.'

'Cracking animals,' agreed Derek.

In the UK, all coloured pig breeds declined in popularity post-WWII as demand increased for white-skinned pigs and leaner bacon. Consequently, breeding companies that emerged in the 1960s favoured the white breeds. Like other threatened species, rare breed livestock with indistinct looks and relative 'normality' were less likely to attract attention and conservation efforts tended to focus on more distinctive and 'attractive' animals such as the spotted and multi-coloured Oxford Sandy and Black pigs.

'Bev was a great believer in the Oxford Sandy and Black but the rare breeds society wouldn't recognise it. But it was,' said Bryan.

In 2014, the RBST recognised them as a 'minority' rare breed. By 2017, with less than 500 breeding females registered in the UK, they were re-categorised as 'at risk'.

When my dad went to Hatfield in 1987 all the pigs were looked after by Lorraine who worked alongside Steve Horrocks and Pete Chisholm.

'I know Steve very well,' said Pete in an email, 'I also know Lorraine well too, although I haven't seen her for some 20 years plus, we were all part of the HMP Hatfield family at one time.'

The prison service gene bank included other pig breeds notably both Wessex and Essex pigs.

'You've got to go back in the genes to find out what breeds that there are today are crossbred,' said Bryan tapping his head. 'That kind of knowledge is up here and goes with them when the farmers die.'

Maurice, whose speciality was pigs, told me that the Wessex and Essex were barely distinguishable from each other, only the presence of two white front trotters on the Essex told them apart.

In the mid-1950s the short-lived Pig Improvement Development Authority advised that because of low numbers the two county breeds should be combined into a new breed, the British Saddleback. Maurice still has a 'soft spot' for Saddlebacks because they were the breed he had as a herdsman before he joined the service.

'Very motherly, friendly, you could do anything with them,' he said, whilst conceding that Gloucester Old Spots were soft as well but he thought that Saddlebacks were particularly responsive to human contact,

'The ones I had would come up to you and almost chat to you.'

First and foremost, Maurice is a pig man so when I spotted a copy of *Practical Pigs* magazine while queuing to use the cash machine in my local post office I bought it and presented it to him before we

Inmates tending Wessex Saddleback pigs and a White Boar at HM Borstal East Sutton Park, Kent.[10]

started chatting about the prison farms. He immediately flicked through to the back of the magazine and scanned the list of herds and breeders. I saw him smile as he found what he was looking for, a herd with the HMP 'Colony' prefix, 'Colony Freiston', based in East Anglia, most likely at North Sea Camp where they kept Middle White and Large Black pigs, both considered 'endangered' breeds by the British Pig Society.

The prison service bought the majority of its commercial breeding gilts and boars from the Cotswold Pig Development Company which also helped the service export breeding pigs to Europe. In 1992 the Prison Service News reported: 'Farm staff at HMP Standford Hill have taken a first step into Europe, with the export of thirty-one breeding pigs to France. The pigs trotted into the history books as they headed off on their French blind dates, becoming the first ever export of pigs to the European Market arranged by PSIF (Prison Service Industries and Farms). Standford Hill's pig unit has some one hundred and eighty breeding sows, from which over six hundred and fifty gilts (female pigs that have not farrowed a litter) are supplied to other prison farms. Some four hundred gilts are also sent to Cotswold Pigs, a commercial operator which has just received the Queen's Award to Industry for pig technology. Cotswold Pigs were behind the request for the export gilts, reflecting high standard of pigs bred at Standford Hill. Standford Hill farm staff hope the export order will be just the beginning of their move into the European Market and feel that it truly reflects the hard work and dedication needed to achieve the necessary high standards.'[11]

Bernard explained that the Cotswold Pig Company were looking for somewhere for British Saddlebacks to be housed because they wanted to own the gene bank but didn't want to look after them anymore,

'So I took them at no cost to the prison service.'

In 2002 the Cotswold Pig Company was acquired by JSR Newsham Limited (now known as JSR Genetics).

'In fact,' confessed Bernard to Derek, Maurice and I, 'it's a good job Cotswold went bust because the pigs the service have got belonged to the Cotswold Pig Company. Jesus,' he added, 'I could probably end up inside before I have finished this.'

We all laughed with him.

'So, what will happen to those pigs now?' I asked thinking of the Saddlebacks at East Sutton Park.

'They'll get eaten won't they.'

'The gene bank will be lost,' stated Maurice bluntly.

'It was former Farm Manager Jim Partridge who brought the Portland sheep in,' acknowledged Chris McGown. Similar to the Spanish Merion breed of sheep, in the sixteenth century there were more than four thousand Portland sheep on the island but by the mid-1970s they were on the RBST's 'critical' list as there were none left on the island and only sixty-six on the mainland. Jim bought the last remaining flock and spent two years persuading the Home Office to take them on.

'You don't want any breed to die out completely and that's what would have happened if they had been allowed to carry on like they were,' said Jim on a video supplied to me by Howard Morse.[12]

The video showed donkey-jacketed and Wellington-booted inmates like Alan John nurturing the Portland sheep till they numbered five hundred.

'It is a great achievement… time flies by when you are out here. There are not enough hours in the day time goes so quickly.'[13]

A slow growing breed with distinctive fox brown legs and faces, there is no such thing as Portland lamb as they are not ready to eat until they are two years old but Portland mutton has an illustrious history having been a regal favourite, served to King George III whenever he visited his friend, John Penn, governor of the Isle of Portland from 1805 until his death in 1834. Legend says that the horned sheep swam ashore in 1588 from a fleet of Spanish Armada wrecked off the coast but the curator of Portland museum, Frank Clafton, thought this was unlikely since, 'sheep don't swim.'[14] But he may have been wrong.

In 2013 sheep were videoed swimming ashore after having been cut off from the land by a rapidly rising tide at Morecombe Bay. After a fifteen-minute swim they reached the land, 'and carried on grazing as if nothing had happened,' attested Ian Joseph, an onlooker.[15]

By 2014 the RBST had downgraded their rating of Portland sheep from 'critical' to 'at risk'.

All the rare breeds maintained by the prison service referenced the Hollesley Bay Colony Suffolk Punch stud through the use of the prefix

'Colony' to denote their HMP origins. The 'Colony Carr' herd of Lincoln Red Cattle was started at Hatfield prison in 1986 with three animals, with the name playing homage to both their prison heritage and the waterlogged, bog-oak filled Carr that constituted much of the prison's agricultural land.

According to my dad 'the Lincoln Red is a quiet, amenable and willing character, but also a highly efficient grazer which has made its mark across the world – thriving happily on poor quality grassland.'[16] Similar in colouring to Red Ruby Devon cattle, the Lincoln Red is robust and resistant to disease and their easy-going nature made them particularly well suited for handling by inexperienced inmates. Bred from what was, in 1926, the second largest breed of pedigree cattle in England, the Lincoln Red Shorthorn, Lincoln Red cattle are currently classified as 'vulnerable' by the RBST.

Bernard laughed as he recalled a radio interview with my dad about his Colony Carr herd of Lincoln Red cattle. 'We'd done a couple of radio shows at the Royal Show and from there they talked about this, "Breakfast on the Farm" so we had to find somewhere where the governor was happy and we could get someone to talk. So these two girls come early in the morning and we go to show them round the farm and it's pitch dark and Bev says, "This is my prize Lincoln Red bull." But you couldn't see anything! You know when Bev retired we gave him a black bit of paper with two white eyes on it.'

'That was Bev's bull,' laughed Maurice.

The names of rare breeds often reflect their place of origin which helps to maintain a sense of local distinctiveness and place identity. Aside from the Suffolk Punch horses that were widely distributed across the prison service, most rare breed livestock was kept as near as possible to where they came from, for example, Portland sheep on the Isle of Portland, Greyface Dartmoor sheep on Dartmoor, Gloucester Old Spot pigs at Leyhill in Gloucestershire. HMP Stocken along with Ashwell, Oakham and Rutland prison, had White Parks, a rare breed cattle that was endemic to the area.

'As Stocken Hall was a big, country house they fitted,' said Maurice adding, 'We tried to put them all in their proper places.'

Although rare and heritage breeds may not have great commercial value, their strength of association with a region or county is a valuable cultural asset. If it wasn't possible to place a rare breed in situ they were moved to a prison farm where there was a governor willing to accommodate them and staff with the appropriate livestock expertise which is why my dad ended up with Lincoln Red Cattle at Hatfield prison in South Yorkshire.

The 'most English of breeds' in the prison service was the British Lop pig that originated in Cornwall but was allocated to HMP Kirkham in Lancaster. When the RBST was established, the Lop was listed as one of six rare breed pigs, now there are eleven on the list. The British Lop is the only native British pig breed to have an associated breed society, the British Lop Pig Society. According to the Society's website the Lop is long and white and looks 'quite normal'. 'Generally docile and easy to manage and hardy enough for outdoor systems the Lop grows readily and will finish with a well-muscled, lean carcass at pork or bacon weights. The dams are prolific and make good milky mothers. Long thin lop ears that incline forward over the face and touch the end of the nose. A large frame and long body... Pure white skin and straight silky hair with no grey markings or wrinkles.'[17]

At Kirkham, Farm Manager Graham Palmer initially introduced twelve female Lops and two boars. Unlike hybrids, pedigree Lops produce two litters each year of about eight to ten piglets. The Lops were suckled for five weeks, matured with feed produced at Featherstone prison before being slaughtered and consumed within the prison canteens. A newspaper article provided by Howard reported: 'Sadly, Lops – pink, short-legged and heavy-bodied – are not regarded as commercial because they lay down fat easily. But judges at the Annual Show of the RBST held at the Royal showground Stoneleigh, last September admired the three Kirkham contenders who trotted off with prizes. Star of the Show was the gilt *Sunshine II* who grabbed the British Lop Championship, Inter-Breed Championship and the Pairs Championship. An impressive result for the prison's first show entry which put the Prison Service in the Champion League.'[18] But amongst British Lops, which themselves were rare, the rarest of all was the Ben Boar line.

Steve Horrocks was instrumental in saving the Ben Boar from extinction.

'At Oaklands Farm there was *the* only one left of that blood line. That is how rare it was. We crossed it with the other lops. That's how serious it was.'

Steve would liked to have kept Highland cattle at Kirkham but they got majestic Longhorn cattle instead. From two Longhorns Kirkham formed an award-winning herd of rare breed suckler cattle, called the 'Kirklan Longhorns'. 'Kirklan Jura, a Longhorn heifer who was tended by prisoners took top honours on the day winning both the Breed and Interbreed Championships. In 2009 at the Longhorn National Show at Stoneleigh, Kirklan Hirta, a senior heifer, sold for 2,700 guineas (£2,835) and was top price on the day for senior Heifers. It's fair to say that the herd is now as much known for its prison residency as it is for its quality.'[19]

When my mum and I visited Steve at his home he asked if we'd like to see the Longhorn cattle that he'd bought after he retired from the service. We eagerly agreed and clambered over a five-bar gate leading to a field opposite his house. As Steve cast a proprietorial eye over the cattle they acknowledged his presence by interrupting their grazing, swishing a tail and tilting their exaggerated horns in our direction. My mum and I were a little apprehensive but Steve remained incredibly calm. When we left, he pressed a folder into my hand full of newspaper cuttings and pamphlets, training manuals and magazines which he'd collected over the years. They included articles about the Longhorns and the British Lops, awards for bat and wildlife conservation and a published letter from a prisoner describing his experience of working at Kirkham.[20] One of the articles noted that produce from the farm was being sold through their own farm shop as well as directly through the wholesale market. 'The cows and calves are coming on in leaps and bounds. It's amazing to see such wonders thriving, and at one with mother nature. It makes me feel right at home, and with stock farming your work is never done, so it's not for the work-shy or faint-hearted. I'm just grateful to be working with two good gaffers, and a good bunch of boys who are characters too, with personalities that could bring sunshine into most people's lives, disproving the myths that all convicts are bad.'[21]

Despite the genetic, therapeutic, commercial and PR benefits of keeping rare breeds, some dismissed the rare breeds as a farmer's affectation.

'Really they did it because they liked it,' argued Phil.

And to some degree he was right. The farm staff took a great deal of pride in saving livestock from extinction, from producing high quality meat, eggs and milk products and from creating a positive public profile for the prison service, particularly through showing and selling their rare breed livestock at local, county and national agricultural shows and sales. But Phil's view was,

'Nice example, a nice thing. Prisoners enjoyed looking after them. No future. You can't make a business out of looking after Suffolk Punch horses. They are about the last stud of Suffolk Punch Horses in the country. They were used by breweries a bit but even that declined so there was no commercial market so we got some publicity out of it, mainly local shows in the Suffolk area. We were spending a lot of money looking after Suffolk Punch Horses. When the population is going up and they say you have got to manage a bigger population then you think well we are probably better off looking after prisoners than Suffolk Punch Horses.'

In 2007, only a couple of years after the prison farms and their rare breed livestock had been disbanded, the Food and Agriculture Organization of the United Nations (FAO) established a Global Plan of Action for Animal Genetic Resources, the first internationally agreed framework to protect and support the sustainable use, development and conservation of livestock genetic resources. It recognised that genetic resources were essential for food security, sustainable livelihoods, human well-being (nutrition) and cultural heritage. Whilst the FAO recommended the establishment of national gene banks, like those in Finland, it acknowledged that this would require institutional systems, government support and technical capacity. Interestingly, the FAO emphasised that to maintain and strengthen animal genetics it was necessary to not only keep accurate records in herd books but to chronicle the knowledge of the increasingly rare breed who look after them.

8

On show

'Everybody has won, and all must have prizes.'
Lewis Carroll, *Alice's Adventures in Wonderland*[1]

It took me a while to negotiate an automated telephone information system that assumed I required a guided tour or the hire of a wedding venue but eventually I reached the archivist at Nottingham's National Justice Museum. Appropriately enough her name was Bev Baker. I explained that I was writing a book about the history of farming in the prison service but a search of her database using the term 'farm' resulted in only four items, all from Dartmoor: a list of Galway cattle, horses and sheep plus a register of field crops and cropping. I wasn't surprised as Dartmoor was the first prison farm to be established in England and Wales and the site of the Farm Museum.

I asked Bev to search for specific farms, helping to spell Hollesley Bay for which there was only a sports programme but she only found two reports, one from Lancaster prison dated 1995 and another for Lancaster farms dated 1997. I must have sounded disappointed.

'We keep photographs in a separate archive,' she offered.

'Is there anything about Suffolk Punch horses?'

'Horses on show – Suffolk Punch stud.'

'Is it dated?'

'No.'

'Any 'Farms and Gardens' photographs?'

It was Bev's turn to be surprised, 'two hundred and eighty-eight photographs mostly 50s, 60s and 70s. Dartmoor, Camp Hill and Eastchurch.'

'Has anybody ever requested to see them?'

'No,' she said so I arranged to visit.

As I waited for Bev to meet me in the foyer of the Galleries of Justice I noticed a huddle of visitors listening to a smock-frocked guide who drew their attention to the banded, human-shaped frame swinging above their heads. Necks straining, the guide said,

'The people of Leicester complained about this gibbet. It wasn't that they objected to a deceased convict being placed inside and displayed in Saffron Lane as a warning to others, they objected to the crowd of twenty thousand who came to see it!'

Bev escorted me into the archive where I found six brown folders laid out on the table, each containing a selection of mostly black and white photographs, some uncatalogued and undated. In the Dartmoor folder I was intrigued to find the photograph below whose inscription read: 'The moorland pasture at Dartmoor is peculiarly adapted for sheep, and a large number is reared on the farm, of which the one in the picture is a capital specimen, and has won several prizes for the King (Queen crossed out) at agricultural shows.' The monarch amendment suggested that the photograph was taken around 1901 when King Edward VII ascended to the throne following the death of Queen Victoria. Photographic evidence that, for over one hundred years, showing has been an integral and celebrated part of penal institutions in England and Wales.

Sheep on moorland pasture near Dartmoor prison.[2]

Royal interest in Farms & Gardens activities persisted. Howard recalled that in 1987, when the Queen attended the Norfolk Show, she paused to ask Hollesley Bay Colony's stud groom, Bruce Smith,

'Who owns *Colony Orchid*?'

'Technically, Ma'am, I suppose you do.'

Stud groom Bruce Smith with award winning 14-year-old Suffolk Punch mare, *Colony Orchid* and her foal *Charlie*.[3]

Howard added, 'There's a sequel to that story. At the Norwich Show the same horse got champion and the Queen was handing out the cups again and it is alleged that she said, "Again Bruce?" After that when he went back to the stables the other members of staff put up a guard of honour and bowed.' Howard laughed, 'it makes a lovely story!'

'When the Queen attended a centenary celebration at HMP Leyhill the horse got tired and just laid down. There's a photo somewhere of the chap who was looking after the horse looking rather embarrassed.' Unfortunately, that photo wasn't in the National Justice Museum archive.

Maurice met the Queen on several occasions,

'We met her at the Royal Show and she was interested in the farms and what we were doing. Our exhibit for the Royal Show had a miniature village with a river, a bridge, duck pond and animals. We put on exhibits of what we did: there was a big, open chest freezer with products in it like bacon and vegetables and a video running about school visits that we had. The Queen was interested in the educational visits, the animals and the village. It was designed by four of us: me, Bernard, Jeremy Fallows and the manager at Ford where the animals came from.' Then he added somewhat candidly,

'We designed it on a bit of paper in the office, similar to how we designed the Chelsea Flower Show exhibition!'

In 1989, the centenary of the Ministry of Agriculture, Fisheries and Food (MAFF) and the official 'Food and Farming Year', the Prison Service Industries and Food (PSIF) teamed up with the Rare Breed Survival Trust (RBST) to put on an exhibition at the Asda Festival of Food and Farming event held in Hyde Park. The festival was described by Lord Carter as, 'the biggest event of its kind in London since the Great Exhibition of 1851.'[4] Over three days, 940,000 people, almost double the anticipated number, visited the festival.

Visitors to the PSIF/RBST exhibit tended to assume that the knowledgeable and engaging person describing prison produce to them was a member of staff. Some visitors, including those that expressed the view that *they* should be locked up without a key, were most surprised to hear, 'Actually, I'm an inmate.'

Maurice was delighted when the Queen's equerry decided that she should visit the PSIF/RBST stand.

'The first thing she did when she got out of view of the general public was to lift one knee, undo her handbag and redo her lipstick, no mirror, nothing,' said Bernard admiringly adding,

'And it wasn't because she'd been kissing Maurice!'

Amongst the exhibits were rare breed ducks, red-haired Tamworth pigs and a fine Suffolk Punch mare with a recent foal. While Maurice chatted to the Queen, a Cat. D prisoner from Ford fed polo mints to the pigs to keep them docile.

'But the Queen,' said Bernard, 'had this green, two-piece suit on with white buttons.'

As she leaned over the makeshift pen a beady-eyed Tamworth smartly nipped off what it thought was a mint!

Seated around a table at Maurice's house overlooking Torbay, Derek, Maurice, Bernard and I laughed heartily.

Farms & Gardens' staff were encouraged to step up their attendance at shows following a call in the late 60s for the department to build their public profile. 'It was vital to supply fresh fruit and vegetables all the year round and to have the gardens and playing fields as an example of which to be proud… It was noticeable that in programmes, on television for example, about prison, farms and gardens were not mentioned. Farm management needed to sell itself, firstly to other Departments and secondly to the public.'[5]

'I've never yet at any of the shows found members of the public who know that we grow our own food,' said Chris Coveney, 'but they all think it's brilliant and give it a double thumbs-up.'

'Showing was an add-on,' said Maurice. 'We used to put up exhibits at shows, not just take the animals to show them. We'd do exhibits to try and spread the word.'

To raise public awareness of an institution defined by impenetrable high walls, a series of booklets were produced in 1972 that profiled the activities of Farms & Gardens and the department began to actively court coverage in the local press with the goal of featuring on radio and television. In 1974, the first episode of *Porridge*, starring Ronnie Barker as petty criminal Norman Stanley Fletcher, was aired as a BBC sitcom centred around a fictitious, category C prison, HMP Slade. Fletcher was given 'special duties' by the governor, mucking out the pigsty on the prison farm in the first episode, *New Faces, Old Hands* whilst his cellmate, a prisoner called Evans, ate the governor's copy of the *Farmers' Weekly*. When Fletcher was caught taking bets over which hen would be first to lay an egg in the second episode, *The Hustler*, he lost various privileges including working on the farm.

After a one-off remake of *Porridge*, built around a storyline about Norman Fletcher's grandson being sentenced for computer hacking and imprisoned within a 'modern' rather than a Victorian jail, attracted

4.4 million viewers in September 2016, the BBC announced it would commission a new series.[6] It will be interesting to see whether horticulture or the prison farms will feature.

'Most news about prisons is pretty grim,' concluded Big Rob, 'and suddenly here was a positive. We showed at Stoneleigh Royal Agricultural Show year after year and people would come onto the stand and say, "I didn't realise we did all of this. Is this what goes on in prisons? Fabulous!"'

After highly publicised escapes in the early 90s, including from the special secure unit at Whitemoor, the Prison Service set about rebuilding its public image with the help of the Farms & Gardens. 'We did a lot of shows in the back end of the 80s early 90s when we started to push the rare breeds forward,' said Bernard.

Howard created a series of short films about outward facing Farms & Gardens including *Farms Review* from 1992 that showed inmates operating modern milking, mowing and fertiliser spreading machinery as well as harvesting lettuce, capsicum and celery from a polytunnel with overhead irrigation. His video also featured a whole collection of vintage tractors including one that was being started with a match! Howard stressed that restoring vintage tractors and machinery was an activity that created interest and enthusiasm amongst inmates.

At Hollesley Bay Colony, Howard recorded two Suffolk Punch horses hauling a road sweeper whilst other horses galloped to the fence. It is, he added: 'Another damp and dismal day not suitable for photographic work' then stressed how successful the stud has been at many shows. A mare with a one-day old male foal was brought out for a walk by an inmate and the farm staff were pictured with heavy radios hanging from their belts.

Whilst at the 1992 Royal Show, Howard profiled a typical Farms & Gardens exhibition stand: against a backdrop of trophies, certificates and rosettes, a shiny, recently restored tractor; amongst a feast of vegetables and flowers of every hue, examples of prisoners' milking attire and churns. Turning his lens towards prison-bred livestock he captured menthol craving pigs from Hewell Grange who'd won the reserve challenge cup for best Tamworth pigs, Kirkhams' Champion British Lop, prize-winning Highland cattle from Dartmoor and, amongst many awards for Usk (YOI Prescoed), a prominently displayed

Challenge Trophy for best group of Berkshire pigs. 'Just a few that reached the top in their classes,' he narrated proudly before explaining that Usk had already scooped two 'firsts' for Berkshire pigs and a Very Highly Commended in the bacon carcass section at the Royal Smithfield Show.

The Japanese Ministry of Agriculture was so impressed with the quality of Usk's livestock at the Royal Smithfield Show that they paid over £1,000 for six Berkshire pigs to be exported to Japan to widen their genetic base. Particularly valued for its leanness by the Emperor, Berkshire pig is marketed as kurobuta or 'black pork' in Japan.[7] At the time Maurice said, 'This shows we are as good as anyone else in what we are doing.'[8]

Building on their international export success, a promotional leaflet from 1994 quipped: 'If you would like to help some stock escape by purchasing your replacements from us, please contact Bernard Feist.'

At the same time as animals and produce were being shown at agricultural shows, flowers were exhibited at prestigious horticultural events such as the Chelsea Flower Show. In 1991 HMP Leyhill exhibited a garden made up entirely of edible plants. It symbolised Leyhill's role as one of five national distribution centres for food within the prison service and 'The choices provided by the Prison system: a fruitless return to the old ways of life or a developing progression through growth and change to a new way forward,' according to Estates Manager Jeff Goundrill.[9] A small circle built of hard Dartmoor stone surrounded by prickly and bitter plants represented 'the initial difficult stage for an inmate coming into prison… the second… built of softer Portland stone… represents the middle part of a prison sentence and the plants here are more palatable... The pathway at the top of the circle leads to a large door representing the way back into the old system. The third and largest circle illustrates the freedom of an open prison... the more tranquil surroundings are represented here by a circle of mellow Cotswold stone… the plants now are much softer and sweeter, more pleasant to taste, offering real choices for a better future.'[10]

Leyhill was an open prison that prided itself on being progressive and humane. 'In typical Leyhill style Governor Nick Wall formed a committee of staff and inmates to devise their entry... Estate Manager Jeff Goundrill said: "It's amazing how this has pulled staff and inmates together.'"[11] The opportunity for Leyhill to exhibit at the Royal Horticultural Society's Chelsea Flower Show was aided by garden designer and Chelsea gold medallist, Jane Fearnley-Whittingstall, who lived a few miles from Leyhill and used to buy fruit, vegetables, cakes and Christmas trees from the prison's farm shop. To raise awareness of Leyhill's delicious home-grown produce, Jane acted as a go-between to the Royal Horticultural Society and Leyhill, endorsing the prison's application and guiding Jeff and his team through the process of preparing and building a Chelsea garden.

'The whole project made me very happy,' said Jane.

According to the Leyhill Board of Visitors: 'We are convinced that ventures such as this, which allow inmates to work within the community, represent a major advance in the rehabilitation of offenders and... we are both pleased and proud that HMP Leyhill is at the forefront of such activities.'[12] The following year, 1992, Leyhill's *Here we go round the mulberry bush* was rewarded with a silver medal.

On the page of notes about what my dad and Maurice thought should be in a history of farming and gardening in the prison service were the words: 'Belamy' (sic) and 'Windelsham'. The former referred to The Conservation Foundation established by David Bellamy and David Shreeve in 1982 to promote positive environmental news, awareness and action and the latter to the Windlesham Trophy.

The Windlesham Trophy was established by the former chairman of the Parole Board, Lord Windlesham, as an inter-establishment competition to encourage garden excellence.

'I liked old Windlesham,' said Phil, 'he was an interesting character.'

Regional managers like Howard Morse chose which prison in their area had the best-kept garden and put them forward to be judged by the Royal Horticultural Society. After HMP Preston, the inaugural winner in 1984 won three times in the first five years of the competition, steps were taken to stop them winning.

When Lord Windlesham became too infirm to present the main prize, an old bell from a 'Green Goddess' fire engine, the honour passed to the director general except, 'I used to go out because Martin Narey didn't do the Windlesham trophy,' said Phil. 'But I knew the people who were involved in gardening and I rather liked what they were doing. It suited me,' said Phil.

'They would take me out to Whatton in Nottinghamshire, who in 2015 won the trophy for a record seventh time, making it the most successful prison in the competition's 31-year history, which had superb gardens; Everthorpe, winner in 2009, where they had done some really good stuff with natural gardens – sustainable stuff a bit out of the ordinary; and Sudbury who won the Windlesham four times. There was really high standard of gardening, really good quality work. Really keen and knowledgeable gardeners and there were jobs. It was something you could do with convictions.'

Then he added, 'You've got to watch it because if you train someone to be a bank manager they can't get a job in it.'

In March 2016 I met with Norma McCloughlin, head of operations and Deb Boydell, an administrator at NOMS, both of whom were well-informed about the Windlesham. They told me that the criteria for this year's Windlesham Trophy had just been agreed and two new categories had been included because, as before, the same prisons seemed to be entering and winning the competition. 'Best newcomer' and 'something about a small area,' possibly something to do with 'hydroponics' they thought. I emailed Chris Coveney, as he was in charge of the criteria, who explained that the two new categories for 2016 were: 'Best initiative garden' such as one created in partnership with other departments or an outside organisation and 'Best use of recycled materials to create a horticultural area or feature,' an inaugural prize won once again by HMP Preston.

Livestock and horticultural shows were an opportunity to bridge a divide between those who judged and those who were judged.

'The show people themselves used to welcome prisoners because they knew that if they needed anything doing in the arena the prisoners would be only too pleased to do it especially at the local shows, not so much at the big shows,' Maurice conceded.

'When I was at Usk and we were at the Monmouth show we always had an 'arena party' who doubled up as the people who looked after the animals. They'd help with the show jumping, putting it right. And the people in charge were only too pleased to have free labour. The organising committee use to feed them. It was all *community work*.'

But there could still be prejudice.

'One particular day, I'll never forget it, I was in the farm office and ten lads from Usk who had been stewarding in the main ring were about to be dismissed when a police car arrives. There was *loads* of goods missing and the *first* people they thought about was the borstal boys! As it turned out it wasn't them, thank goodness, but that showed you what you were up against.'

Showing, both agricultural and horticultural, provided inmates with an opportunity to fulfil 'normal' outside roles. 'Between May and August 1995 an estimated 860,000 visitors to agricultural and flower shows across the country were given the opportunity to see the kind of work being done in their local prisons and to talk to staff and prisoners... Prisoners from Hollesley Bay acted as an arena party for the Suffolk show and a floral display, made on request at the prison, decorated the President's marquee... Hollesley Bay's famous Suffolk Punches took time off from giving groups with special needs tours around the prison to win the Four-in-Hand cup. At the Royal Show Hewell Grange won a gold medal for their garden *The Good Old Days* and their Tamworth pigs also picked up a 1st, 2nd and 3rd in competition. East Sutton Park won three awards with their five Saddleback pigs and Hatfield marked the 100th anniversary of Lincoln Red cattle by winning Reserve Supreme Champion, Female Champion and a first prize. At one of the most prestigious events of the year, Leyhill prison won the coveted Tudor Rose Award for best garden at the Hampton Court Flower Show... It was officially opened by Esther Rantzen and Director General Derek Lewis.'[13]

Maurice wholeheartedly embraced publicity associated with showing as he believed it benefited both the department and the institution.

'There was always a regard for Farms & Gardens irrespective of whether governors really liked it or not as they could see that it was something that added to the value of the 'nick', certainly in the 70s and 80s because it got reasonably good publicity.'

When I asked Big Rob, the last remaining Farms & Gardens employee at head office, how else the prison service was represented outside of the Farms & Gardens he replied,

'Very little. Maybe the dog teams and that was it.'

When I asked Maurice he gave a one-word reply,
'Nothing.'

'I think the shows were wonderful for the staff,' Howard concluded as he passed me a red box file that Isobel asked me to write Howard's name on. The box contained various articles and newspaper cuttings that they were happy for me to copy along with DVDs and photographs.

As exhibitors, farm staff and inmates developed a range of professional and transferable skills including proficiency in livestock handling, customer relations and communication skills.

'The first Lincoln Red we showed was a young heifer and I didn't really know what was involved,' said John Glover, 'I'd been to shows and seen what they get turned out like. Well, I did shampoo them but I didn't realise that they clipped their coats and all that. So the first few shows I went to we were placed bottom at every show.'

But their placing was not simply a consequence of inexperience.

'I think to start with because we were the prison service they didn't think we would take it seriously.'

John and my dad paid very close attention to how the commercial stockmen prepared their animals. But no matter how well-bred or presented HMYOI Hatfield's cattle were, they failed to win any top prizes.

'Bev and me we didn't go there to 'play' at it, we went there to bloody win. And if you do something like that you either do it right and go for it or don't bother. If I asked Bev for a litre of shampoo he'd bring back ten litres. There was no shortage of materials, we 'ad everything we needed. There was never any scrimping with anything. We had proper leather halters from a local saddler and proper straps that you 'ad to have when they were tied up in case they got away.'

After several unsuccessful shows, John decided to test out who or what was being sanctioned. He swapped places with a stockman called Graham, who showed Lincoln Red Cattle belonging to a renowned Lincolnshire breeder, Mr Bembridge, to see if it was the animals or the prison service that was being judged. They each led the other's animal and whilst Graham got placed in the top three showing a prison service bred Lincoln Red, John failed to pick up a rosette!

Gracious and philosophical, John said,

'Well you've got to start somewhere haven't you? Eventually at the Lincoln show we couldn't have done any better. We won Supreme Champion there with a baby heifer and the reason we got it I think was that it was a totally outside judge and it came down to me with this baby heifer and this young bull and he took us to one side and he said, "To be honest I can't really tell much difference between them but I believe that the future of Lincoln Reds is in the female side so I am giving it to the female." And I don't think it had ever been won by a female heifer before, especially a young one.' Modest as ever, John conceded, 'That young heifer, I didn't show her, she showed herself.'

After winning their first supreme championship at the Lincolnshire Show with *Colony Carr Hazel XI,* their two-year-old heifer, Bev said, 'It was all down to the inmates and stockman for their efforts.'

Whenever Bev and John went to a show they were always accompanied by an inmate who for weeks beforehand would help prepare the livestock: grooming, trimming and halter training the animals.

Prison farm manager Bev Wright, with stockman John Glover (second right) and two inmates.[14]

'We went through quite a few different inmates showing and we had some good ones, some brilliant ones. We had to pick one that would behave himself whilst we were there. I must admit that the lads that we took to the shows were quite good, very good actually and we very often let the lad put the white coat on and he led something to show and they must've loved it,' recalled John.

'They were just as proud as the farm managers,' said Bryan. 'If they got a rosette they were over the moon but if they didn't get a rosette they still weren't disappointed, it was that pride, it was the first time that they could lose and not be worried or angry about losing.'

Christine noted that the prisoners took pride in everything associated with showing including the prison farm produce displayed on prison stands.

Showing taught inmates a variety of social skills not least how to share a confined living space with staff! Steve recalled that at shows he would bed down in a sleeping bag on the straw alongside the livestock and inmates. Bev and John preferred to sleep in a caravan.

'Bev loved his little caravan with all the wood inside,' recalled Sarah Croft.

'Bev and I used to have one end and the inmate used to have the single bed up the other end,' said John.

'We 'ad this inmate and he did wake us both up one night and he's going, "Mr Wright, Mr Wright, *please* Mr Wright", and Bev says, "What the bloody hell do you want?" "You're snoring Mr Wright, I can't sleep, I can't sleep." We 'ad this curtain and he'd pulled it across thinking that was going to stop it,' John laughed.

Another inmate who was 'into his bodybuilding' chose to sleep outside the caravan.

'Just laid on the ground,' said John.

As far as Maurice knew, nobody ever reported an inmate trying to escape from a showground.

One night whilst Bev and John were sleeping head-to-toe, three of the commercial Lincoln Red stockmen: 'Cammy', Graham and Charlie, dropped some beer through the window of the caravan onto Bev's head. He jumped up so fast that the middle of the bed collapsed. Faced with a broken bed Bev ousted the inmate and made him sleep on the floor whilst an uncomplaining John had to make do with the broken bed.

'Another time the other stockmen came along and altered the legs and the bloody caravan went up while we was in it. I mean it was all fun we didn't mind.'

Showing was a way of introducing inmates gradually back into normal, everyday routines,

'Bev would cook for the lad because he'd have to have something to eat and we all ate together,' said John.

'I took three lads to a show and they were uncharacteristically helpful, volunteering to get up early to milk the cows,' said Steve. 'It took me a couple of days to realise that they were getting paid 15 pence per gallon for the milk and getting nine gallon out of this cow and pocketing all the money!'

Chris Coveney recalled taking two inmates from East Sutton Park to the Royal Norfolk show,

'We took a caravan down because there was only accommodation for men so Lorraine and the two girls had a caravan and I was in the stockman's quarters. We did all the showing and they invited the girls to the stockman's party at night and they ended up serving behind the bar and they had a whale of a time. I mean nowadays they would all have a fit but at the time it was *brilliant* and these two girls, one was a fashion designer and the other was a legal secretary, so they wouldn't likely be doing it again.'

On reflection I wasn't sure whether he meant re-offending or going to an agricultural show!

'At the Lincoln show we always had a BBQ, that was always a good evening,' said John. 'At the Royal Show one night, I mean if the bosses 'ad found out there would've been real trouble, but they 'ad a bull race – they jumped on the bulls and rode round. Well the bosses would've jumped up the wall if they'd known what they were doing but they didn't.' Laughing he added, 'Bev and I didn't do it ourselves but we were there.'

'There was one that amused your dad. There was this man he showed Lincoln Reds and he was the owner, I can't remember his proper name but they used to call him "Squaddie" because he was a squadron leader. You could tell he'd been in the Air Force, very smartly dressed and just his manner you could tell he was. He had like the old type suitcase and he kept his tack in there and obviously before he come to the show one of the cattle had put its foot through it. He still used it but it 'ad a hole in it. And we were at the Royal Show and you know you had to carry the water to give the cattle and your dad was walking by and he stubbed his toe on the suitcase so he poured the whole bucket full straight in and it *really amused* Bev.'

Lorraine also recalled my dad's sense of humour and fun,

'He was a jolly man. Sort of what you would expect as an extra who could do Father Christmas. Easy to get on with, fun and loving his job and loving his animals and he loved his showing. He was a gentleman, a very gentle, kind person.'

'I have many happy memories of the fun and good times we shared at the various Lincoln Red events,' wrote Mike Winterbottom, a fellow member of the Lincoln Red Cattle Society, 'I will miss both his witty company and wise counsel.'

'There wasn't anyone else like Bev,' said John, 'I mean he was like the owner manager and compared to the others none of their bosses you never seen them until the day and they'd just watch, they'd just receive the prize so that was quite a bit different with your dad like.'

Prison governors, even if they differed in their support for the farms and showing, were often more than happy to escape the confines of the

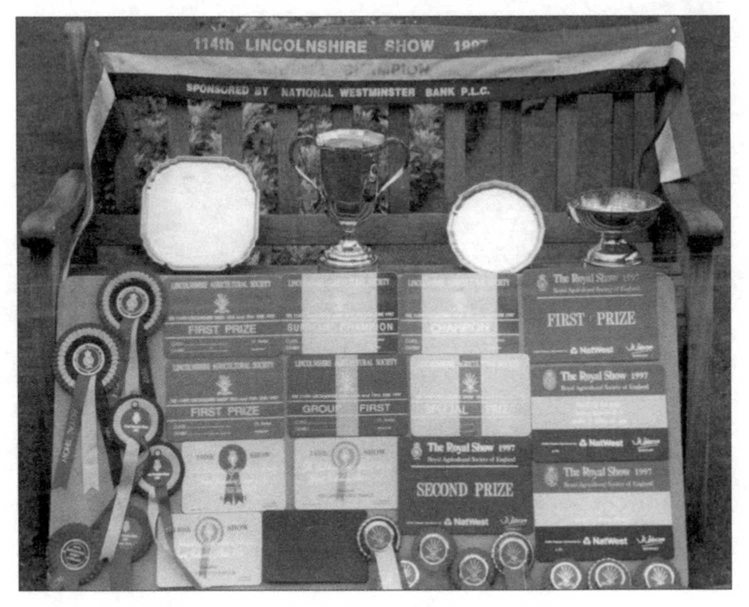

Trophies and rosettes awarded to the Colony Carr herd of Lincoln Red cattle in the mid 90s.[15]

prison institution and enter the winner's enclosure to accept trophies then display them in the public foyer of their prison. They also appreciated the contribution that prize money made to the prison's cash account. Rosettes on the other hand were usually pinned up in the farm office.

Did showing get the recognition it deserved? I asked Big Rob.

'Maybe because some saw it as "not ideal use of public money" but it was good PR.'

'Inevitably I'd say, *No*,' concluded Maurice. 'We got the publicity through the farming press and we always made sure that Prison Service News had the information and to be fair to them, they often published it. But I don't think it got the recognition from politicians that it deserved.'

I asked Phil Wheatley the same question. He acknowledged that showing provided a positive media profile for an otherwise opaque institution but he was disparaging about local rather than national coverage.

'It tended not to be in national newspapers. Some odd exceptions like Leyhill gardens got national newspaper attention. But if you look at most of the national news coverage about prisons it is bad news.

My dad Bev Wright (left) receiving the trophy for Champion Female Lincoln Red at the Lincoln Red Cattle Society, Autumn Show, 23 Oct 2010.[16]

Local news coverage is different. We were always able to get much more positive news at the local level. Hearing that your local prison was doing something interesting and had won something is OK.'

This photograph from the Lincoln Red Cattle Society archive was accompanied by: 'The Colony Carr Herd was formed in 1989 & had some very successful years of showing, using prisoners to work with the cattle, providing what must be one of the best forms of rehabilitation. The Colony Carr Herd was dispersed in 2002.'

At my parents' house, a long line of red herd books that catalogued the entire breed, doubled the size of my dad's book collection that otherwise consisted of *Countryman* magazines and a few sea faring novels. Bev served on the Lincoln Red Cattle Society Council for several years before and after his election as President of the Society in 1999. In 2010 he was appointed Patron of the Society.

'His commitment to the promotion of the breed was above and beyond the call of duty as he and Ann travelled miles to stand by a pen of cattle and talk, in his engaging way, to all who cared to listen,' attested Jayne.

Bev Wright, President of the Lincoln Red Cattle Society in conversation with HRH Princess Anne.[17]

Eventually, having proved their ability to breed and show champion livestock, Bev and John were considered worthy enough to become judges.

'The last show that I judged at was Woodhall Spa,' said John, 'but blimey I didn't realise how big it was; the number of cattle and my head was spinning by the end of the day and I thought, "I don't know whether I want this." I think I was on the wrong side. I think my thing was showing the cattle really. Well it was I felt, a bit of an honour to be asked, if nothing else.'

My dad loved judging. Unfortunately, despite scouring second-hand shops, we were never able to find a black bowler hat large enough to fit his head so he wore a trilby instead, an upgrade on his usual flat cap. A champion breeder and showman whose knowledge of butchery helped him appreciate the quality of the animal from the inside out, he was always scrupulously fair in his judgement of both animals and people.

After selectively breeding and successfully showing Lincoln Red cattle for the prison service, my dad bought a small number of the Colony Carr herd when they were auctioned in 1999 and established the Bevann Herd. Somewhat controversially, he added to the Bevann Herd when the Colony Carr Herd was dispersed in 2002.

Bernard said, 'It was a bit like bargain hunt they can't bid for their own. It's very difficult sometimes to separate 'the job' from your own feelings.'

But Maurice, ever a staunch supporter of my dad, stressed that Bev hadn't contravened prison policy, so long as he was the highest bidder. At the same time, there was little appetite amongst other Lincoln Red breeders to bid for cattle that Bev wanted to purchase.

'Bev had some big successes in the showring,' wrote Lincoln Red Cattle Society Secretary Jayne Borrows, including repeatedly winning the junior bull title at the Lincolnshire Show with bulls called *Beverley Zeal* and his progeny *Bevann Gallant.*[18]

But as the progeny lines within the Bevann Herd included *Hannah*, I hoped that my dad wouldn't confuse his family and animals too closely, otherwise I might be served up!

When I met up with Maurice, Bernard and Derek for the second time, it was at the Okehampton Show in Devon. On my way to find them

I watched as a group of sheep were judged by a dishevelled older lady who looked like she rarely emerged from the depths of Dartmoor. She wore a full length 'dry-as-a-bone' style coat and something akin to a trilby hat. I couldn't help noticing that she had a beard. She took her judging duties very seriously, peering at the back end of each sheep, pursing her lips, pulling back the wool before sweeping her hand across its back and giving it a hearty pummel on the buttocks. Understandably each sheep baulked and the handlers had to give a countering tug on the halter to prevent them from spinning away. After a quite a lot of huffing she resolutely took a blue rosette from her box-holding assistant. There were smiles all round as the rosette would add value to the winner's breeding stock.

The first person I found was Derek, fervently form-filling at the back of a small white tent, looking very dapper and sporting a VIP badge. He was animatedly conferring with another official about forms that should have been filled in by competitors but hadn't been. Fortunately for the entrants, Derek and his co-judge agreed that they had enough information to proceed without disqualifying anyone. Before I left Derek kindly loaned me a badge that would allow me access to the VIP tent and apologised that it wouldn't entitle me to a free lunch. Later, as I waited with Derek to hear who'd won the vintage tractor competition he took me to one side and gave me some sad news. He'd been diagnosed with cancer.

Back in March 2013 I replied to an email from Jayne on behalf of the Lincoln Red Cattle Society asking about Bev's state of health as he'd recently stepped down as President of the Society.

I wrote:

Thank you for your lovely message for my dad, Bev. He really appreciated it. You will be relieved to know that I am not writing (at this point) to tell you that he has passed away.

I had a chat with him last week and we would like to know if the Female Champion Lincoln Red class at the Yorkshire show has a trophy or not as he would like me to arrange a 'memorial' trophy on his behalf if possible. As you will know, he has had some success over the years breeding Female Champions in particular and as he has lived in Yorkshire for the last 26 years it would be particularly apt to provide a trophy for this category. I was also wondering if the Female Champion class had got a trophy at the spring/autumn Lincoln sales?

He has asked me to make something 'different' for the trophy! In other words, he is looking for something other than a regular cup or plate…

Jayne replied:

I am so relieved to hear that Bev is still with us. I do hope he is comfortable. It sounds like he is being his usual very thoughtful and generous self! I do hope too that Ann and all of you are coping okay; having been through what you are going through I have a small inkling of how devastating it is!

I have approached the Great Yorkshire Show Society and await their reply. I'm afraid I'm not holding out an awful lot of hope as we did try to present them with one of the LRCS (Lincoln Red Cattle Society) trophies from the Royal Show which they turned down. But you never know, they may change their minds. A question they may ask is whether the trophy would be their property or property of the LRCS – these days it's all to do with insurances.

You also enquired about the Trophies at the LRCS Spring & Autumn Shows – an arena that saw one of the Bevann Heifers capture the Champion Female Trophy recently. We have the Bettinson Punchbowl for the Champion Female in the Autumn; your Dad won that in its inaugural year of presentation. In the Spring Show we have The Parkes Perpetual Trophy for the Champion Female.

Just a passing thought: we have trophies for the top breeding sires – easy enough to do as they produce many offspring (at least we hope they do); but we don't have a trophy that recognises the top breeding female. As I say it's a passing thought and I'm not sure what the qualifying criteria could be – I am sure your Dad would have some excellent ideas! A couple that spring to mind are: number of shows she's won in the year and number of her offspring that have been shown, points awarded for position in their respective classes, could include direct descendants i.e. granddaughters & grandsons, but not nieces or nephews? Where they have to compete with a bull for overall Champion they should still qualify if they are Reserve at that Show (some Judges prefer bulls to females). As I say this is just a passing thought…

I'll let you know as soon as I have a response from the Great Yorkshire Show.

Please be sure to pass on our very sincere thanks for such a generous offer – do hope we can fulfil his wish!

Please also give both Dad and Mum my love.

My very Best Wishes to you and your family too!

Chat soon
Jayne

The following day Jayne sent another email:

Hello Hannah,

I am very pleased to advise that the Great Yorkshire Show have agreed to your request. They say they will be very pleased for the Lincoln Reds to have a Trophy to present to the Champion Lincoln Red Female.

I hope this will please Bev and you.

Look forward to hearing from you.

Kindest Wishes

Just as Jayne had hoped my dad beamed with pleasure at the news that at the next Great Yorkshire Show, a trophy bearing his name would be presented to the champion female. As his daughter, I knew that this would make him very proud.

9

Where there's muck...

'No profit grows where is no pleasure ta'en.'
William Shakespeare, *The Taming of the Shrew*

Highly profitable, Farms & Gardens received an £8 million grant from the UK Treasury in 1992 and turned over more than £35m. Four years later prisons were spending a quarter of their catering budget on purchases from the veg preps which guaranteed a market for prison produce. As both Farms & Gardens and the catering department were funded by the Treasury they exchanged credit rather than actual cash. Consequently, there was no mechanism for production or transportation costs incurred by Farms & Gardens to be covered when a prison exceeded its 'non-cash' allocation and demanded extra milk, meat or vegetables from the veg preps.

Profitability within Farms & Gardens was not new. In 1948/49 the Farm Section, as Farms & Gardens was called at the time, generated an £11,000 surplus based on an income of £86,000 and annual expenditure of £75,000.[1] Throughout the 1950s there had been a 10 to 15% year-on-year increase in profit.

One of the reasons why the prison farms became so profitable was the early adoption by farm managers of systematic and accurate record keeping, data analysis, planning and budgetary control. Initially, this took the form of an annual Farm Management Report which also formed the basis for decision-making both at the level of the individual establishment and nationally, with staff at Head Office aggregating the data and balancing the books across all the prison farms. To identify exactly what crops and farming methods were most likely to return the highest gross margin per acre, a system of management accounting known as a Trading Account was introduced in 1953 and extended in the late 60s to include the value of amenity work (such as mowing lawns, maintaining sports fields and sustaining conservation areas like wildflower meadows).

In 1968 when genial Peter Stevens took over from authoritarian John Wiley as chief manager, he set about introducing procedures that accorded with the redefinition of farm managers by Head Office as: 'a head of business, a good economist.'[2] As the scale of activity increased, and in response to the 11th Report of the Parliamentary Estimates Committee,[3] Peter brought in the National Agricultural Advisory Service (NAAS), which was rebranded as ADAS (Agricultural Development and Advisory Service) in 1971 and whose remit was to teach (or help) farmers to make rational decisions. Each farm manager took as a starting point data published annually by ADAS that specified typical agricultural output by region, for example, litres of milk per cow in the East Midlands. The targets set took account of local conditions such as the (often poor) quality of the prison farm land and, in consultation with the prison governor and the regional manager, specific requirements such as employing inmates and supplying food to the prison dietary. In the early 70s, 'Standards of performance represented targets for the Manager to aim at. These were to present a challenge to the Manager but he had to guard against the setting of targets which were difficult or impossible to achieve. Such targets only bred frustration.'[4] But Peter Stevens' effort paid off; twenty-five years later, ADAS concluded that prison produce 'represents standards typical of best commercial practice.'[5]

Peter also oversaw the introduction of 'Management by Objective', a scheme piloted within the Farms & Gardens in 1971/72 and subsequently implemented across the entire prison service. Although not formally evaluated, the introduction of Management by Objective coincided with increased productivity and quality outputs which enhanced the status not only of management practices within the Farms & Gardens Group but also of the Group itself.

'When Management by Objective came in that gave a bit of a lift,' declared Maurice.

'It was very popular and used not just in the prison service but in *all* the other government departments. I mean I used to give talks about Management by Objective to all sorts of people including the Council of Europe.'

However, then he said, 'Perversely it might have started our downfall because it was very popular. It made me wonder whether

Farms & Gardens got too much publicity, whether we were outstripping our use.'

'Seen as *too good* at what you were doing?' I asked.

'I don't know,' he mused.

Farms & Gardens proved economic, productive and efficient. In 1971 they employed 2368 inmates and over the next three years profitability increased from £60,000 to £400,000. Farming within the prison service flourished in the mid-1970s. 'Eight years ago many people had considered that farming in the Prison Service was declining, they were obviously wrong as Farms & Gardens had gone from strength to strength,' stated Mr Beck, director of industries and supply in his closing address to delegates at the Farm Management Conference at Seale-Hayne College, Devon in July 1976.[6] Delegates at the time included Maurice who was regional Farms & Gardens manager for the northern region.

By 1977 Farms & Gardens were reporting a £1.5m profit.

'Profit was simply a measure of efficiency and clearly good quality work and training could not be provided by an inefficient and unprofitable unit. It was considered that the wider rehabilitative aspects of farm and garden work was in fact a bonus which had long been recognised and supported officially,' stated Peter Stevens, chief Farms & Gardens manager at the annual Farm Management Conference.[7]

A year later, even though the value of production increased by 14% to £6.8m, Farms & Gardens reported a £200,000 reduction in profit as fixed costs increased from £1.9m to £2.4m, mainly due to overtime paid to staff employed on hourly contracts. However, the department was still exceptionally profitable compared to industries, the department that ran the prison workshops and reported a £2.8m loss in 1978. However, the business-like nature of Farms & Gardens proved costly. Behind the scenes politicians began to discuss whether any of the department's land holdings, that had significantly increased in value, should or could be disposed of.

In 1982 Maurice interviewed my dad for the position of farm manager at Gaynes Hall in Huntingdonshire, 'By which time we were very well acquainted.' According to Bryan Wakely, there was a unique working relationship between them.

'I don't know what your dad had on Maurice but Bev could always walk on water. There were times when Bev had a rough time but you knew he was always going to come out alright.'

Maurice was Bev's mentor and life-long friend.

'Bev would ring me up if he wanted to know anything about the history of Gaynes Hall,' said Maurice.

It was unlikely that my dad was calling to find out about Oliver Cromwell who lived in one of the estate houses in the early 1600s, or about the Grade II listed Georgian house that once housed the governor and which, along with 20 acres, was being marketed for £2.2m in late 2016. Our quarters by contrast were more modest, a semi-detached set back from the conker tree-lined approach to the borstal.

My dad and I playing with our kid goat 'Gem' with Gaynes Hall borstal in the background.[8]

When travelling from London to visit prisons in the northern region Maurice would drop in to see my dad.

'Gaynes Hall was a place that I'd served. If I was going up north, I'd call in there for a cup of tea. I'd normally get there about 10 o'clock, dive into the farm manager's office, have a cup of tea and a chat and then be on my way so to speak, that's how we used to operate. Bev and I just chin-wagged really, sat there and passed the time of day. It was very informal. We'd talk about cricket, about football, we'd talk about what was going on. Then there were formal visits when you had a day with him going around the farm looking at the livestock, seeing if there was money that was needed for something.'

Whilst Oliver Cromwell lived at Gaynes Hall for 21 years, we only stayed for 9 months, leaving shortly before the borstal closed in 1983. Between joining one school in the spring and another in the autumn I spent the summer learning to sail on nearby Grafham Water. In November, we moved to Tadnoll Mill Farm attached to The Verne on Portland and I enrolled in my tenth school. Unfortunately, I was set according to my ability to speak Latin and German, neither of which had been offered at any of my previous schools. It took me three years to prove able enough to join the top set.

Maurice knew that Bev was one of the farm managers whom he could rely upon to do a good job. According to the Staff Inspection Report (1985) managers like Bev, 'showed greater enthusiasm and commitment than others and this was often translated into a more challenging approach in the work. They were for instance more willing to diversify, experiment and try new ideas and methods when enterprises were not performing well; appeared to set higher standards both for themselves and their staff; and last but not least seemed to be more aware of the need for, and benefits of, tighter financial monitoring and control.'[9] These staff could be called upon to take up 'detached duty', work on other prison farms across the country, and they were usually promoted quickly.

When farm staff applied for a promotion they applied for a grade rather than a particular job or post. Jason Errington recalled his boss Graham Norwood saying, 'We're having a new post, Farm Manager 4, like a bottom rung manager but the problem is you're a craftsman and you can only jump two grades when you're in the service.' Graham suggested an innovative solution, 'Apply to the advert as if you don't work for the service.'

'I got it. Maurice gave it to me! He offered me Wellingborough YOI, I was 22 and my wife was 20. There was a lovely big quarter with a long back garden but it was looked over by one of the wings. As we went in the garden they all went, "Wha' hey," so I said to my missus, "I'm not that bothered, let's just say we don't want it."' Jason who was still hoping for a career in the RAF turned it down.

'Which was a bit unheard of?' I guessed.

'Yes. Then I got a phone call. There's another option at HMP Blantyre House. I looked on the map and Blantyre was in the Weald of Kent quite near Goudhurst so I went down there and Goudhurst was nice so I took it.'

At HMP Blantyre House they said to him, 'I can see you in 20 years' time in charge of Farms & Gardens, you know standing there in your wellies with snot dripping off your nose!'

Such was the importance of the appointment of farm managers for the success of the Department of Industries and Farms that even when Maurice became an area manager in 1991 he still retained personal responsibility for their appointment.

From Blantyre House, Jason did a stint of detached duty at Standford Hill on the Isle of Sheppey in Kent. When he subsequently applied for a promotion he was offered a permanent position on the island but was reluctant to accept it.

'My wife and I didn't want to bring the kids up on the Isle of Sheppey but I didn't know how to get out of it. I said that I was going to turn the job down because my wife didn't want to go and I was told that if I didn't accept it I wouldn't go anywhere for five years.'

There was an audible lull.

'That was what I was told. And I came back with, "I've never done agriculture. I'm a horticulturalist. I'm a nurseryman by training." And they said, "Well we'll send you to college." All of my avenues that I was trying to say, "I don't want to go" were being closed off!' said Jason laughing.

'So, I said, "We'll go. We'll do two or three years there and something will come up." *Fifteen years later!*'

Jason recalled that it was Maurice who'd recommended his transfer.

'Imagine my disgust when you made me go to Standford Hill!'

'I can. All good training though!' said Maurice.

'I think that's how you sold it to me then,' laughed Jason.

I looked at Maurice, 'You probably raised your eyebrows just like that too!'

'In modern parlance, 'career planning'!'

We laughed and I remembered Bernard, who took over from Maurice as head of Farms & Gardens saying,

'He had a way of getting you to do stuff by calling you 'mate'!' and Bryan Wakely who'd said,

'You knew your number's up and you'd be moved somewhere you didn't want to go because he had plans for someone else. It was the worst thing he could call anyone!'

Income from amenity services, such as mowing grass and tending herbaceous borders within the confines of the prison, formed a key component of the profitability detailed within the annual trading accounts of Farms & Gardens. Amenity costings were calculated by the Property Services Agency and based on comparable prices charged by the relevant local authority. These costs were contained within a memorandum of understanding between Farms & Gardens and the governor of the individual establishment. The memorandum detailed not only the cost but also the type of service provided, for example, the area to be mown, the type and quantity of bedding plants to be supplied, the number of hanging boxes planted or the type of flower displays that Farms & Gardens would provide for public and communal spaces such as the prison reception or the chapel.

Despite a request in 1973 for amenity accounts to be published separately from farm accounts this wasn't realised until 1985.[10] It took a long time to disentangle amenity services from the overall farm accounts because repeated clipping and manicuring of lawns provided an important source of revenue for farm managers. Mowing, according to Bernard, was one of the most profitable activities undertaken by the Farms & Gardens department,

'We had a great system on how to mow lawns. I went to Leyhill and Eddie Chambers my predecessor made a million-pound profit on mowing grass! I think our grass acreage was about 90 acres (36 hectares) and he had 1,900 acres (769 hectares) down.'

According to Big Rob amenity costing sheets created a 'struggle' even 'rivalry' between grounds maintenance and the farms,

'Though it was not heavily spoken about,' he added.

As costs associated with the maintenance of grounds were claimed as a cost saving,

'All of the horticulture work was shoved into the pot to make the thing profitable. There was grass to mow and edge, sports fields to mark and drain and all of those things were costed and the gardens always used to know that it was their efforts that was holding the farms up but at the same time the farms would have none of that,' he laughed,

'It was one of those things that Bernard Feist and I continued to spar on.'

Despite having been profitable since 1976 and 'more than useful' to the Directorate, Farms & Gardens were never able to reinvest any of their profits.[11] 'It was what was called "A&A": Appropriation in Aid which basically meant profit but you had to dress it up differently for government because we spent tax payers' money!' exclaimed Big Rob. Almost twenty years later, in 1995, although the income generated by Farms & Gardens through sales to customers outside the prison service totalled £2.68m, all of it passed directly to the Treasury.[12] Items that contributed to the £2.68 million included: fresh milk sold to Milk Marque, excess pigs and vegetables over and above that required to supply prison kitchens, surplus animals and equipment, rare breed animals, sales to staff and prize money. Everything other than milk and pigs was dealt with at an establishment level by local management.

In response to European and national calls for a free agricultural market outlined in the 1992 MacSharry reforms to the Common Agricultural Policy, the savings generated by using prison farm labour were never credited back to the farm. The only beneficiary from this system of funding was the Treasury.

In 1988, while money for running Farms & Gardens was managed from headquarters by the head of Farms & Gardens, Maurice produced a report (a copy of which Maurice has tried to find in his loft but which currently eludes us) that showed how farms could be self-financing.

'When I came back from America I wrote a paper that showed how over a period of time you could make the farms and gardens self-sufficient. If the money that we made each year in A&A (Appropriation in Aid), which was about £4m per year, was given back to us then the money that we asked for could become a reducing commitment.'

Maurice's paper demonstrated how prison farms could benefit from economies of scale, a consequence of each area having multiple establishments in 'clusters' that could work cooperatively to source and supply food locally. He envisaged Farms & Gardens becoming a stand-alone business, akin to a community interest company. But what he was proposing was twenty years too early for the service. His ideas were never formally implemented.

'They were just not interested.'

Although the income from the farms reduced the overall costs of running the prison it couldn't be 're-used' by the prison farm, they couldn't plough back their profit and, because they were Treasury funded, they couldn't apply for any external grants. Unlike commercial farms that could draw up plans for activities across the medium- or long-term, prison farms had to work within timescales set by the Home Office and their political bosses. This put prison farms at a considerable disadvantage compared to their commercial counterparts.

'It takes two or three years from the time a calf is born for a cow to come back into the herd again,' explained Bryan so farm managers requested funds based on a 5-year livestock breeding programme.

'The prison service was on a one-year contract. It all stopped at the end of each year. The budget was for twelve months.'

'When I became a regional manager,' said Bernard, 'the Midlands used to produce the best litreage per cow which used to really upset these 'farmer types'.'

'It's only because he bribed the managers and the cowmen,' joked Maurice.

'It was mathematics! You needed a lot of cows between March and January. If you have a lot of cows for 11 months but you divide it by 12 months – it was about mathematics it wasn't anything about…,' Bernard paused so Maurice nipped in and finished his sentence,

'A wing and a prayer.'

Under pressure to fit with annual accounting cycles,

'You spent it or you didn't,' stated Bryan, 'you couldn't take the money over so you always started the next year with less budget than you had had the year before so the governor had got to think how he was going to spend the money that year.' Governors were making annual requests to the Treasury for funds and making local decisions about how to spend the money allocated to their establishment.

'Farms & Gardens were trying to plan, to have a strategy for five years, but the prison could only do a strategy for one year because that was all the budget it had. All it knew was that next year the budget was going to be less,' said Bryan. In addition to the annual financial cycle the situation was further complicated by a lack of synchronicity between the 5-year farming cycle and the typical 4-year political time frame.

'If farm mangers didn't get what they needed then they'd moan and the governor might say, "Farms are always moaning", which didn't help them attract cash for the maintenance or modernisation of their buildings and equipment,' said Maurice.

Despite despatching produce daily to London's twenty-seven prisons, the farm manager's offices at Standford Hill consisted of what had been

Photograph taken at Eastchurch (Standford Hill) in Kent in March 1970 with an inscription on the reverse that read: 'Mr Russell (Head cowman) in the modern mechanical milking dairy.'[13]

semi-circular homes built for RAF officers in 1938. Former hangars that had been used for aircraft assembly lines acted as cold storage for up to 800 tonnes of potatoes and processing and packaging units for root crops. A similar veg prep at Lindholme was described by Phil Wheatley as,

'Almost medieval. It was unheated, there was water everywhere.'

Limited maintenance budgets led prison farms to make do and mend.[14] Technically, building construction and maintenance was the responsibility of the Department of Works but farm staff tended to be reluctant to employ them as Works frequently charged more to erect a building than it would cost a commercial farmer. At some farms, staff went to great lengths to be independent from 'the Works'.

'We didn't want to know the Works. We were happy to do the work ourselves', said Bryan.

Standford Hill was a large site with historical buildings many of which were listed. 'Classic example, Standford Hill. Wright brothers flew the plane and it was where veg prep was so it was listed and listing,' joked Bernard.

'We had to put a new roof on but works said, "The new roof will cost the same as building a new wing so what do you think we are going to recommend?" That was our problem. We never had the key people on our side because we were too much of a family and looked after ourselves. We were not looking out making sure that the Works Department was on our side and happy to spend money on us. The prison roof was going to come before the farm roof.'

At HMP Usk, staff and inmates chopped down mature trees from within their own forests, planed them into planks and used them to build temporary sheds and barns. But the self-proclaimed self-sufficiency of Farms & Gardens according to Big Rob contributed to an ever-frostier working relationship developing between the two departments, 'There was always conflict. That might be too strong a word but antagonism, between works and farms. Very rarely would you find examples where they worked in complete concord with one another. For some reason, it didn't work. I suspect it was because most of the people who worked in farms were farmers and farmers out of necessity have to be self-sufficient therefore they could make do and rig something up to make it work. But it is worth noting the rivalry between works and farms.'

'Because the Works Department wouldn't maintain the buildings Farms & Gardens got in the habit of paying to have them repaired or a new building put up which shouldn't really 'ave happened because it took money away from other things,' said Chris Coveney. 'When they started doing that works said, "Well over to you" and that got out of control when they had to build proper sheds and environmental stores.'

'Is it any wonder that the Health and Safety Executive threw their hands up in horror at safety on farms because some of the, "It'll do," said Big Rob.

'So here I am standing on an elevated bucket of a tractor trying to fix a cable or whatever. It happens. And so do the accidents unfortunately.'

When an incorrectly installed two-way valve on a slurry tank at Featherstone failed, my dad slipped on the effluent and sustained a debilitating ligament injury that left him with a permanent limp. Following extensive surgery and a long period of rehabilitation his solicitor advised him to take the prison service to court and seek compensation. He never did because he couldn't afford to engage a barrister.

An area that regularly involved the Works was the upgrade of quarters. Newly appointed as a farm manager at Featherstone, my dad became eligible for central heating so a Works party that included an officer instructor and a handful of inmates spent a couple of days installing radiators. A few weeks later, our neighbour failed to investigate when our doorbell sounded like it was malfunctioning and thieves made off with my mother's engagement ring, the meagre contents of my piggy bank and the only item of any worth that my dad had inherited from his father, a double-linked, double gold chain that had once belonged to his grandfather. Word about the stolen goods circulated within the prison but nobody was apprehended. When my dad tried to claim on the household insurance the underwriters refused to pay out because we'd allowed prisoners into our home. Thereafter my dad insisted that works refurbish our quarters before we moved in.

In 1982, the year that Her Majesty's Inspectorate of Prisons was established, Farms & Gardens was turning over £13m and returning a

£2.46m profit. At that time five prisons: Featherstone, Standford Hill, Hollesley Bay Colony, Kirkham and Leyhill, had major farms or gardens and generated more than half the profit. Normally, Maurice had to argue fervently for funds from the Department of Finance which, at that time, was not especially profit-oriented but during the 1980s Maurice had the support of the head of Industries and Farms, Joan McNaughton.

'She was the only person who had faith in me,' he said. 'She always maintained that our financial systems were *way* in advance of what anyone else was doing.'

At the end of the financial year if there was money left over in the prison budget there would be a Prisons Board meeting and Joan would ask Maurice if he could make some money.[15]

'If the answer was, "Yes" and it always was,' said Maurice, 'she'd give me the money to buy for example, one hundred cows for £50,000 on the understanding that I would turn that £50,000 into £100,000. It was an easy thing to do. At that time, you could get out and buy more cows. We had a big milk quota so you could sell the milk and you not only had the value of the animal, you had the milk as well.'

With an excess of milk, Maurice saw an opportunity to add value by introducing simple, low cost processes to turn the milk into cheese and yoghurt.

A pioneer, Maurice introduced organic agriculture within the prison service, seeing it as an opportunity to replace costly agrichemicals with abundant inmate labour. He also supported the installation of renewable energy generation, motivated principally by it being 'good business' rather than benefiting the planet. Maurice pushed the department and those working in it to adapt, innovate and diversify. Howard recalled approving finance for a small trial conducted by Bryan Wakely to develop an auto mixer to add nutrients to tomatoes grown on volcanic rock wool. Deemed successful, 'Eventually a big system went in.'

Despite the relatively high permanent farm staff costs incurred by prison farms compared to their commercial counterparts, some competitors felt that the low cost of inmate labour reduced prison farm production costs and enabled prisons to unfairly undercut other suppliers. Maurice said that labour costs were related to skills in the 1960s.

'So where did Farms & Gardens come in?' I asked.

'*One from the bottom!*' exclaimed Maurice.

'One from the bottom?'

'*Yes*. The bottom one was the cleaners!'

'*Don't put that down*!' exhorted Jason.

'Toward the end,' said Maurice, 'we made a tremendous amount of progress on that. A lot of people like former Director General Chris Train didn't have that perception of us, they thought we had greater value.'

'Did that persist into the 1980s?' I asked.

In 1982 2400 inmates, out of an average daily prison population of approximately 44,000, were working within the Farms & Gardens Group. Ten years later an 80-person farm management team supervised the training and education of 3500 inmates every year who were typically paid £3 to £5 a week, in credits not cash, an amount that compared favourably with the £2.69 paid to a casual agricultural worker.

When Maurice decided that he was going to supply the entire prison service with yoghurt he saw it as an opportunity to create a product that would, like prison Industries, be able to offer real wages to inmates. Unfortunately, 'He went into a bit of an 'arms race' with Industries to be the first organisation within the prison service to offer real wages to inmates,' explained Chris Coveney. Unable to cover ongoing costs, the yoghurt venture folded.

Although introduced by Maurice, the original idea to produce wine can be attributed to Chris Train, director general of the prison service between 1983 and 1991 who thought it would be 'nice' to serve prison service wine at official dinners. Chris was 'an old-fashioned Whitehall mandarin', with an interest in farming since his youth. Amiable and supportive, Chris was a strong advocate for prison farms and particularly fond of the Suffolk Punch horses.

To deliver his wishes, Maurice found a prison farm in Kent, East Sutton Park, that was near the largest vineyard in England and therefore likely to have the best climatic conditions for cultivating grapes. To kick start production, vines were planted on a south-facing slope and Lamberhurst wines were employed to make HMP wine. When Lamberhurst folded so did the prison wine-making venture and although Lamberhurst would go on to reinvent itself and become one of the largest and most successful English wine makers, the vines at East Sutton Park withered.

In 1983, the annual value of production in Farms & Gardens reached approximately £14.6m as law and order took on a special significance in preparation for a UK general election. Attention started to shift away from profitability back towards the provision of purposeful work. In April *The Reorganisation of the Directorate of Industries and Farms* was published in which the aims and objectives of Prison Service Industries and Farms (PSIF) were clearly stated but they didn't include being profitable.[16]

The 1983 reorganisation required the Department of Industries and Farms to 'explain and demonstrate to others precisely what it is doing and for what reasons... and work more closely with the Service.'[17] But whilst clothing and textiles, engineering and woodwork, the planning and services group, finance group and management control and information systems, all underwent a detailed review process, Farms & Gardens did not. However, the report noted, 'We have allowed a considerable gulf of misunderstanding and communication to grow up between Department of Industries and Farms Headquarters and Department of Industries and Farms' staff in establishments.'[18]

The main consequence of the reorganisation for Farms was that they lost direct control over the supply of prison labour. A new position was established, head of inmate activities, who decided the number and category of inmates allowed to work outside the walls. In a conference speech delivered in 1984, a prescient Maurice, recently appointed head of Farms & Gardens said, 'Hopefully work will not become too unfashionable in the establishment and hopefully we will continue to feed the inmates.'[19]

By 1985 the financial value of produce supplied by Farms & Gardens to the prison dietary amounted to nearly £5m. The price of the produce supplied into the kitchens was set following comparisons with a range of wholesale markets with the difference between the wholesale market price and the cost of production producing the paper surplus for the farming operation. As the directorate aimed to be profitable in the widest sense, much of the farm produce was consumed within the establishments but inter-establishment nominal charging and a lack of reconciliation within each establishment caused difficulties in identifying the real costs and benefits to the Farms & Gardens. Like other parts of the Farms & Gardens it was difficult for the five veg preps to generate income to reinvest in equipment as running costs were high and they received inter-establishment nominal charging rather than an actual cash surplus for the produce they supplied to other prisons.

From 1985 onwards, to make ends meet, there had been what Rob Haslam called a lot of, 'robbing Peter to pay Paul, which was a case of make do and mend with the tractors that you've got, and we'll take that capital money and put it into something else and so on and so forth.'

'We used to have meetings to finalise what this establishment was growing and what that establishment was growing and bring it all together to see what you've got to put into the veg prep. But you always kept some money in your back pocket so if there was a problem at a particular prison you could solve it', said Derek.

'It took a little while to move the money out from the centre. We only gave them seeds and chemical money to start with. We could juggle it', agreed Bernard.

'We were heavily stretched and that was the unfortunate reality of the demise of the veg preps. Run that past Bernard,' added Big Rob so I did. I emailed Bernard and asked him whether money earmarked for the veg preps was used elsewhere and whether that had hastened their demise. He replied that repairs were a running cost and suggested that the main challenge to the viability of the veg preps was a change in dietary preferences. 'The cooked meal three times a day was a thing of the past, and pasta and pizza were replacing meat and two veg.'[20]

Some headquarters staff, including Maurice's 'very blunt' right-hand man, Tony Gilchrist, began to question the authenticity of the costing figures that were being presented,

'At the moment farm programmes are not completed accurately – completely false figures were being given. This was bad budgeting. In the future we would use computerised costings.'[21]

Tony had moved quickly from Senior Farms & Gardens Manager to Head Office where he took up the position of head of personnel within Prison Service Industries and Farms (PSIF) working closely with Maurice.

'He used to lay the law down. He would give someone a rollicking and then they'd come round and talk to me', laughed Maurice. 'He was very loyal. I could discuss anything with him and it wouldn't go outside. He was one of the few who bought into what I was all about and to be fair to him whether he totally agreed or not he stuck with it through to the end of his career. He could see the way that I wanted Farms & Gardens to evolve. I gave him the responsibility of recruitment at the lower level and he did not make many mistakes in recruitment of estate staff. If I wanted anything doing that was not nice like investigations into staff stuff like that he would do it. Some people might say that I used him too much.'

To help the bottom line Maurice realised that he could add 50% to the value of milk by making cheese.

'When I first came to East Sutton Park in 1990 we made mozzarella and ricotta cheese,' explained Lorraine Coveney.

'The cheese we made was really nice,' said Bernard.

'*Really* good,' agreed Maurice.

'We used milk to make the mozzarella and the whey to make ricotta. We did that for three years. Eventually we turned out a good product and it was selling well but it wasn't making a profit,' said Lorraine.

Although well intentioned, the cheese-making venture went sour for a number of reasons. First, there was a shortage of milk as East Sutton Park only had 33 cows so the service had to buy in extra milk from the Milk Marketing Board. This meant that they paid a premium for a product that if they had had more cows on-site, could have been supplied at nil cost. Second, as this was a specialist endeavour they had to bring in cheese-making expertise from outside; this increased their production costs and crucially, exposed them to business practices that were incompatible with Home Office procedures for procurement. Bernard and Maurice described what happened.

'The bloke we were dealing with was an Italian,' Bernard confided. 'He had a restaurant down in Brighton in the Lanes. So we go down to Brighton this Saturday morning and we get into this restaurant and it is all laid out for this big dinner so I said, "I would like the table cleared. We can't have dinner with you." So they cleared the table but this place was so *dark* and Jim, another member of staff, had a calculator that was solar powered and it wouldn't work.' Bernard laughed at the memory.

'We negotiated who was going to pay who what and because it was all in Italian lire, it was millions! We did have a cup of coffee with him when we finished. But it became a big legal problem about who owed who money.'

To be honest, at that time I didn't really understand what Bernard was alluding to but at a subsequent meeting with Maurice it became clearer when he said, 'This person got himself into problems with the justice system in Italy.'

Mo asked, 'How big was the lump of parmesan that you came home with?' Maurice didn't hesitate, 'Oh *massive!* I thought what have we got into?' He paused, 'Those are the bits of my life that I want to forget,' he added wryly.

A third reason why the cheese-making venture soured was poor communication. At the initial press launch attended by the then Director General Derek Lewis, rather than asking farm staff, who knew all about the cheese plant to answer questions from the media, the service appointed a 'dreadful' former prison marketing manager to respond, a man who liked to argue that the idea to make cheese had been his. As the TV cameras rolled the marketing manager claimed that the service had got a big sale for the cheese in London.

'Are you saying that you are selling this to Harrods?' asked the interviewer. To the incredulity of the farm staff standing nearby the marketing manager said, 'Yes I am.' But he wasn't!

Finally, following a routine inspection of East Sutton Park in 1993, the prison inspector questioned whether the cheese-making venture was an appropriate use of public funds. To address his concern, the prison service arranged another press conference, this time attended by the prison governor and Maurice's recent successor, Bernard Feist. The farm staff expected Bernard to explain that the prison farms had realised that cheese-making was unprofitable and they would be closing down the plant. To their surprise Bernard stated on national TV that not only would the cheese-making plant cover its costs but that it would be profitable within the next ten months. As Bernard walked out of the studio a member of the East Sutton Park farm staff asked him, 'Where did you get those figures from?' Bernard just smiled and said, 'Do you know where you are going to be in ten months?' Within seven months, under the directorship of Derek Lewis, Bernard had taken up a new position as head of industries.

'He didn't care. It left us with this white elephant. The governor had gone and Bernard had gone.'

With devolution of budgets to the individual establishment, losses that up until then could have been absorbed at a national level were now being passed down to the establishment and in this case, being firmly attributed to the Farms & Gardens. The new governor, faced for the first time with responsibility for establishment finances, was not prepared to pay for capital investment in a venture that he regarded as peripheral to the core role of the prison, looking after prisoners. As it had taken three years for the prison service to develop their product, the machinery started to wear out even before the cheese reached the prison dietary. Despite researching and setting up a modern production facility that enabled inmates to acquire agricultural processing skills and produce high quality outputs within an emerging market that were beginning to sell well, the new governor decisively closed down the cheese plant.

'Everyone knew it was a dead duck,' said Chris Coveney. 'We were like lambs to the slaughter.'

Around the same time that Maurice sought to diversify into cheese he looked into the prison service becoming one of the first producers of biomass fuels. At Hollesley Bay Colony and the other veg prep units (Stamford Hill, Leyhill, Lindholme and Kirkham) there was a big problem with waste.

'They were spreading water and starch (from processing potatoes), they had a lake of starch. We even had an agreement with the Works Department at Leyhill that we could put waste down their pipes to the sewers but then they did some homework and they realised that the starch would muck up the bio bacteria in the cess tank so we couldn't do it. No-one thought of that one and that cost us thousands. We could spread some of it. We had about 80 acres but the land got saturated and it had to be hauled away,' added Bryan.

Maurice visited various biomass farms and manufacturers and researched the equipment and processes necessary to reduce the spreading of slurry on fields. He saw turning manure into biomass as a way to reduce groundwater and surface water pollution. As an ash, the burnt manure, unlike the raw material, was free of pathogens, viruses and disease and had much less odour. Being more consistent it was easier and safer to handle than runny slurry which, as my dad found to his cost, could cause serious injury.

Maurice wanted to use the processed manure to heat the greenhouses where the salad crops were grown,

'We had so many greenhouses it would have saved a fortune.'

The idea was to heat the greenhouses during the winter months when animals were housed indoors and the manure was easy to collect. As all the animal manure required storage, disposal and treatment anyway this was a way for the service to literally make money from muck. There was also the potential to use the biofuel to produce hot water for use in the dairy or generate electricity to cool and refrigerate the milk.

To finance the initial installation and running costs of the biomass plants Maurice requested a 10% increase in his annual budget. But the Prison Board P9 Finance Division would not support the investment. Ahead of its time, Maurice interpreted their refusal to invest in the development of value-adding and cost-saving processing skills as a lack of institutional support for farmers within the prison service.

The story was similar for attempts to introduce organic farming. In the mid-1980s there were very few organic farmers in the UK despite an emerging interest amongst some supermarkets to stock organic food. In 1991 the Soil Association announced that it was looking for places to trial organic gardening so three small establishments volunteered to trial organic farming including HMP Drake Hall. The idea was to grow produce without the use of routine pesticides and herbicides, the use of which had doubled between 1961 and 1988 despite the publication of Rachel Carson's *Silent Spring* in 1962 and the premature mortality of farmers such as my uncle Bid and Maurice's dad.

Although for commercial growers it was generally costlier to grow organic produce, within the prison service the availability of low-cost labour offset the additional costs of hand-tending market garden crops like salad and small root vegetables. Bernard recognised that Farms & Gardens had an opportunity to be at the forefront of organic production but to be successful the prison farms required the co-operation of the prison caterers.

As the season progressed the organic gardens became 'untidy' and the size and shape of the produce became less regular. Prison caterers associated the irregular look of the vegetables and salad crops with a loss of quality. The misshapen veg arrived in the kitchens at a time when catering skills were being eroded. Caterers and inmates were losing interest in preparing ingredients that involved checking for the presence of bugs or extensive scrubbing. There was a reluctance to adapt recipes to the availability of seasonal raw produce; instead there was a demand for ready-to-eat meals. At the Farm Management Conference in 1991 it was noted that 'organic food had not so far proved its staying power and that there would be resistance to the produce from caterers on the grounds of cost and appearance.'[22]

In the face of resistance from caterers more interested in expedient, cheap food than quality produce, Bernard reluctantly ended the organic pilot. The timing was unfortunate. Only a few years later in 1995, the UK government introduced the Organic Aid Scheme to subsidise the cost of the two to five years it took to convert to organic production. This led to a significant rise in organic agriculture and in 2008, *The Clink*, the first inmate staffed restaurant opened to the UK public serving organic food produced in prison greenhouses.

In many ways these projects were ahead of their time. In the late 1980s organic produce and carbon savings were not yet part of the general narrative of agriculture, nor were they deemed necessary or desirable at either a policy or institutional level. These projects required capital investment that the service was either unwilling or unable to fund even though it would have increased efficiency and reduced costs in the medium-term. Furthermore, they were hampered by long-running animosity between different prison departments, keen to demonstrate their relevance within a rapidly evolving prison service. All of these factors contributed to the stifling of innovation and diversification.

Maurice had long argued that as Farms & Gardens were being compared with local and national farming standards, accounts should include an element of 'training loss'. Unlike commercial farms, prison farms had high staff costs because they had to employ enough staff to fulfil agricultural duties as well as ensure an adequate staff to inmate ratio for effective inmate supervision and training. Staff were often paid more than their commercial counterparts because they had to have suitable horticulture or agriculture skills and qualifications and qualities that made them suitable for working closely with inmates. These higher staff costs impacted on prison farm profitability.

'Profit is always tricky to do when you have got prisoners, you have to have additional supervision so you have got more cost. So it was unfair and unachievable,' lamented Big Rob.

Crucially, because Farms & Gardens had long been operating as a professional business, individual farms were able to account for costs as well as their profits.

'When I was farm clerk it was run as a business,' said Sarah. 'Every audit trail was in place and everything was done correctly and we knew exactly what we had on the computer. That was how he had always run it. Bev liked things to be organised.'

'Because Farms & Gardens was ahead of the game with Farmplan it was the only organisation that could actually lay out a budget plan,' explained Chris Coveney.

Farmplan was a computerised whole farm accounting system developed from DAISY (Dairy Information System) designed by Professor Richard Esslemont at the University of Reading in 1979. It was also instrumental in Maurice meeting Mo for the first time. Their paths crossed when Farms & Gardens became an early adopter of Farmplan and Mo was tasked with conveying data to the university.

'We shot ourselves in the foot really because we kept on going on about the profit, profit, profit that we were making and it came back to bite us on the bum because Industries were going on about "Employment and Training" and making a huge loss,' said Chris Coveney.

'Because of Farmplan, Farms & Gardens were the *only* organisation that could devolve the budget because they knew exactly what they had. Industries couldn't because they didn't really know what they had and who was doing what, what they were making or how much work they had. It was crazy. Industries had warehouses full of chef's check overall cloth to make clothing and they were all wearing white but they kept ordering it and they didn't really have control over it. But that is what Farmplan did for us. We were too open. It was too easy for us to lay a sheet out and say, "This is what we have, this is how much it is going to cost to repair the buildings." But again, they were not playing fair because they were expecting Farms & Gardens to pay for all the buildings and maintenance yet Industries was all paid for by the Works. They kept saying, "Well you are making all this profit you can pay for your own buildings," but Industries couldn't say that.'

Consequently, Farms & Gardens were the only organisation within Prison Industries that could devolve budgets to individual establishments, all the other Industries retained control over their own pot of money.

In 1990, as head of Farms & Gardens, Maurice managed a £15m annual budget, an 80-person management team and a temporary workforce of 3,500 prisoners. Although Farms & Gardens was the largest and most profitable prison industry, Maurice was a Grade 6 civil servant, paid the same as the heads of Catering and the Works department.

Governors found themselves overseeing farm managers who controlled the largest budgets within the establishment. At New Hall, Pete Chisholm managed £500,000 and the farm manager's budget at Lindholme, which included a veg prep, was in the region of £3–4m per annum. Devolution to individual establishments increased the power of the governor, who took charge not only of prisoners and security but, 'All the Industries, all the Farms, all of the education, absolutely everything', announced Big Rob. But many governors didn't know how much it actually cost to run their prison. When Derek was at Dartmoor the governor had a million-pound budget, 'No handle on it. Frightening. 80% of that was staff costs.' Phil recalled,

'I used to run a prison without knowing what they cost. I got bits of things like 1,000 cabbages without knowing what they cost to produce and I think that meant that we were not efficient in the way that we used the country's money.'

By the early 1990s the prison service as a whole was being criticised for poor planning and management but the farms were operating well and going from strength to strength. 'In conclusion it was stated that there was a feeling that too many people judged the Prison Service by its failures, but it would be sad indeed if such a thoroughly professional organisation as the Farms & Gardens were so judged.'[23]

It was widely acknowledged that Farms & Gardens provided inmates with healthy and therapeutic work as well as creating 'an atmosphere of trust and responsibility between inmate and staff which was much more difficult to achieve in closed conditions'.[24] Given their all-pervasive nature and the huge contribution they made to the overall profitability of the establishment, governors, especially those who had no farming knowledge, relied heavily upon farm managers. But there were some people within the service who envied the success and positive profile of the prison farms and others who found it threatening and unpalatable to have farmers occupying the office next to the governor and being effectively second-in-command. Some felt that farms had an over-inflated view of themselves and in accordance with the maritime origins of the prison service, they felt that farms needed taking down a peg or two.

In 1993 all farming and horticultural activities were integrated into Prison PSIF, an organisation controlled by Prison Enterprise Services (PES) from Home Office headquarters. Budget and staffing decisions were controlled centrally with the aim of maintaining a national approach to the provision of food for the prison service and the upkeep of its horticultural estate.

The change of name of the annual farm conference in 1993 reflected the subjugation of Farms within Enterprise Services. What had been the Farm Management Conference became simply a Management Conference and there was no longer any room in the schedule for farm walks or farm visits. Nevertheless, there was optimism about the future of the Farms,

'I didn't get any hint that it was likely to decline', said Howard when he retired from the Service in 1993.

'We should have had a better working relationship with industries. Farms & Gardens and Industries? No. Farms & Gardens. Industries. The two might have been in the same building but they weren't together,' insisted Bernard.

A further reorganisation in 1994 did bring Industries and Farms together but split the organisation into work supply and technical. The position of chief of Farms & Gardens disappeared and Bernard moved to head up work supply whilst Jeremy Fallows took over as head of technical. Bernard's appointment as head of industries rekindled old animosities between Farms and Industries, as the most powerful positions were given to people within the tight-knit Farms & Gardens group.

Once in post, Bernard decided to 'sort out' the Textile Industry whose staff included Norma McLoughlin, head of operations for Public Sector Prison Industries when I met her. Norma recalled meeting Maurice in the early 1990s when prison service headquarters where based at Lunar house in Croydon. At that time Maurice managed 250 staff, approximately 50 of whom were based at Lunar house. In March 2016 the number of staff at NOMS headquarters,

'Are 50 for everything, for everything. So that is the scale,' said Norma. 'And now we,' she added meaning Farms & Gardens, 'are down to one.'

Norma enquired about the wine-making at East Sutton Park and said that there was a rumour that there were still bottles of HMP wine squirreled away.

'Yes, but nobody seems to know where it is. I'll ask Bernard,' I said.

'He'd know where all the skeletons would be buried!' laughed Norma.

'Trust me,' wrote Bernard when I emailed him, 'it's not worth hunting down. It was horrible!'

10

Making the grade

'If a man does not keep pace with his companions, perhaps it is because he hears a different drummer.' Henry David Thoreau, *Walden*[1]

For Maurice and his staff, the principal reason for operating prison farms with prison labour was to inculcate 'a real work ethic'. Between 1974 and 1983 inmates employed on farming and ancillary work (for example, forestry) rose by a quarter from 2,000 to 2,611 despite the number of prison farms halving from thirty-five to seventeen.

'I had an inmate,' recalled John Glover, 'he was only a young lad and he worked with me on the cattle. You know he said to me, "I've never worked a day in my life but I've got so used to getting up and coming down here to Misterton Carr Farm, when I leave I may look for a job." Whether he ever did or reverted back to his old ways I don't know.'

To reduce costs and ensure there was plenty of work, the prison service bought very poor quality land that was especially difficult to cultivate. Big Rob recalled a former Home Secretary requesting the purchase of marginal land near Birmingham but on inspection saying, 'There's not nearly enough hard work on this farm. We can give that one back. We need much harder work.' Consequently, they rented Frankley farm from Birmingham City Council instead.

'There were hundreds of acres of gorse and the Home Secretary was delighted. There was a huge land clearance programme and prisoners were having life and death struggles with gorse bushes for years and years.'

Unlike commercial operations that could buy premium farmland or hire and fire as desired, prison farm staff had an obligation to provide work suitable for anyone allocated to them, willing or not. Although levels of pay between prisons and outside industries were similar it was unrealistic and inappropriate to expect the same level of productivity. Jobs had to be able withstand interruptions from visitors such as family or probation officers or attendance on educational courses or rehabilitation programmes.

'No matter what things you try and do the thing that you have to get it down to is that you are dealing with prisoners,' said Jason Errington. 'You're going to get someone coming in who's not going to work and he'll stop the bloke next to him working and you've always got to bear that in mind. What you make is a by-product of what we are trying to achieve; rehabilitating, training and introducing the prisoner to a work ethic. The product is just incidental.'

'When I went to Exeter,' said Derek, 'I had the sheep as well, 300 Exmoor Horn sheep and 80 Ayrshire cows, pedigree Ayrshire cows. A lot of the workers there I could have left the milking to them, within a month you'd get them trained up and they were like *workmen* you know. I had a good bloke number one on the sheep, he'd been there six times, he was done for shifting stolen goods, not a *real* criminal really but he was on the sheep and he could shear as well.'

As Farms & Gardens work was planned and carried out on a long-term basis the Department provided employment for a full working week throughout the year; such continuity was more difficult to achieve in other industries. 'Farms and gardens can be much more resilient than workshops absorbing fluctuations in the population of an establishment and more readily offer scope for prisoners to be fully occupied, in the open air, rather than be left unemployed inside an overcrowded establishment.'[2]

Between 1970 and 1981 the average working week for prisoners reduced from 26 hours to 21.5 hours, meaning that the total number of inmate hours worked almost halved from 21.7m to 11.6m. Nevertheless, inmates tended to work longer hours on the farms than those allocated to industries such as catering, workshops or the laundry, who started later, finished earlier and took longer breaks. A typical working day for inmates on the farms started at 0830, followed by lunch between 1140 and 1300 and an afternoon session that ended around 1640. For prisoners working on the land, their day was often extended by travelling long distances to the farm, for example, Tadnoll Mill Farm was 16 miles from Portland's The Verne.

Other industries tended to employ more prisoners than was strictly necessary to do the job which meant that each person had less to do. A Brunel University study conducted in 1992, that focused heavily on industries inside the walls, concluded that prison work and training didn't help prisoners obtain employment after release or help them avoid re-offending.[3] Importantly, horticultural and amenity placements had additional costs such as rent, utility charges and capital equipment depreciation, unlike education or physical training places that were costed on teaching hours alone.[4]

Farms were not only expected to occupy prisoners, they were also expected to teach social and practical skills and provide opportunities to gain formal qualifications to enhance the prospect of taking up a job on release. In 1971 following the establishment of the National Test Proficiency Council, the first formal Farms & Gardens training for inmates was established with ten inmates at Kirkham prison attending a day release class at a local college. This was quickly followed by the introduction of an agricultural training course at Gaynes Hall.

'There was a brick shop, a plumbing shop, the farm, the welding shop and the lads would go into the plumbing shop or the painting and decorating shop or whatever and learn the trade and then they'd get a certificate like an apprenticeship,' explained Steve Horrocks.

Gaining qualifications could motivate inmates, reduce the amount of supervision they required and help them find employment on discharge. Formal qualifications were likely to increase their rate of pay. Statistically, whilst 60% of prisoners without any qualifications are likely to be re-convicted one year after release, this reduces to 45% for those with a qualification and for those who find work, the recidivism rate reduces substantially to between 5 and 22%.[5]

In 1976 136 inmates working on the farms gained proficiency certificates and 21 passed their City & Guilds in agriculture certificate. Two years later 228 inmates were awarded proficiency certificates. The number of inmates gaining qualifications might have been higher if the structure of the initial courses had been different; as examinations were only held once a year some trainees had already left custody. However, it was not long before arrangements were put in place for inmates who had been released to take the examination at external centres if they wanted to and those in custody could take them on site because the prisons themselves became test centres.

Transferable skills could also help inmates find and keep employment post-release and thereby reduce the likelihood of reoffending. Eleven prisons including Leyhill, Featherstone, Ashwell, Dartmoor, Kirkham and The Verne had machinery repair workshops where inmates refurbished old tractors. As we looked through his extensive collection of photographs and videos, Howard Morse called upon his prodigious memory,

'The blue tractor is a DOE DD tractor in Essex.'

Some of Howard's photographs were used to promote Farms & Gardens which often stressed the variety of jobs and opportunities on offer 'in ancillary activities such as estate maintenance, the repair of agricultural machinery and equipment, the processing and marketing of produce and the manufacture of jam, pickles and other articles of food. It creates links, at a number of establishments, with vocational training through farm and horticultural training schemes organised in conjunction with the Education service.'[6]

Farms & Gardens' policy focused on using 'modern methods and management techniques'[7,8] to develop prisoners' practical and transferable skills. 'The range of skills required in agriculture is such that it offers employment to persons of varying abilities as well as providing a promotion ladder from navvying to such crafts as dairying, stockmanship, tractor driving, plant and shrub propagation. Achievement is largely up to the individual but no inmate is left unaware of the skills he may acquire or of the scope for particular interests which he may develop and which he may be able to pursue, should he prove able and worthy of the responsibilities involved.'[9]

'Our prisoners knew how to dig, knew how to handle a JCB, knew how to handle a dumper and a tractor,' said Bryan.

'The gas people would come in and offer them employment because not a lot of people out there today want to get down a manhole or into a pit and start digging with a pick and shovel and at the same time operate a JCB.' Through 'provision of a steady working day, farms enabled inmates to develop commitment to a job, encourage a sense of responsibility, learn new skills and acquire a degree of self-confidence and achieve a sense of self-respect.'[10]

'We were the only part of the prison that would take an inmate off the street, give him six weeks training and give him a £50,000 combine to drive,' said Maurice.

'It wouldn't happen anywhere else. But senior management and the inspection team used to 'poo poo' that.'

Tractor driver Baker (Estate Hand) supervising an inmate in the farm machinery repair shop at HMP Kirkham in Lancashire in March 1970.[11]

Farms & Gardens had a long history of collaborating with external bodies such as Young Farmers' Clubs (YFCs) to develop basic literacy, numeracy and technical skills. YFCs, farm training classes and correspondence courses were integral to the running of prison farms since 1952 when six borstals had YFCs.[12] In time, every borstal with a substantial farm had a YFC linked to it. Through the YFCs it was possible for inmates to associate with young people outside the establishment, participate in competitions and fulfil positions of responsibility such as becoming a member of the local YFC committee.

Gaynes Hall was typical of a borstal with a farm and a YFC. 'The boys sent to Gaynes Hall in the late 1960s are, in general, in the 18 to 20 age group, healthy and of good intelligence. They are the sort of boys who have the best chance of succeeding in their borstal training... Gaynes Hall have a branch of the Young Farmers' Club and visit other clubs in the district... All these activities are good in themselves but, more important, they let the community see and know the boys and prevent the boys from feeling hopelessly rejected before their adult life is begun.'[13]

Maurice recalled running the YFC at Usk in the late 1960s where the 'borstal boys' took part in 'social, public speaking, judging, everything and as a reward the farm staff used to take them out for an evening,' which was how they ended up on the town in Newport 'picture house' in 1968.

Maurice and the farm foreman took a group of about 20 'lads', all YFC members from Usk borstal, to watch *Shane*, an American Western that, appropriately enough, told the story of a drifter and retired gunfighter who turned up in a small Wyoming town with the hope of settling down as a farmhand.

'The staff to inmate ratio was not particularly high,' said Maurice, 'so we got them in a row, he sat one end and I sat the other. We watched the film and thought *this is brilliant,* no problems at all. But when we got up and went out through reception there was *all* these coppers.

Borstal boys from Hollesley Bay prison in Suffolk on an outing to a local cinema.[14]

The boys had been nipping over the back of the seats and going out on the town! They'd come back in again before the film ended. We hadn't noticed *a thing*!'

An undated PSIF video made by Howard showed inmates smoking and sharing a laugh with farm staff whilst working out the optimal number and size of cabbages to pack into wooden crates.[15]

'I used to say that people who look after the animals, drive the tractors or plant the seeds, if you give them the confidence to add up or make up the rations there's always an educational element to all that they did: maths, methodology, everything was there, it was like a practical classroom for them but a lot of what I said fell on stony ground,' said Maurice adding, 'Some took it to heart.'

In 1990 the National Vocational Qualification (NVQ) level one agriculture was introduced with the first complete level one certificate being gained by an inmate from HMP Verne, Portland. A year later an amenity horticulture NVQ was also introduced. Eventually, inmates could complete NVQs on site at all establishments. According to Bryan,

'NVQs should have been the best thing to happen to farms. If you had an NVQ level in hairdressing it was exactly the same skills that you needed do building or agriculture. They were transferable skills like handling money or meeting and greeting people.'

Whilst an inmate at one of the last remaining prison farms, East Sutton Park, Amy Cullen gained a NVQ – Level 2 Diploma in Work-Based Agriculture.

'The practical skills that I have gained while working on the farm are vast. From repairing fences and tractor driving to livestock management, handling and care. It really has been all encompassing. I have no idea what the future holds for when I am released from prison, but I have no doubt in my mind that it will involve working with animals and utilising the skills which I have gained here on the East Sutton Park Farm.'[16]

However, some staff fought against the introduction of NVQs.

'They were frightened because they had to go and sit a test themselves. Some, like Bev, didn't have to take a test because they had a depth of knowledge, five or more years' experience. But if you were only employed for two or three years you had to do a training course and sit an exam. Sit. Exam. Writing? They didn't want to do it,' declared Bryan.

Bev had excellent management skills and he was an accomplished farmer but like Bryan, he found writing challenging and he had few formal qualifications. Both men were naturally left-handed but from an early age my dad had been forced to write with his right hand. Consequently, his writing, a random mixture of upper and lower case, was difficult to decipher. But illegible handwriting was not uncommon amongst staff, particularly farm staff. As Bernard said,

'You could never read Phil's writing. You'd get his handwritten bit and what his secretary had typed underneath.'

When Bernard retired from the prison service in 2010 he received a farewell card from Phil. On it he'd written, 'I will miss you.'

'I think it said, "I will," it might have said, "I have,"' joked Bernard adding, 'My handwriting is bad but Phil's was worse.'

Bryan described Bernard's writing as, 'Appalling. Spider writing,' and noted that Bernard relied on his assistant, a man called Geoff Peters, 'as his pen pusher, his writer, his scribe.'

But Bryan conceded that 'Bernard's comprehension of the language was very good.'

'Bev's squiggle or writing was like my squiggles writing' noted Bryan who was taking notes when he met my dad for the first time.

'Do you know you've got the same problem as I've got?' said Bev.

'Have I?' enquired Bryan.

'Yes.'

'And that was it, we said no more. And the sad part about that was I did thirty-one years in the prison service and I never admitted to it for twenty-six years. It was only in my last five years I was strong enough to say, "I am dyslexic." I was recognised, having enrolled for a degree, and from the Department's point of view then I had to put on my form 'dyslexia' as a disability. I had the word spelt out and I kept it in my pocket.'

Ironically, 'Mr (W)right the righter' as my dad was widely known, who was neither a reader nor a writer, featured on the front cover of the prison service recruitment journal for fifteen years. He was photographed posing in front of a wall lined with books in the library at the Wakefield prison officer training centre shortly after he joined in 1975.

Never formally diagnosed as dyslexic, my dad relied on his wit, charm and audio technology to communicate. Like Bryan he was indebted to support staff particularly clerks like Sarah.

'I just filled in the bits that I couldn't read and he'd say, "Yeah, that's fine." He had his own style and you got used to it!'

Bryan said, 'There was a good bunch of ladies in the typing pool. They gave me a Dictaphone. When we got rid of the typing pool and we had computers that helped me because with two fingers you can't go fast! You soon realised when you went to a new prison that you had to hunt out and find that person who could help you on the admin side and it could be anybody. In fact, when I was at North Eye I found a deputy governor of all people you know.'

According to the Scottish National Farmers' Union, dyslexia disproportionately affects 25% of those working in agriculture compared to 10% in the general population. Bev and Bryan's undiagnosed dyslexia made them reluctant to apply for senior positions within Head Office.

'I didn't want to go because I knew that my problem would make it difficult for me because you have so many reports to write,' said Bryan.

Interestingly, when I met Chris Coveney at Head Office in December 2015, he explained that his staff were very lucky if they received a written email from him, he too preferred to communicate verbally. Amongst the prison population an estimated 40% are dyslexic so delivering education and training through practical rather than classroom tasks suited staff like my dad and the inmates they supervised.[17] Ultimately, my dad's dyslexia meant that he was never going to write this book but as his close friend Chris McGown stressed,

'Your dad always worked around the corner!'

In the late 80s and early 90s the Staff Personal Development Report was introduced and Bev was recruited to train senior officers and middle managers about the new system. He was expected to prepare and deliver a formal presentation to prison officers who'd been released from their duties on the wings to attend the compulsory training courses held in 4- or 5-star hotels around the country. Undeterred by his dyslexia he developed a presentation style that was based on his personality. After taking to the podium Bev would often be met with 'What do you know? You're a *bloody farmworker*'. A charming, consummate professional he'd undercut all the venom by making them laugh.

Back on the farm Bev relied heavily on his farm clerks to maintain the farm ledgers and stock records, prepare orders for purchases of stock, process invoices for payment, compile quarterly estimates and prepare the annual Trading Account. Sarah started working with Bev in about 1993 when his former secretary Jill went on maternity leave. When Jill returned to work, they job-shared which pleased my dad because he was very fond of both them.

'Bev was wonderful to work for. It has got to be one of the best jobs I've had, even when he made me count the sows. I used to love the little piglets but when it came to counting the sows he'd say, "Get in there and count them." We used to do that every quarter and I don't think there were many other farm clerks who had to do that but we had to do it. We would have a year-end Farms & Gardens seminar when all of Yorkshire and Humberside would get together and they'd name and shame if people did not get their returns in on time. We weren't allowed to be on the 'name and shame', we had to be on time. When he was at Hatfield we knew everything, we knew exactly what animals of what breed we had, it was run like a proper business.'

'He was a businessman,' agreed Chris McGown,

'They found that out when he went up to work in London. They found out just how much of a businessman he was and they were a bit frightened of him some of them. And I think they tried to keep him away from people that he might influence. I know that 'feared' is not the word but people were very cautious.'

When my dad joined the prison service, my mum was advised that he'd 'never be the same again, it will alter him.' Already used to discipline and authority having served in the merchant navy, he'd adapted easily to the routine of prison. A 'true professional' according to Maurice, Pete Chisholm said that Bev, 'taught me to engage my brain before opening my mouth. He took a strategic overview rather than wading straight in.' But as Sarah commented,

'I wasn't exactly scared of him but I was dubious because if Bev shouted, everyone knew about it. I was never on the wrong side of him. That wasn't somewhere you wanted to be. If he thought he was right, then he wouldn't back down. Once it was resolved, majority of the time, that was it, sorted. No hard feelings.'

Christine corroborated Sarah's experience,

'I always remember him as saying exactly what he wanted, when he wanted it, how he wanted it and that was him, he had his opinion and that was it. I mean we had lots of discussions about whether his cows were worth more than other cows on the farm plan and he made sure that they were in the right category, the right value and all the rest of it. That was him. He was not afraid to say something. He was very honest.'

'He was who he was, not what people wanted him to be,' said Bryan.

'He was quite a bluff sort of character,' noted Rob. 'He was a big farm manager and I was just "the boy", the technical boy in head office of very little consequence. To say he didn't exactly make friends easily was not fair because he always was willing and helpful and he always had a smile on his face. He was usually amused at something that was going on, that was going wrong. He found some amusement in that.'

Whilst it's been acknowledged that 'The positive value staff gain from prison work is often missing from traditional accounts of the prison officer,'[18] the experience of prison and civilian staff working on the outside of the prison remains largely undocumented. From my discussions with former and current Farms & Gardens staff, it was evident that they felt part of a team, a family of farmers who valued and supported each other.

'It was like a family,' confirmed Chris Coveney, who was seconded to NOMS HQ to take care of land based activities after Big Rob retired.' When I updated Pete on progress with the book, he emailed,

'Great to see all the names of people, all of which I know, 'twas a family affair the prison farms once upon a time.'

'We were close knit,' said Jason.

'It's the only organisation that I've known that's a family,' agreed Bryan,

'No other organisation had a family like we did. We had all the problems of a family but it was a family.'

'It wasn't just the farm managers was it?' prompted Christine.

'No, all the staff, the admin staff as well,' he affirmed diplomatically.

'Having my 21st birthday at Hatfield, it were wonderful,' said Sarah.

'This officer 'ad found a blue teddy made by an inmate in a needlecraft class and they'd give it to me. I felt like I belonged. It was a really lovely day. I loved working in Farms & Gardens and everyone did seem to get on with everyone else. We were a team, we really were. And if there was a problem Bev was there and he'd go out and sort it out and that's not always the case. I've never worked since then as part of a team where if you'd had a bad day they'd say, "life happens" and give you support.'

'The sad thing is that Bev would have enjoyed going round and meeting everyone,' lamented Lorraine.

'Best I can do is to be here instead,' I said.

Chris Coveney added, 'You must find everywhere you go that there isn't anyone in the Farms & Gardens in the prison service who isn't passionate about farms and gardens and working with prisoners and stuff?'

I agreed, 'It's incredibly positive.'

'Everybody is really passionate about what they do, even the lazy ones!' exclaimed Chris, 'If you asked the officers, it would be a very short book!'

'That's because if you love the animals you care for them,' said Lorraine, 'Agriculture, even horticulture, is more of a life-choice than a job isn't it? Particularly the livestock side of it.'

But then she added, 'Gardening, possibly not.'

My dad loved his animals, they were treated like family. Rather than pictures of his wife or children, his wallet contained photographs of prize-winning Lincoln Red cows and his dog.

'Farms & Gardens,' said Big Rob, 'it was like a family. As with all families there are characters and falling outs and you really need to include that.'

I knew what he meant. During my dad's last few years in the service he suffered harassment and bullying and, as I heard from his former colleagues, he was not alone.

In 2004 new grades like head of teaching were brought in. People who'd never worked in a prison before and had little, if any, knowledge of agriculture or horticulture were appointed to manage the farm staff.

'I'll never forget having a huge row with this woman who was almost as powerful as a deputy governor,' said Steve.

An inmate tending plants in a greenhouse at Kirkham prison in Lancashire.[19]

'She'd been put in to get training back in. They re-opened all these workshops that were opened in the 80s and shut in the late 80s. I'll never forget they said, "You're a manager F, a very senior position and you're wasting your time with animals, you should be leading on the training." And I said, "No, I'm a senior farm manager *because* of my knowledge of agriculture, that is my specialism," and she wouldn't have it. She said, "A craftsman can do all the work that you do." In the good old days, the farm manager was thought highly of for being the head of the farms but they just didn't want to know. They just didn't understand. This head was only interested in learning and skills. For example, we had a greenhouse and there were twenty prisoners working in this huge, two-acre greenhouse, biggest greenhouse in the prison service at Kirkham.'

'We produced 18 tonnes of tomatoes out of that greenhouse. The veg prep would take so many and the surplus would go to a wholesaler. And on a Friday we had to get all those tomatoes picked and on the wagon by 3pm. Not maybe. We *had to* by 3pm. And she's going on about training,

"I want ten of your men out of that greenhouse for training."

"You can't have them. We have to get those tomatoes out." I said.

"That'll have to wait."

"They can't wait, they'll go off. You either want production *or* you want training, you can't have both. Come to the greenhouse and have a look with me."

"*No*."

'She didn't understand and she didn't come anywhere near the greenhouse. You have to get ready for harvesting, get them packed and get them away. She wouldn't have it. I started to become disillusioned then. That's why I left. They didn't care about the farms. All she was interested in was,

"If you don't do training, then shut it down."'

11

A fresh start

'Grown-ups love figures... When you tell them you've made a new friend they never ask you any questions about essential matters. They never say to you 'What does his voice sound like? What games does he love best? Does he collect butterflies?' Instead they demand 'How old is he? How much does he weigh? How much money does his father make?' Only from these figures do they think they have learned anything about him.' Antoine de Saint-Exupéry, *The Little Prince*

Attendees at the 1980 Farm Management Conference, held in the Abbey Hotel in Great Malvern, Worcestershire attributed the beginning of the end to the May Committee Report, commissioned in Autumn 1978 and published in 1979, across what became known as 'the winter of discontent' due to the prevalence of industrial action amongst public sector workers.[1] 'The evidence submitted by the Government to the Committee will be read by historians and can be seen as a Domesday Book of the Prison Service,' said Mr Neale OBE, newly appointed director of regimes and services.[2] The *May Report* was an independent inquiry into the state of the British prison system: the living conditions of prisoners, alleged drug use and brutality, the state of relationships between staff and prisoners as well as between prison officers, governors, outside specialists, Prison Department officials and the Prison Officers' Association (POA) who wanted pay parity with the police. Some commentators at the time questioned the independence of the report, suggesting that it was a means to legitimate the Home Secretary William Whitelaw's policy on prisons.[3]

The *May Report* focused on industrial relations and made a series of managerial recommendations that resulted in changes to pay and allowances, the reorganisation of senior management at headquarters and in the four regional offices. David Faulkner was charged with putting the recommendations of the *May Report* into effect. He suggested the creation of a new administrative post, director of operational policy, which he fulfilled between 1980–1982, overseen by Director General Dennis Trevelyan who, according to Faulkner, 'had a 'normal' Head Office administrative background.'[4]

The *May Report* led to a redefinition of Prison Rule I (para 4.26) centred on positive custody, elimination of cell sharing and better sanitation for prisoners (although it would take thirteen years before 'slopping out' was ended in 1994). It called for a greater degree of unity and identity within the prison service: 'Change must look different as well as be different or prove damaging to the Service,' advised Mr Neale OBE.[5] Meanwhile, Chief Farms and Gardens Manager Peter Stevens congratulated farm managers, 'for achieving, he thought, the only bouquet in the May Committee Report. Modesty prevented him from reading it aloud but advised anyone who had not seen the note to refer to paragraph 4.32 of the Report!'

However, the following section in the Farm Management Conference proceedings stated, 'A good year indeed was 1979/80 for Farms & Gardens with only one cloud on the horizon which called for comment and perhaps clarification. Delegates, he said, would be aware that a series of meetings was underway to consider whether any of the Department's land holdings should be disposed of and this may have given some cause for concern about future job prospects.'[6]

To check what Peter Stevens was referring to I ordered the page containing paragraph 4.32 from the online National Archive and received a notification saying that I could purchase and download the *May Report*. However, there was also a 'Note to Customer' stating that they couldn't find a reference to Cm 7673 (even though Cmnd 7673 was written on the front cover of the report) or a paragraph 4.32 which left me somewhat confused!

The *May Report* precipitated a reorganisation of the Prison Department with regional industrial managers and their staff being removed and a departmental working party being set up to reappraise the role and function of the Directorate of Industries and Farms (DIF). In terms of size and influence DIF should have been called Directorate of Farms and Industries but the decision to put industries first was, according to Maurice, just a matter of making the name and the acronym easier to say. There was he said, 'just friendly rivalry and banter' between Industries and Farms whereas the relationship between Farms, Education, Works and Catering was often more fraught.

Up to this point both Industries and Farms had been providing services *to* the prison service, the main difference being that Industries, with the exception of quarrying on Dartmoor (that was undertaken in collaboration with Works), was situated inside the walls, and farms were outside the prison walls.

A firm of management consultants, Arthur Young McClelland Moores & Co were brought in to review DIF activities with a view to improving management systems, organisation and efficiency, and in doing so became the first outside company to report on the organisation of the prison service.[7] Around the same time, a Staff Inspection Report published in 1985 noted, almost as an aside, that the requirement for the service to farm prison land had never been formally established.[8]

'We thought we had better be a family,' said Maurice, so in the late 80s the four core activities, ordered in diminishing importance: keeping inmates secure, feeding them (Catering), housing them (Works) and occupying them (Industries and Farms) became integrated within Prison Service Industries and Farms (PSIF).

Many I spoke to attributed 'the start of the end' to limitations imposed on overtime associated with *Fresh Start* or the *Next Steps Report* as the policy was more formally referred to outside of the prison service. The *Next Steps Report* had four themes: focus on the 'job to be done', have the 'right people', maintain 'a pressure for improvement' and take on more of the role of delivery. The seeds of the policy were sown with the election of Margaret Thatcher as Prime Minister in 1979 and the establishment of The Efficiency Unit, headed by Derek Rayner, joint managing director of Marks and Spencer, whose express remit was to identify ways for government departments to save money. Within the prison service, *Fresh Start* prioritised changes in staff pay. 'The first modern restructuring of the Prison Service management and working arrangements began with a policy known as *Fresh Start* in 1987... in a five-year phased programme it terminated the overtime culture hitherto enjoyed by prison officers to the extent that by 1992 all prison officers would be salaried and working a 39-hour week.'[9]

1987 certainly marked a 'fresh start' for us as a family. After five years at Tadnoll Mill Farm, the longest we'd ever lived in one place, my dad was promoted to farm manager 1A at Hatfield whilst his opposite number, Mike Pengelly, transferred to Tadnoll. Such transfers were commonplace. Jason recalled moving his family from county to county, Norfolk, Kent, the Isle of Sheppey then Sussex,

'Once I did Ford I said that's it I'm not moving again. I've moved my family so many times and I don't want to move anymore.'

As my dad and Mike had exchanged jobs, they were expected to swop quarters but my mum refused to live 'in the sticks' at Misterton Carr Farm so they settled into a house that nestled in the armpit of two motorways, directly opposite Hatfield prison instead.[10] My parents left my sister and I behind but to claim the moving allowance for dependent children my best friend and I pretended to be sisters. During our cursory visit I met Pete Chisholm, John Glover and Lorraine Coveney for the first time.

At the 1991 Farm Management Conference, 'Mr Wright opened the session by taking the audience back to June 1987 and the introduction of *Fresh Start* at Hatfield, bringing with it the new area of inmate activities.'[11]

Officers were on overtime until *Fresh Start* put them all on a 37-hour week with no overtime,' said Steve Horrocks. 'They needed to

An Officer Instructor inspecting salad crops at Hewell Grange, Worcestershire.[12]

reduce overtime and that was the start of the end. They couldn't get enough inmates out and the staff to inmate ratio was poor.'

'*Fresh Start* was the first 'nail in the coffin' for farms,' he concluded.

It took a while but eventually all members of the Prison Officer Association (POA) agreed to support *Fresh Start*. At Wandsworth the governor 'locked-out' all the POA members who refused to sign up to a unilateral shift policy, the strike lasted from 29 January to 8 February 1989.

'We didn't have an officer out on the farm anymore,' said Steve. 'The vast majority of open prisons just wanted large parties to do work on the farm and they'd send one officer but without an officer they reduced the numbers of prisoners allowed out.'

As officer instructors were removed, farm staff received training in the management (and constraint) of inmates and began to take over disciplinary roles, supervising as many inmates as they felt comfortable with in ways that they felt worked.

'They used to want us to have more prisoners per member of staff to be more cost effective. Every member of staff was supposed to have twenty prisoners. But if one of the farm staff is going to go out ploughing he can't take twenty prisoners with him in the tractor.'

According to Steve, the prison service response was,

'"Well, don't do the ploughing."

We said, "We've got to do the ploughing," but we couldn't get through to them.'

My dad and his co-presenter, the newly appointed head of inmate activities at Hatfield, Hazel Lydon, 'realised that to ensure success a training exercise would be needed to enable the new Head of Inmate Activities (HIA) to understand exactly what went on 'down on the farm'. The Farm Manager's responsibilities to the HIA, and his acting-up in the HIA's absence – chairing meetings etc. – was outlined and the fact that the Farm Manager had become more involved with the overall management of the establishment… Working with the HIA… had enabled the farms to gain a higher profile within the regime and the culmination of this had been the Farm Manager's elevation to functional head in his own right. Mrs Lydon also began her session by referring to *Fresh Start* and her appointment as Head of Inmate Activities. Her introduction to Farms & Gardens, and in particular the

Lincoln Red Bull – she had not realised how big they were – was recalled.'[13]

It was unusual for there to be co-presenters at the 1991 'farm walk' but Bev and Hazel Lydon's decision to share the floor reflected a new development within the service. In the future, farm managers would be reliant on the head of inmate activities for the allocation of prisoners, and it was likely that other head of inmate activities would only know as much about cows or farming as Hazel.

Hazel was a psychologist and she got on well with my dad. Widely regarded as a 'fixer', my dad arranged for me to meet Hazel so that I could learn about opportunities for psychologists within the prison service. Hazel was one of the first of a new type of prison employee, a graduate who would be fast-tracked through the service, becoming governor in charge of Acklington, Frankland and Belmarsh before becoming the head of Women & Young People's Group covering twenty-five prison establishments. My dad admired Hazel but like many fast-tracked university graduates she had little or no direct experience of agriculture or horticulture. As Jason noted, in the absence of experience, this led some operational staff to make decisions based on 'pre-conceived ideas about farms and gardens'.

I was due to graduate from Sussex University with a degree in psychology at a time when graduate job prospects were the lowest they'd been for twenty years. I appreciated my dad's intervention but having moved repeatedly and attended ten different schools, I associated a career inside the walls with insecurity.

'It's given me a good living so I can't complain,' said Jason. 'I won't think that I've wasted my work time because I've enjoyed what I did,' but he didn't want his children working on the wings, 'They're just not nice places.'

Maurice had no regrets but when his granddaughter who, having studied criminology at university, sought his advice about working in a prison he said,

'*No, no, keep away!*'

Most Farms & Gardens' staff were members of the Agriculture and Allied Workers Union and their pay and conditions were covered by the Agricultural Wages Board. Farm managers tended to join the Prospect/IPMS union which also represented prison chaplains. Being active members of the farm section committee of the union, Bev, Bernard, Maurice and Derek were all heavily involved in the negotiations around overtime and changes to basic pay for farm staff that were part of *Fresh Start*. They saw it as an opportunity for farmers to directly influence policy makers.

'You got to know what was going on and you got to meet people, high ranking people,' noted Bernard.

Seasoned negotiators, they enjoyed their work with the union,

'One of the advantages of the unions was that it gave you a chance to deal with ministers, you could make a little bit of a mistake,' and 'learn how to operate in their presence,' explained Maurice.

Bernard elaborated,

'The biggest plus *ever* was when we had the Max Jenkins report on farm gradings and they had come up with one farm manager pay grade of 1A. We spent this night, us as the union, the official side, and Ivor Gough chairing the meeting. I said, "We are quite happy to sit here all night until we have got this sorted out," and my colleagues were looking at me thinking, "What the hell is he going on about? We've got nothing else to say!" So then we said, "We're going to have to call it to a halt because Maurice has got to go to a football match!"'

Maurice laughed heartily at the recollection as Bernard continued,

'Well they had to agree to an adjournment and reconvene two days later. If they'd called our bluff! It was a good bit of negotiation. We baffled Headquarters because we kept telling them they needed new 1As and old 1As. We got them so tied up in knots Max Jenkins said, "One manager 1A" and we landed up with six.'

I recalled a letter from the IPMS union addressed to 'Mr B Wright – Farm Manager 1A' that I'd found amongst photos and certificates of prize-winning Colony Carr Lincoln Red cattle in a red plastic crate stamped with 'HM Prison Farms' in his back garden shed. Dated 1998, creased and with a mouse-nibbled edge, it expressed 'concerns about the way Bev was treated when the farms at Hatfield came under the management of Lindholme.'

Bev made regular trips to London on union business and he was a frequent visitor at prison headquarters. As part of the restructuring of the prison service, the Home Office announced in February 1991 that its headquarters would move from London to Derby so that it would be at the centre of operation rather than policy. The transfer represented the largest move of Home Office staff away from London; 700 jobs would be relocated from London and 800 posts would be filled locally. An advance party was scheduled to have moved by 1994 and the main move was to occur in 1995. In anticipation of the move to Derby, Maurice gave Bev and a couple of other farm managers temporary contracts at London headquarters so that they'd have relevant experience and their chances of satisfying the Derby recruitment board would be enhanced.

Faced with the prospect of my dad becoming an assistant area manager and therefore able to buy and live in his own home for the first time, my parents bought a heavily discounted ex-service house in a housing estate in Nottingham. However, their ambitions were thwarted. In October 1992, at very short notice, Home Secretary Kenneth Clarke cancelled the move to Derby and announced that the prison service would become an agency instead.

In April 1993 the UK Prison Service and the Scottish Prison Service became executive agencies within the Civil Service. Although the move to agency status has been attributed to the publication of the Lygo Report in 1991,[14] it also coincided with American consulting firms, like PA Consulting Group, identifying the UK Prison Service as a potential market to develop their performance management systems based around targets and key performance indicators (KPIs).[15] Executive agencies were expected to operate as businesses, be highly efficient and profit-oriented – something that Farms & Gardens had been achieving for years. To meet KPIs certain internal services including prison catering, education and external court duties were set to be contracted out.

Clarke scuppered my parents' ambition to live in their own home and left them with a 'dead duck'; an empty house in an area of Nottingham known as the 'burglary blackspot' of Britain.[16]

'Bev wanted to go back out in the field,' said Maurice, so he carried on managing the farms attached to Hatfield YOI.

As head of Farms & Gardens Maurice made it his mission to visit every one of the 147 prisons in England and Wales. He is only person to have done so. Charismatic, able, strategic, innovative, modest and everyone's 'mate', in 1991, in recognition of his achievements, Maurice was invited to apply for the newly created position of area manager, a post that would require him to manage prison governors and ensure the delivery of national policies within each establishment.[17] Many, including Bryan Wakely, were saddened by Maurice's appointment as it took him away from the farms, although he still retained his position on the promotion board for farm foreman and upwards. Maurice became the first non-governor ever to become an area manager.

'Ever?' I asked Bernard.

'There was Amy Edwards after him. And she didn't survive.'

Maurice remained an area manager until he retired in 1996.

'The North governors, Yorkshire governors would all say that you could not wish for a better bloke to be your manager but don't buy a second-hand car off him! That was their view of him,' said Bernard.

Unfortunately, some politicians and senior managers within the Home Office opposed Maurice's appointment and their opposition was rooted in farmer stereotypes and prejudice that Lorraine had rather understatedly described as 'not a good perception.'

'The governors wanted a governor,' recalled Maurice, 'they saw me as an outsider. I wasn't even a prison officer.'

As Maurice took up his appointment, foot and mouth disease broke out across the UK. At Lowdham Grange in Nottinghamshire all their native breed Dairy Shorthorn and Ayrshire cattle had to be destroyed. Dairy Shorthorns are now so rare that their survival depends on embryo transfer into surrogate mothers.

At his first monthly area meeting with governors, Maurice's credentials for the area manager position were questioned until Harry Crew, the governor at Askham Grange, a prison for women in North Yorkshire, stood up and said that in his opinion if somebody could take responsibility for supervising the slaughter of hundreds of animals for foot and mouth then he could take responsibility for running prisons. Maurice appreciated Harry's support and told me that he and Mo still receive a Christmas card from him, the only card they receive from former governors in his area.

To ensure that he was acceptable and accepted in his new area manager position Maurice volunteered for every form of training on offer including anti-terrorism.

'I made it work. They fast-tracked me through incident, control, adjudications, hostage taking, I did the siege negotiation course all those sort of things.' In due course Maurice became 'Gold Commander', able to commandeer national resources: police, army, air force, if he was on duty when a significant disturbance occurred at a prison establishment.

Maurice described an incident when he was called to deal with a group of inmates who were holding a prison officer hostage in a cell. Verbal negotiations failed and it looked like the officer's life might be in danger so Maurice decided to break the officer out by drilling through the adjacent cell wall. All the prisoners were evacuated from the wing and, to conceal the noise of the drilling, Maurice authorised a delighted Air Force commander to scramble a fighter jet to practice very low level flying over the prison. His ploy worked and the officer was recovered unharmed. In the end, Maurice was highly commended as an area manager.

'He did an excellent job,' said Phil Wheatley.

But in 1994 Maurice suffered a serious car accident on the M11 that left him unable to drive. As he was expected to travel within the Yorkshire region his wife Mo became his chauffeur for two years.

'She never got paid for it. Joe Pilling, the director general, said, "What are you going to do?" and I said, "Well my wife can drive me with my car." He thought about it and said she could hire a car.' Maurice paused.

'I could've put her on an establishment payroll and paid her. *I never did it.* I missed a trick!'

I laughed, Maurice was as canny as my dad!

Gradually, prisons and the prison service were reconfigured to fit with a private sector business model. Prisons started to employ auditors and accountants and place greater emphasis on good presentation skills.[18] In England and Wales what had been known as the 'farm walk', become the Prison Enterprise Management Conference, the first of which was held at Keele University in 1995.[19] Attended by Director General Derek Lewis and his soon-to-be-replacement, Richard Tilt who, at the time, was director of security and services and 'good,' according to Maurice. There was only one 'Agriculture and Horticulture Session', led by Hugh Johnstone, Bernard's Deputy and soon-to-be what Maurice called, 'diluted form of Farms and Gardens head after it had all been sold.' The conference focused on finance, management and lessons learnt from the USA.

Initially, prison governors had, '*No* accountant, no financial wizardry or understanding at all. He had really got a mountain to climb. And he had to tackle all of this stuff,' said Big Rob.

To get a handle on efficiency the service brought in professional financial advisors.

'PSIF had its personnel people and its accounts people. Row after row of accountants for every prison and a team of half a dozen accountants centrally doing all the number crunching and suddenly they employed 100+,' he said.

As private sector accounting tools, prison ratings and KPIs were introduced, emphasis shifted away from macro issues such as the roles of prison in society, alternatives to imprisonment or general criminal justice issues to the success or failure of the individual establishment.[20] Around the same time, Chief Inspector of Prisons Stephen Tumim (1987–1995) who understood 'that institutions are about people before processes' and 'had little time for performance measures and other management tools. Did a place feel right? Were the staff enthusiastic? Did prisoners walk with a spring in their step?", published his *Doing time or using time* report.[21,22]

It looked like there might be a return to the situation that existed prior to the late 60s when prison farms were run independently of each other, each having its own bookkeeping system and no liaison between the farms. As budgetary devolution to individual establishments occurred, farms' books could no longer be balanced by moving money between institutions. In an attempt to save costs governors started, 'undercutting the prison next door,' said Chris Coveney. The air of cooperation that Maurice had inculcated and encouraged came under threat.

'What kept you together?' I asked.

'Sarcasm,' quipped Bernard.

'I think,' added Maurice, more seriously, 'we all shared the same outlook and everything else, you know, the same goals.'

The prison service had to rapidly recruit senior managers who could understand the demands of operating as both a public institution and a commercial operation and farm managers fitted the bill. Used to adapting to rules and regulations set by external bodies for health or animal welfare, many farm managers effortlessly took on operational roles that required them to meet and exceed targets for product quality, quantity, timeliness, profit and price, often at short notice. In addition to presenting coherent accounts and communicating effectively with a wide-range of people including prison officers, royalty, politicians, union members and the media, farm managers understood how things worked, Bev especially so. Having been an officer, 'he knew how to do ducking and diving,' remarked Bryan.

Consequently, farm managers, based on their experience rather than formal qualifications, were promoted above and beyond an agricultural role to fill the role of business managers. At HMP Ford in 2006, Jason found himself with a supportive female governor who recognised his capabilities and gave him additional responsibilities; he ended up overseeing 91% of the prison budget and deputising for her.

'She used to say, "Jason you are running the prison, if you need me I'm on call." And the first time I did it I had a prisoner jump off Bognor pier and try and drown himself. I had the police ringing me up at 8 o'clock at night and I am thinking, "Why am I doing this?"'

Between October 1995 and January 1996 Brian Pollett, governor of Blantyre House, chaired a review of the agricultural and horticultural activities in the prison service.[23] In addition to Brian Pollett the review team consisted of fourteen men including five farm managers one of whom was my dad. Neither Maurice nor Bernard Feist were part of the review team as Maurice had retired and Bernard didn't become head of industries and farms until later that year. The aim of the review was to 'examine and provide the basis of maintaining the existing and foreseeable agricultural/horticultural activities within the prison regime'. It focused on the provision of employment opportunities for prisoners, meeting the dietary requirements of the prison service, maintaining amenity, sports and conservation areas, developing internal and external sales opportunities and addressing staff and prisoner training needs.[24]

The *Pollett Review* team interviewed governors and farm/amenity staff, distributed a questionnaire to farm managers attending the annual conference at Newbold Revel in autumn 1995 and another to governors whose prisons included major agricultural and horticultural activities. The team met five times at the Croydon headquarters to discuss the results and collate the report.

Sixty-three percent of governors at establishments with farming and horticultural activities who completed questionnaires considered farm and gardens activities met their requirements for the provision of purposeful work and training.

'In some of the prisons the farm was the farm and the prison was a bit of inconvenience,' explained Maurice, 'but that was the wrong way to go. You've got to be an integral part of it. If the governor *needs* you and *sees* you as an asset, then that's going to help.'

Farming and amenity work was described as 'a complex and varied operation that included less well-known activities such as quarrying, lawn mower repairs and the rearing of rare breeds.'[25] The amenity workgroup was valued as a way to employ 'inadequate or difficult prisoners who cannot easily be deployed elsewhere'[26] and its popularity amongst prisoners meant it could be used as part of an incentive or earned privileges programme.

However, the *Pollett Review* team also noted that the complexity of farming and amenity work 'causes analytical difficulties which clouds the issues of its position, relevance and value to the Prison Service.'[27] Unfortunately, none of the team, not even my weather oracle dad, could foresee that this was not a passing cloud but the start of a storm.

12

Nails in the coffin

'When all this is over', said the swineherd,
'I mean to retire, where
Nobody will have heard about my special skills
And conversation is mainly about the weather.'
Eiléan Ní Chuilleanáin, *Swineherd*[1]

In 1991, Chris Train, the longest serving director general was succeeded by Joe Pilling, a career civil servant who joined in 1966 and had been director of personnel and finance since 1987. Joe became the first director general to set out a moral framework for running the prison service. Emphasising the development of inmate responsibility and self-respect, he stressed that, 'people are sent to prison *as* a punishment, rather than *for* punishment.' He thought that prisons 'should take more calculated risks with inmates to allow them to develop a sense of personal responsibility' and that could be encouraged by minimising time spent in cells.[2] On a visit to headquarters, the newly appointed Home Secretary Kenneth Baker was told that inmates could be incentivised to leave their cells and enter the workshops in three ways: being at the front of the food queue, an extra video, or permission to hear the racing results![3] In 1992 Kenneth 'Ken' Clarke replaced Kenneth Baker as Home Secretary and the following year he was succeeded by Michael Howard whose 'Get tough – lock them up' speech at the Conservative party conference was anathema to Joe Pilling's penal policy.

In the couple of years preceding Joe Pilling's appointment, the prison service had a run of bad press.

'If you hear people speak about the good old days it wasn't very professional and as a result simple things like suicide, escape rate, abscond rate, rate of violence, the number of serious incidents, riots, were endemic. North Eye was burnt to the ground (1986), there were a whole wave of disturbances: Strangeways (1990), dispersal riots, major riots at Gartree (1973), Albany had significant events (1972), Hull was a really bad riot (1976), after I left,' added Phil Wheatley.

In response to the disturbances, increasing emphasis was placed on identifying and quantifying outcomes like escapes at the expense of less easily defined, intangible, qualitative outcomes like developing a sense of belonging or attachment to an animal or another human being.

'The important thing for me is, what are your outcomes? What are the things you are meant to do? We are not supposed to have escapes,' emphasised Phil. 'We are supposed to keep prisoners safe so that they do not kill themselves. We are not meant to have major disorders and we are not meant to have major drug use inside. Those are hard-edged things that you can count and if we are having less of them then things must be improving and that is what we are being paid to do. And if we are having a lot less of them and paying less money, then we are probably becoming efficient or more efficient.'

To achieve this the prison service moved 'towards a managerialist mode of operation, particularly in the creation of objectives, targets and standards, with the introduction of a general performance culture and some centralisation of procedural aspects of performance.'[4]

Qualitative assets such as the therapeutic benefit of livestock or the contribution of the farm staff were increasingly overlooked as resources were diverted to delivering core services, keeping prisoners secure and keeping them safe, inside the walls.

'Governors thought that they were going to be dragged down by the cost of farms and gardens that were not delivering their core business especially when they had to ensure that prisoners would be safe outside the wire on the farms,' explained Bryan.

'You are the governor, you have a budget, and you have to run a safe and secure place. Hit your targets. We don't tell you how to do it from the top,' said Phil adding, somewhat derisorily,

'We moved away from the idea that you could weigh your piece of bread and say, "I have lost half an ounce and I've been diddled."'

All capital expenditure on farms was frozen. Ivor Gough, farm manager at Standford Hill explained resignedly, 'New accommodation for the inmates was more important than new homes for the pigs.'[5]

Kenneth Baker introduced the Criminal Justice Act in 1991 which marked the end of the state prison system by enabling private sector administration of prisons. Within a year the first two private prisons, The Wolds in Humberside and Blakenhurst in Worcestershire, were opened. Both were financed and controlled by private security firms and built on former agricultural land within the prison estate. Blakenhurst was built on farm land at Hewell Grange and The Wolds was built on the Home Farm at Everthorpe. Home Farm had housed a piggery and dairy unit as well as pasture and arable land. Whilst the pasture and arable land were irreplaceable, the piggery and dairy unit were rebuilt at Everthorpe's more distant farm, Woodlands. For the farmers within the prison service the loss of agricultural land was not a cause for celebration.

Most large-scale farming enterprises relied heavily on subsidies under the common agricultural policy to make them viable. As these subsidies were production-based, the more acres or animals you had, the bigger the subsidy; therefore, the bulk of the subsidies went to larger holdings. As their agricultural land was requisitioned or sold, acreage reduced and so did the subsidies. Farms & Gardens adapted by focusing on activities that were better-suited to small acreage. But as neither pigs, poultry nor horticulture received any subsidies this further impacted on their profitability and viability.

Many small family farms, such as those that John and Lorraine grew up on, were being bought by large agri businesses, but as the size of a typical land holding grew, the number of local abattoirs dwindled, a situation that was exacerbated by the introduction of EU regulations governing animal welfare standards. Until the 1990s every town had its own slaughterhouse which benefited the animals and the meat as shorter distances meant less stress in transit. Where there was no local abattoir, for example, on the Isle of Wight, commercial and prison livestock travelled long distances to be slaughtered. Loaded into a horse box, the prison stock was ferried to the mainland before being driven 50 miles to Guys Marsh, near Shaftesbury in Dorset, where they rested overnight before being re-loaded and transported to the abattoir.

As local slaughterhouses closed, Farms & Gardens had to absorb the additional transport costs. These could have been offset if they could have reduced the frequency of deliveries to caterers but a lack of capital investment in kitchen facilities meant that there wasn't adequate freezer space to accommodate more than a week's worth of meat.

From 1 January 1991 Crown property had to meet new Welfare of Livestock Regulations that covered lighting levels, fixtures and fittings, the provision of space and dry areas for bedding and calving, the housing of sick or injured animals and ventilation. To meet these and other new regulations covering food hygiene, environmental and waste management required major capital investment but it wasn't forthcoming. Unusually, Onley prison farm near Rugby closed because of poor management and concern about animal welfare,

'At Onley, they were doing such a bad job and the governor was so scared he was going to get sued for animal cruelty that he got rid of the lot. Governors are always risk averse and if there is something going on, then they shut it all down. That is why Onley went,' explained one of my interviewees.

Many smaller farmers left the industry as farms were consolidated to achieve economies of scale. Outbreaks of disease such as foot and mouth and BSE furthered the exodus from agriculture. In the founding countries of the European Union the agricultural labour force declined from 12.8 to 3.7 million between 1960 and 1997 and the number of farms fell from 6.8 to 3.8 million. In the UK 87,000 farmers and farmworkers stopped working in agriculture between 1993 and 2001 as average net incomes from farming plummeted from £80,000 in 1995/6 to £8,000 in 2000 and just £2,500 in 2001.[6] Although £2,500 was an incredibly low amount, the reality was actually worse, as this figure didn't include any salary paid to either the farmer, their spouse or other family members.[7] In 2000 2.1% of the national workforce (217,700 people) worked in agriculture, and by 2005 this had fallen to 1.8% (177,000 people).[8]

Dairy farming was particularly badly affected as the pound increased in value against the euro by approximately a third between 1996 and 2000 and a serious outbreak of foot and mouth disease in 2000/01 resulted in the slaughter of tens of thousands of livestock. At the turn of the new millennium the number of dairy farms in the UK was 70% less than in 1970.

'You look at how many dairy farms were shutting at the time we were shutting ours,' said Bernard. There was a pause.

'That's right,' conceded Maurice.

'The industry was just contracting,' agreed Derek.

Farms & Gardens had long prided themselves on providing

meaningful work for prisoners but as 90% of prisoners were coming from and returning to an urban environment, it looked increasingly unlikely that agricultural skills per se would enhance their chances of employment post-release.

'The problem,' said Bernard, 'was that the outside industry was declining so what were you training people for? The figures that we quoted at the time were if there are 30,000 people disappearing out of agriculture every year why train people for agriculture when amenity horticulture was increasing by 30,000 a year? That was the argument I put to the Treasury.'

Bernard realised that the Prison Board had made up their mind that farming outside the walls was untenable.

In terms of size and productivity the prison service farms peaked in 1992 but following Michael Howard's appointment as Home Secretary in 1993 tougher and longer sentences resulted in courts sending more offenders to prison and longer mandatory minimum and maximum sentences. The prison population mushroomed but the availability of inmates to work on the farms plummeted. Changes in sentencing were accompanied by changes in the profile of offenders, a steady increase in the number of lifers and more people incarcerated for violence against the person, drug and sexual offences especially following the introduction of the Sexual Offences Act 2003. Between June 1993 and June 2012, the numbers of prisoners in England and Wales almost doubled from 44,246 to over 86,000.[9] As the prison population increased it became increasingly difficult for the prison service to be self-sufficient in food. Farms & Gardens owned 1,400 breeding sows and produced enough pork and bacon to feed 47,000 inmates but Bernard and Maurice agreed that once the prison population went over 50,000 they could no longer produce enough food given the amount of land they farmed. In 1996, as Maurice retired, the decision was taken to end commercial pig farming. It marked the beginning of the end for the prison farms.

Inmates had always been subject to risk assessment prior to working on the farms; arsonists were never allowed access to highly combustible materials such as straw, but the criteria for being released to work outside became more stringent in the mid-1990s. Those in charge of

Farms & Gardens were faced with a serious shortage of suitable labour,

'There were a lot of places where they had a farm attached but they didn't have any labour because they couldn't get the labour out the gates,' explained Chris Coveney.

To address over-crowding the judiciary started to sentence only more serious offenders to prison which meant that there were less Category D prisoners available to work outside. This exacerbated the labour problem for farms since most of them were located at open prisons where Category D prisoners could be used in relatively unsupervised conditions. Prison farms that were attached to Category C establishments began to suffer from labour shortages because insufficient numbers of Category D prisoners were available to take up the employment places. A shortage of prisoners led to an increase in the cost per employment place on farms that could only be offset by generating more outputs and therefore income as noted by members of the Pollett Review team.[10]

'If you're not doing your core business, how can you have a business?' asked Bryan. As the core business of the farms was, 'cost-effective employment of prisoners and the provision of required products at competitive prices,'[11]

'That was the downfall and we never recovered after that,' he stated bluntly.

Additionally, and importantly, inmates who'd served two-thirds of their sentence, who might otherwise have been moved to less secure establishments with farms, became eligible for home detention curfew (HDC) or 'tagging'. Many of the inmates who were suitable for tagging were inmates from open institutions who would normally have been let out to work on the farms.

'The real killer blow was HDC,' stated Big Rob.

'We were employing hundreds, probably thousands on farms and in comes HDC with the Labour government I think. The governor, to get all the 'brownie points' from his line manager, would say, "I am going to free up all these places in the prison so I will send them all down the road with bracelets on their ankles." Instantly the number of prisoners working on farms went through the floor. As a result, the farms couldn't justify their existence. There were probably 200 working on Hollesley Bay alone and after HDC there were probably 200 working across the entire prison farm service.'

'They've had a lot of problems with the Cat. D, the open prisons, about getting enough prisoners into them,' noted Deb Boydell, a current member of the Public Sector Prison Industries (PSPI) project team, 'because if they are eligible to go to an open prison then they are eligible for tagging anyway and they would rather be tagged and out.'

Whilst in 1996 there were 1047 prisoners employed on farms, by 2001 the number had reduced by three quarters to only 249.

HDC was accompanied by ROTL (Release On Temporary License).

'Essentially a test, a tick box exercise that said this person can go home (or not) or can go out to work on the farm,' explained Big Rob, 'and it was the same piece of paper. *Exactly* the same piece of paper.'

Norma and Deb agreed that ROTL was a key cause of the decline in prison farming,

'To be able to put them on a farm you had to be able to ROTL them out. They brought in electronic tagging and a lot of ROTL stopped in terms of working outside because they got released anyway and sent home on a tag. Lots of other things, but that was one of the big things,' said Deb adding, 'There are very few that actually meet the new criteria for a ROTL. It is quite a lengthy process to get someone on a ROTL. By that stage, they are likely to be released on tag or released completely.'

To meet the needs of livestock, prison farms had always had to have sufficient staff and equipment available for times when prison labour was in short supply, for example at weekends and in the evenings but a lack of inmate labour led to staff being overworked,

'We didn't get any long-term prisoners on the farm anymore so we couldn't train them to go tractor driving, for example, which put more emphasis on the staff doing the work,' explained Steve.

'We only had four or five prisoners at Werrington in Staffordshire. That was the beginning of the end if you didn't get the prisoners out. Quite a few prisons struggled.'

'When I left Hatfield in 1992 we used to have twenty lads working at Misterton. If we managed to get five inmates out to work on the farm at New Hall it was good,' said Pete Chisholm, 'but the reduction in inmate numbers meant that closure of the farms was inevitable.'

There were many nails in the coffin for prison farms in England and Wales. A decrease in the number and type of inmates permitted to work outside the walls was one of the most significant. Norma, head of operations for Public Sector Prison Industries, who remembered both Maurice and Bernard, emphasised that the prison service could only justify paying staff to do agricultural or horticultural work if it occupied prisoners,

'If there were no prisoners there was no point in doing it.'

The impact of low inmate numbers was exacerbated because the farms were designed to be labour intensive with manual rather than automated processes. Major capital investment was required to operate with a significantly reduced prison labour force.

'The farms,' said Bernard, looking to Derek and Maurice for agreement, 'became a "management problem" for governors.'

Maurice cleared his throat and clarified that the source of the problem was not the farms per se but the use of delegated budgets by the governors together with allocation to local cost centres. Farms was one cost centre, others included education and catering.

Bernard continued,

'Governors were finding that this bit of land out there which was very nice for them to go and walk around if they had a bad afternoon was now causing them a management problem. There was a lot of pressure from them through the area manager system to not have farms.'

Derek shrugged his shoulders and Maurice, who'd also been an area manager crossed his arms.

'In some ways, I think that we actually caused some of our own problems,' said Bernard. 'The Farms grew a treat. And you can see, whichever way you like, the people who were managing them then were prepared to do *anything* and they didn't need a lot of guidance.'

Maurice, keeping his arms folded said softly,

'Not guidance but help and support.'

'For whatever reasons,' continued Bernard, 'and I suppose some of it was about pounds in your pocket, people needed more guidance as we got to the 90s really.'

Maurice didn't interrupt Bernard,

'And there wasn't the same *commitment*.'

'When Maurice, yourself and himself were there,' said Derek referring to my dad, 'They were committed to the job. It didn't matter if they had to turn out in the middle of the night, whatever.'

Months later, in March 2016 I received an email from Bernard that re-iterated Derek's view,

'The farm managers at the end were not like your dad and others of the eighties and nineties.'

Their level of commitment depended on how they and their role was valued as much as the support they were given by governors and heads of inmate activities.

'In some of the prisons the farm was the farm and the prison was a bit of inconvenience,' explained Maurice, 'but that was the wrong way to go. You have to be an integral part of it. If the governor *needs* you and *sees* you as an asset, then that is going to help.'

In Hatfield prison where my dad worked with Hazel, morale remained high but elsewhere it faded.

Phil 'arrived near the top' of the prison service as assistant director of custody in 1992 when the UK Prison Service and Scottish Prison Service became executive agencies.

'I didn't feel like I was 'of HQ' until prisons became an agency.'

Prison catering and education were amongst the first services to be contracted out.

'From that point onwards we just got more commercial awareness and more conscious of how we use money so all the decision-making was much more on a business case approach; are the benefits we are getting from it worth the expenditure? We are more inclined to think what investment will this really need, not just up-front investment, but continuing investment. We'd become a more professional group of managers. Before you'd have found people saying, "Well, we have prison farms, they produce food for the prison, we need them," without thinking, "How else could we get food? What is the value of the farms? Can we invest that money differently?" That wasn't in the business case at all. They just thought, "They are there, so we have to do it."'

At the top, Ken Clarke appointed a former television executive, Derek Lewis, to replace Joe Pilling as director general of the prison service.

In his own words, Derek Lewis was 'a private sector outsider brought in to change the service.'[12] He was 'a good guy,' said Bryan kindly, who, 'brought a very *commercial* approach,' emphasised Big Rob. Maurice, who'd recently been appointed area manager, 'got on alright with him. He rang me up one Saturday morning, something had happened at Thorpe Arch and he said, "I want you at Thorpe Arch at 8 o'clock." Of course, he was new and I thought I'd better turn up but he used to do that, he would suddenly appear at random places so I used to ask his secretary to let me know if he was coming to Yorkshire then I could pre-empt him and be there.'

As Maurice needed a base in Yorkshire he rented a small holiday home near Wetherby situated within a farm that for many years catered for academics and other senior prison staff visiting the area. Behind the main farmhouse was a large, empty agricultural building that the owner said he might convert at some point into another holiday let although somewhat incongruously it was guarded by a pair of Rottweilers. When he retired Maurice gave up the tenancy. A week later the police raided the farm and unearthed a massive hoard of looted silver and valuables hidden under a fake floor within the barn.

'It must have been a tip off,' said Maurice, amused that the farmer ended up serving time in HMP Wolds.

Derek Lewis had limited experience of farming and was unlikely to have paid much attention to the farms until a chance encounter with Pete Chisholm, soon to be 'enterprise manager' at New Hall prison looking after the workshops, health and safety, the kitchens and the farms. As Derek was returning with his wife and two daughters from a family holiday in Scotland he decided to turn off the M1 at Wakefield and call in at New Hall.

'Well Pete saw this as a golden opportunity and he took Mrs Lewis and the Lewis children around the farm and showed them what was going on, the cows, didn't dwell on the marvellous effluent system that I had installed at great cost,' added Big Rob laughing.

'He showed them the dairy and the pigs and when Derek finally came out his wife and children said, "What a marvellous job the prison farms are doing." From that day on the new director general was much more amenable to the farms!'

Unfortunately for the farms, in 1995 Michael Howard rather sensationally sacked Derek Lewis and replaced him with Richard Tilt, the first director general to have been a former prison governor. Within a year of the 1996 Pollett Review, and under Richard Tilt's direction, a small team consisting of Bernard, two Prison Enterprise Services

(PES) staff, Jeremy Fallows and Hugh Johnstone (newly appointed head of agri business), plus a former PES accountant, Ian Burley, undertook a second review of agriculture within the prison service. This review, known as the Prison Service Agri Business Review (PSABR), was carried out between October–December 1996, shortly after Maurice retired from the service. PSABR aimed to 'address the scale of assets involved and the operating and financing methods of the current agriculture/horticulture activities within the Prison Service and their effectiveness.'

The PSABR considered all known physical and financial data and information available including the Pollett Review, land agent Brown and Co's survey of 28 prison service land holdings[13] and ADAS's[14] assessment of financial and operating systems, produce quality and pricing.[15] However, the PSABR did not include any reference to the report produced by Maurice Codd in 1988 that outlined how prison farms could be self-financing.

The aims of the PSABR were: to set clear goals and objectives for the next ten to fifteen years, until 2011; to reduce the cost of employing prisoners on agri business activities by 68% from £2,491 to £788 per annum or 52p per hour; to reduce staff numbers by 30–32 but only through natural wastage; to directly manage at least one prison farm under Private Finance Initiative (PFI) and oversee 'pump priming' capital investment in all but directly managed enterprises. Capital investment at least equal to the value of depreciation in existing assets was to continue in order to maintain existing enterprises.

Bernard's team recommended taking into account the future prison building programme and disposing of 'certain pockets of land' amounting to 710 hectares (1,754 acres) and valued at £3m.[16]

'Basically, what they were doing was *asset stripping*,' said Maurice.

Other recommendations included: ceasing recording output related to ground maintenance as 'production'; over five years, phasing out the growing of potatoes as existing machinery becomes beyond economic repair; saving an estimated £100,000 per annum in capital costs; ceasing pig production for the dietary system except for productive and well-equipped units 'where all progeny will be channelled to commercial outlets'; dispose of dairy herds that cannot 'realise their potential to improve performance in line with commercial averages over the next five years'; reorganise the five distribution centres to include a purchasing as well as distribution function and, with the exception of jam making, discontinue 'the non-cost effective peripheral activities (saw mill, tunnel manufacture, quarrying) which have evolved over the past ten years.'

In 2001 Bernard was attending the prison farm conference at Newbold Revel when the director general demanded his return to headquarters.

'Come and have a soft chair, Bernard,' said Martin Narey.

'I was called in to start the 'modernisation' of the farms,' said Bernard.

'And what did Martin Narey mean by 'modernisation'?' I asked.

'That was our term not his. What he meant was, '*we need to review the farms and close them*.'

'He didn't want to get his hands dirty,' said Maurice, 'He was more distant, more ministerial, he didn't do 'touchy-feely' and I don't remember him going on a visit to any of the farms in Yorkshire.'

'Martin Narey gave us a choice,' said Bernard, 'You do it or we will get some outside contractors in to do it.'

Martin was supported by his newly appointed deputy, Phil Wheatley who described Bernard as, 'one of those people who finds a way of doing things, doesn't tell you you can't do things and he is a very good operator. You couldn't ask him to do the impossible but he was good at making things work. And he is a nice person.'

Phil expressed little sympathy for the wider remit of the farms, 'When you get really tight times you have to think because you are meant to be running prisons should I bother about how many saddlebacks pigs there are in the country or look after 1,000 prisoners properly?'

'In 2001,' wrote Bernard, 'I was asked (told) to review farms. This resulted in the modernisation programme and the creation of the department called Land Based Activities.'[17] At that time there were 21 farms including 14 dairy units across 5,500 acres (2,225 hectares).

Bernard reported to the prison board (chaired by Martin Narey) who recommended to David Blunkett, then Home Secretary, whether to keep or close the prison farms. Staff 'on the ground' felt that the decision to close the farms was the wrong one and some felt that

Bernard could, and should, have tried harder to save them. One of these was Bryan who recalled the minister with responsibility for the prisons saying to Bernard,

'It's your decision. If I was you I'd keep the Farms & Gardens open because there are no savings and one day I think we'll actually need the gardens.'

Ultimately, however, although Bernard was responsible for making a recommendation to the prison board, the decision about whether and how to close them was taken by the board under the direction of politicians.

'To be fair to Bernard,' stated Maurice, 'he was put in the situation where it was, if you don't do it then we will put in someone else to do it. So I think he was doing the best thing.'

Nevertheless, nationwide, a close knit farming family unravelled.

'I was going to say that Bernard was in charge but he was there and I don't know how you want to put this,' remarked Bryan, 'but the reality was that Bernard in the early days had every farm manager as his friend and when the Farms & Gardens closed he struggled to count his friends on one hand, not even on one finger.'

The farm modernisation programme was approved by the prisons minister in February 2003 shortly before Phil became Director General.

'I got involved in the winding down of Farms & Gardens. We did wind them down quite deliberately.'

Bernard tapped into the resettlement agenda. In accordance with his own and Phil's background in horticulture he made the case for an expansion in gardening. He argued that whilst 30,000 jobs had been lost in the agricultural sector, a similar number of jobs were being created in horticulture – mainly grounds maintenance and landscaping. Phil told me,

'You're interested in growing things that you can sell so it drives commercial discipline which is relevant. Even though I am 'sniffy' about the jobs in farming, there are loads of jobs in market gardening and horticulture and landscape gardening. That is a growth area because with the service economy, the very rich, they want their gardens sorting out and they like their bijou vegetables bought locally and they will pay a premium for it.'

Approval was given for a phased reduction in the services' agricultural activities with a corresponding increase in horticultural activity. Ministerial approval came after lengthy periods of consultation with MPs and representatives from DEFRA. 'Following the approval, meetings were held with all of the area managers and governors involved. From these meetings detailed business plans were compiled for each site involved in the programme. These plans were completed by the end of March 2003, a programme plan, timetable and financial plan was completed by May 2003. Treasury gave approval to the planned method for the disposal of farm assets and the reinvestment into horticulture and its formal training. Staff associations, Prospect and TGWU [Transport and General Workers' Union], representing the staff involved, were consulted at all stages; this included a meeting between the unions and the prisons minister. Local union members were involved in the local business planning stage.'[18]

There were two aspects to the farm modernisation programme: the first was to move away from large-scale agriculture that involved few prisoners to people-intensive, small-scale farming and horticulture and the second, to focus on training and accreditation for prisoners, that is, move from working prisoners to training prisoners. The new Land Based Activities (LBA) department ended field scale cropping of both dietary and arable crops and 'phased out' 12 of the 14 dairy herds. Consequently, the internal milk supply ended and replacement contracts had to be put in place for vegetables and milk.

The farm modernisation programme was scheduled for completion by April 2006. Money from the sale of machinery and livestock was set to be invested in horticultural equipment to increase the numbers of prisoners employed and trained in horticulture.

'Friday night, you could hardly squeeze soap on the telly, between all the gardening programmes, so horticulture was seen as popular, if not 'sexy'. So Bernard bless him said, "I think this would be a good idea. We'll take all the proceeds from the sales and redirect it into horticulture either commercial or amenity" and it was seen as the right thing to do. And I wouldn't disagree with that,' conceded Big Rob, himself a landscape gardener.

'You are trying to get offenders jobs that they will enjoy,' said Phil, who headed NOMS from 2008, the year that Bernard retired.

'Can you earn enough to have a decent standard of living is the first thing, can you enjoy it? If you put people into mindless, repetitive tasks the chance is they will be frustrated and think, "Well I might as well go thieving." If a job is interesting, then you are less likely to reoffend.'

A year after Phil left the service in 2010, the Ministry of Justice published *Making Prisons Work* which blurred the distinction between work, skills and learning within prisons. It suggested that prison industries could instil 'disciplines of working life' such as orderliness, timekeeping, working to deadlines, being managed and overseen. Through participation in prison work the inmate had an opportunity to develop life skills that formed 'the fabric of responsibility' underlying a person being a better employee, partner, parent, neighbour or friend.

I asked Phil whether he thought there was any future for horticulture or agriculture within the prison service,

'I think horticulture will be alive and well, you're still going to be gardening, you've still got to occupy prisoners, you've got to have variety and you can still train for series of skills for which there are real jobs out there. Because people are not time rich they pay to have their gardens done. Landscaping needs doing. Because they're not desperately skilled, they aren't growing their plants from seed, so they are happy to buy them which means there are jobs growing them. So there is a whole series of work that is entirely compatible with being an ex-offender and that sort of work is good fun.'

In 2013 72% of 200 horticultural businesses surveyed were unable to fill skilled vacancies.[19] The first *Horticulture Matters* report also found that 70% of 18-year-olds believed that horticultural careers should only be considered by people who'd 'failed academically.'[20]

'Nobody saw the benefit of farming,' said Jason, trained in both horticulture and agriculture, 'and it sort of fitted, but Bernard was retiring and I suppose he gave up the fight. It wasn't worth his while so we ended up with what we ended up with.'

Initially, nine farms amounting to 3,133 acres (1,268 hectares) were ear-marked for sale whilst a further 885 acres (358 hectares) were to be let out, as the land might be required for the building of prisons within 10 years. Two rented farms amounting to 2017 acres (816 hectares) were returned to their landlords. The Suffolk Horses were to be disposed of 'with sensitivity.'[21]

Lord Deben knew all about the horses having been the MP for Suffolk Coast. He insisted that Bernard should meet him in his office in Queen Anne's Gate.

'I need to see you tonight, 7 o'clock because they are going to have a vote in the House of Commons.' But it was late and Bernard couldn't get a security pass.

'Don't worry. We are smuggling you in in the back of the car.'

'This is true!' extolled Bernard, 'We left Queen Anne's Gate in his official car and I am sat in the back between two other ministers and we got to the gate and they waved us in. We had a meeting in the House that finished at half past 8 and the bell went for them to go and vote. He said, "We've finished," and I said, "Yes, if you've finished Sir, then I've finished. But how am I going to find my way out?" "Well, you can find your own way out can't you?" No pass. Nothing!'

Bernard, Maurice, Derek and I all laughed.

'That was John Gummer. For closing the farms, we had something like 27 written MP's questions and 3 oral questions.'

When my dad joined the service, the staff were 'us' and prisoners were 'them' and there was less penal politics. But over time, as security and control took political and popular precedence over justice, 'us' became synonymous with people and practices within the walls and 'them' on the outside became outsiders. Whilst in the early 1970s it had been inmates 'who have found themselves to be out of phase with the pace of modern life and those who in many ways are inadequate,'[22] by the early 2000s those in charge of the service were assessing farm staff in a similar way.

After the farms attached to Hatfield were sold my dad was transferred to the 160 hectare (395 acre) arable farm at nearby Lindholme prison. Built on a former WWII airfield, crops were grown on reclaimed runways and grass standing areas. As the manager of a 3,000-tonne cold store facility rather than two large farms, my dad was demoted from a manager 1A to manager 1. Around the same time at HMP Camp Hill, a Farms & Gardens staff member took the service to an employment tribunal claiming constructive dismissal because he didn't think that the alternative post offered to him was suitable replacement work. He lost his case.[23]

All prison governors were under pressure to save money and in many cases this was achieved by reducing staff costs and looking to outsource services such as catering. The newly appointed governor at Lindholme was known as someone who was prepared to play one man off against another. When he approached the incumbent farm manager at Lindholme and asked him whether he needed all his staff, he implied that he might not need him. To save his own position and that of his closest ally he turned against my dad.

'It was crucifying Bev,' said my mum.

Feeling under-valued and ostracised, like others who have contributed to this book, my dad endured his last few years in the service; a time marred by competition, discrimination, in-fighting and despair. He stuck it out until 2003 when, at 60 years of age, he qualified for the index-linked pension that had attracted him to the service.

Initially farming at Lindholme was expected to continue but eventually all the farming equipment was sold and the land rented out. The land was contract farmed by the Ploughman's Association. In May 2007 Lindholme hosted the European Festival of the Plough, an event that included ex-European Champion, Simon Witty from North Yorkshire defending his title in the 24th European Reversible Ploughing Championships. There was also Heavy Horse Ploughing 'which gives visitors the chance to watch the majestic shire horses at work as these magnificently turned out gentle giants evoke by-gone days when farming was an altogether slower way of life.'[24]

Shortly after the last furrow had been ploughed the veg prep unit at Lindholme closed and the redundant buildings were reconditioned to provide alternative prisoner employment and training such as, forklift driving and hard landscaping courses.

'We could've kept the veg preps going because it was an industry that could've been done within the curtilage of the prison but that required recapitalising,' concluded Big Rob.

Horticulture, that could be undertaken inside the walls, was 'reborn with a glasshouse and other equipment purchased.'[25]

When I met Lorraine, I asked her why she thought the farms had closed. She paused,

'Slight change in government policy in what they wanted inmates to do and they started to put people out to work in the community, which is good for them 'cos they are progressing but there wasn't always the labour force to carry on the same as what there was.'

Then she turned to Chris,

'I think the people at the top weren't bothered, don't you?'

He nodded in agreement.

With high-level political support the farms flourished, but without it they floundered.

'Every few years there would be a move from politicians asking, "Why do we have the farms?"' recalled Howard.

In April 2012, the Chief Inspector of Prisons, Nick Hardwick, concluded that East Sutton Park, which caters for 90 adult and young offender female inmates, produced 'very good outcomes for the women it holds and the public as a whole.'[26]

'The Justice Secretary, the MOJ, the Governors, and sadly (considering how much a part of our daily lives they are) even the Prison Officers will never know, never understand and never realise that for a number of us at East Sutton Park, for *The Farm Girls*, it is not down to their programmes, their initiatives or their incentives that we have found peace in the chaos and disorder that is the prison & criminal justice system, it is in many ways very simply down to the East Sutton Park farm,' wrote former inmate Amy Cullen.

East Sutton Park is a 'half-way house' for female inmates especially those serving life sentences. Like Hewell Grange, inmates at East Sutton Park are housed in a mansion house, in this case a Grade-II listed fifteenth-century Elizabethan manor that overlooks the weald. Over time the main house has been splendidly restored by the prison works department.

'A lovely house,' commented Bryan adding, 'Going to make a lovely hotel. Not good enough for a golf course but big enough for a spa hotel!'

The manor house is surrounded by about 70 acres (28 hectares) of farm land which hosts 50 cows and RBST 'at risk' Saddleback pigs that are returned to the prison farm shop as sausages and pork chops. Given the nature of the property it was decided that the land and house could not be sold separately.

Just days before I visited Lorraine and Chris Coveney in late 2013 the Ministry of Justice announced in the press, rather than directly to staff, that both East Sutton Park and Holloway prison would close but the timescale for the closures was unclear. Holloway had just taken part in the Open Garden Squares Weekend and piloted a project with the British Hen Welfare Trust whereby inmates gained qualifications from looking after ex-battery hens. Two years later it was reported that the women imprisoned in Holloway had notices slipped under their cell doors telling them that Holloway was closing and they would be transferred to other prisons. In 2016 a commercial property firm was awarded a contract by the Ministry of Justice to oversee the sale and subsequent development of the site, part of a £1.3 billion overhaul of UK prisons announced by the former Chancellor of the Exchequer George Osborne.[27]

Lorraine and Chris meanwhile were concerned because the sale of East Sutton Park would not only entail redundancy it would also mean losing their home.

13

Dispersal

'I saw, without knowing it, the last journey of the last threshing machine to the last farm along this road that grew any oats worth threshing: such is the unremarkable way things trundle and clank to an end.' Michael Viney, *A Year's Turning*[1]

'There,' exclaimed Maurice, 'I'm on my high horse now. *It's gone. It's gone.*'

Agriculture, a significant feature of the prison service in England and Wales for more than 150 years, was in terminal decline. As was my dad.

According to Chris McGown, the first prison farm to close under the farm modernisation programme was Portland.

'Why they chose Portland I don't know. We'd just bought enough fencing to fence the whole of the Bill in. And all the gates. We had all prison-made gates.'

Reportedly, the prison farm on Portland closed in 1996 because it was unprofitable. Its closure resulted in Chris being made redundant and the rare breed Portland sheep being rehomed. An *Independent* newspaper article at the time reported: 'Chris McGown, an agricultural instructor who has worked on the farms for 25 years, said: "We will all miss the rare breed Portland sheep. They are an added attraction to the island, but there is a real risk that we will not find accommodation for them here. Some local people have expressed interest, but it's not just a question of buying a sheep. You have to move them around, so you have to have more than one field. We have had a request for four ewes and a ram, but you cannot have just one ram because you'll mess up the bloodlines."'[2] Eventually the flock were accommodated on a community farm established on a former RAF site near the island's Verne prison.

A total of one hundred and ninety-three staff were affected by the farm modernisation programme. Farm staff, who it was stated would not be laid off, were redeployed.[3] The 'emotional' reallocation of farm-based staff required some to undertake additional training to avoid redundancy.[4] Some became prison officers, others transferred to horticulture, industrial or non-industrial work. After his flock of sheep was sold, Dartmoor prison's shepherd, Brian Dingle became a curator in the prison's museum. Housed in the former dairy, Brian tends the artefacts and guides visitors around the exhibits that include a display about 'Mad Axeman' Frank Mitchell, a collection of farm machinery and a glass cabinet with fraying and fading show rosettes.

At Standford Hill a consortium came forward interested in buying the buildings and creating a museum 'showing one of the first flying schools and linked to the Short brothers.'[5]

'When you went into the fitting shop at Standford Hill they had the bits where they used to put the aircraft together,' said Jason Errington who, twenty-eight years after joining the prison service as a stop-gap while awaiting a position in the RAF as a mechanic, retained a soft spot for aviation.

The plans for the flight museum were supported by a local government initiative with oversight from the Office of the Deputy Prime Minister so, to enable them to attract funding, the sale of the farm was delayed, with all of the grassland and some of the buildings let out for one year.[6]

After the dairy herd and machinery were sold in 2006 the service retained 100 acres (40 hectares) of IACS registered agricultural land (eligible for European Commission farm subsidies). Some of this was let on a farm business tenancy and the remainder contract farmed because there was the possibility that either a third prison would be built on the site or nearby Elmley prison would be expanded.

Bernard approved investment in a market garden unit including the installation of polytunnels and the purchase of horticultural equipment 'to enable the further development of certificated training.'[7]

I asked Jason if there was anything at Standford Hill now?

'All derelict. In fact, they've just pulled down some of the old piggery. I thought some of the buildings were listed so I don't know what they've done but all the fitting shop and everything, all gone.'

The Dartmoor prison farm dispersal sale in 2004 attracted two and half thousand people. With the farm's pigs already sold off, Derek Webber oversaw the auction of two hundred cattle, seven hundred sheep, three tractors and other farming paraphernalia.

'Farmers and cattle dealers from across Britain flocked in to bid for the prime Devon and Highland beef cattle from the prison farm. Two shire horses and some farm machinery also went under the hammer, raising a total of almost £90,000. Prison governor John Lawrence is looking to cut £200,000 from this year's £13.6 million budget and pay off a £250,000 overspend from last year. He said: 'I will be keeping the special breeds Highland cattle and concentrating on the dairy herd, possibly expanding it because milk is still profitable.'[8]

The sale raised £250,000 and was marketed as a significant contribution to a wider £500,000 cost-cutting scheme at Dartmoor prison and a way to cut vets and animal food bills. However, most of the acreage at Dartmoor was leased from the Duchy of Cornwall. After protracted discussions with the Duchy officers all but 28 acres (11 hectares) of the farm land was returned at a cost exceeding £500k, a good deal considering that initially the Duchy had requested £2m. Consequently, the sale only raised half the cost of returning the land. The retained land included some buildings suitable for small-scale farming centred around five Highland cattle and twelve Dartmoor ewes. Subsequently, with assistance from Duchy College, a rural activities training building was added.

Four years after the sale, a director at the Eden Project in Cornwall, Howard Jones, 'took the simple proposition that prisoners growing food inside prisons has a marked benefit on health, behaviour and outlook.' A collaboration with Cisco Systems resulted in a prison gardening project being established in a disused exercise yard at Dartmoor prison. 'In an exceptionally bleak environment Eden (in partnership with the prison and other supporters), created fruit, vegetable and healing gardens, with food delivered to local people and schools in Princetown. The programme evolved to become less about a simple prison activity and more of a community enterprise, concerned with resilience and prosperity.'[9] But nowhere on the 'Growing for Life' project website did it acknowledge that Dartmoor prison was where prison agriculture and horticulture had started in 1852, or that for over 150 years it had been the largest prison farm.

Instead the website talked up their own achievements, how they'd 'expanded the programme, across eight other prisons during 2008–2011, drew ministerial attention and then wider public interest when those prisons and ex-offenders, working under the leadership of Howard, the Eden Project, Shekinah and with a number of homeless people, exhibited their commitment at two major Chelsea Show gardens, in 2010/11.'[10]

Abandoning prison farming necessitated the sale not only of the commercial herds but also most of the award winning rare breed livestock that had been competed, shown and sold over many years. The dairy herd and farmland at Tudworth was sold in 2004. 'Due to its location close to both the M180 and M18 the farm attracted a lot of interest from developers.'[11] When Maurice and I visited the site in late 2016 the agricultural buildings were falling to pieces and the silage and slurry pits were full of rubble.

'There'd been a lovely Friesian herd at Hatfield. They sold everything off at auction. Same as up here at Lancaster,' lamented Steve who'd kept the catalogue from the sale of the 155 pedigree cattle from the Lancaster herd on Thursday 11th August 2005 at 11am.

'All the regular dairy cows went to somewhere in Stafford,' recalled John Glover, the former stockman at Hatfield, but the Colony Carr herd were taken to a specialist Lincoln Red cattle sale at Louth.

'I went to tidy them up on the day and I actually took them all into the ring,' said John ruefully. The genetic credentials of the prison livestock that had been enhanced through showing were fully catalogued.

'And some people were asking me about the different ones. The inmates were amazed 'cos Lincoln Reds to most people, one is the same as all the others cos they are all the same colour, but they aren't really. I mean I could go down the field and say, "Look that one come out of that one." Well, you just knew. You didn't have to look at their ear tags or nothing.'

For my dad, John and Steve the sale of their rare breed livestock was 'like cutting off their right arms,' stressed Christine Wakely.

'Your dad didn't *have* to sell the Lincoln Reds *someone* made sure he sold off the Lincoln Reds because the Longhorns weren't sold at Kirkham,' said Bryan. 'Expecting Bev to sell off the Colony Carr herd of Lincoln Reds was very mean.'

For thirty-five years, the prison service leased 500 acre (200 hectare) Frankley Farm from Birmingham City Council on 'an old-style farm tenancy'.[12] But in May 2007 the Birmingham Post reported that 'A change in Government policy meant teaching farming was no longer seen as useful for prisoners as it provided limited job prospects once they returned to the community.'[13] Reluctant to terminate the lease on what had been a run-down farm before prisoners transformed it into what Big Rob described as, 'a far, far better farm, in much improved condition,' the prison service proposed a joint venture with the City Council, a rare breed farm park with working demonstrations for members of the public and school groups. The idea was that the park would be overseen by Tom Houston, the existing farm manager.

'The farm park could have been a self-financing exercise. They had sufficient ground and there was a fair rent. At the end of the day it was a business case,' said Derek.

'Very much so,' agreed Bernard before adding, 'we got rid of it.'

'Wasn't anyone tempted to take it on?' I asked.

'Technically, we couldn't be involved,' explained Bernard.

According to the closing report on the farm modernisation programme three members of staff lived in tied accommodation on Frankley farm including Tom Houston. Birmingham City Council offered the prison service a large share of the sale receipt of the farm (£370k) if they could arrange vacant possession rather than surrender their tenancy so the prison service arranged for the staff to be rehoused.

'Tom got upset because he had to leave Frankley which had been his home. We are in touch now but it was a bit rough for a while,' said Bernard. 'He lives at Hewell Grange. He bought a quarter there.'

To protect the Frankley site from speculative development the council decided to lease rather than sell the farm land. Following a successful funding appeal by the Royal Society for the Prevention of Cruelty to Animals (RSPCA), an animal centre and hospital was built on the site. Now, rather than rare breeds, the site is home to abandoned pets: cats, dogs, rabbits and even rodents – farm 'pests' rebranded as 'furries'.[14]

At Rochester the farm buildings were demolished and the dairy herd transferred to another establishment from where it was sold. Surplus machinery was disposed of at auction. Some of the proceeds from the sale were used to purchase gardening equipment to enhance certificated training in horticulture. Most of the former prison farm land was used for an extension to the M2 and the high-speed rail link but 37 acres (15 hectares) were retained and rented out on a farm business tenancy in case the land was required for 'future building or extension to car parking.'[15]

Similarly, at Littlehay, or Gaynes Hall as we knew it when my dad worked there, approximately 50 acres (20 hectares) were retained and let on a farm business tenancy because, like Rochester and other prisons including: Featherstone, Camp Hill, Wymott, Werrington and Lindholme, new prisons might be built on the site.

Steve showed me the brochure for the dispersal sale of Lancaster prison's four farms: Oatlands, Cookoo, Ridge and Stone Rowe.

'It was sad,' he said.

The brochure stated that the sale would comprise: '109 in-calf & in-milk cows, 30 in-calf & in-milk heifers and 16 maiden heifers.' All the cows with the prefix 'Lancaster' had dams or grand dams with the prefix 'Colony' indicating that they had been bred within the service. Far from merely creating a good first impression, 'The Lancaster Herd,' it went on, 'has operated as a closed herd and has gradually been improved since 1993 by the use of top Semex bulls. The herd boasts an average production of 7,854 litres per cow and a rolling butterfat average of 4.16%.'[16]

Following the disposal of the dairy herd and equipment three of the farms were sold whilst the fourth, Stone Rowe, was developed into a staff training facility for Lancaster prison. Proceeds from the sale were reinvested in a new greenhouse and storage facilities inside the walls to enhance training in horticulture.

Six rare breed Longhorn cattle along with two stockmen who had been at Lancaster were transferred to Kirkham in 2006. Like Lindholme and Standford Hill, Kirkham was built on a reclaimed former airfield. Approximately 80 acres (32 hectares) of IACS registered land were retained at Kirkham 'because they were going for planning permission for Kirkham II and obviously we couldn't sell land that could be identified so we sold 12 acres (5 hectares) in the corner off the sea road and the rest is grass and a conservation area. We kept the Longhorns and the Beef shorthorns and a big PFI (Private Finance Initiative) factory boning out chickens,' explained Bernard.

'By the veg prep?' enquired Maurice.

'Outside the prison,' replied Bernard.

'Is that still going?' I asked.

'It was,' said Bernard.

The retained land was managed in-house. Two acres of dilapidated glasshouses on the Kirkham site were demolished 'to reduce the commitment to commercial production.'

In the early 2000s 150 farmers had converged on Kirkham for the Longhorn Cattle Society AGM.

'It was the week before, 7am on Sunday. I went up to see the lads and there was a lot of end-of-sentence lifers working at Kirkham and this lad comes up to me and it was absolutely heaving it down with rain and rain was pouring off his face and he says, "Mr Horrocks, this is great. I love this. For the first time in my life I've got something to get up for in the morning, to sort my cows out and all that." It was heaving it down and he was loving it. A lot of lads were like that. So much so that the governor put us forward for the Butler Trust Award. To cut a long story short we won in 2009 and went to the palace to get an award and it was all because of what we did with lifers and our big conservation area. We talked about animals and the Longhorns and Princess Anne said, "I must come up to Kirkham to see the Longhorns," and she asked, "Why have you got rid of those Suffolk Punch horses from the Bay? It's awful."' Then, according to Steve she added, 'I like animals better than people.'

From 1938 until 2006, Hollesley Bay had been the most diverse of all the farm sites and the home of the rare breed Suffolk Punch Stud. The disposal of the site was handled in four phases. Phase one saw the disposal of under-used marshlands, a redundant pig unit and the ending of arable farming. Phase two involved lengthy negotiation to find a new home for the Suffolk horses. 'The service owned and maintained the largest stud of Suffolk Punch Horses at Hollesley Bay. There was considerable political and media interest in the future of these horses, we were also mindful that The Princess Royal was patron of the Suffolk Horse Society.'[17, 18]

Princess Royal visiting HMYOI Hollesley Bay April 1991
in her capacity as Royal Patron of the Butler Trust.[19]

'We had oral questions in the House which meant we had to sit in a little box and write the answers,' recalled Bernard.

'Do you know how oral questions work?'

'No,' I admitted.

'You've got to try and guess what the five other questions might be and you write answers to those five questions and then you sit in the little box just in case you've got it wrong. Well, the second question about the horses was "Does this mean that we will lose the Queen's head off the banknote?"'

We sat in stunned silence.

'And that is how it works,' said Bernard adding, 'Unfortunately, and it is still happening now, the horses played too big a part.'

Without hesitation, as soon as he'd finished speaking, he proudly passed around a photo of himself with a Suffolk Punch foal when he was 'at the Bay.'

The Suffolk Punch Trust was set up in 2002 by interested parties to retain the horses, equipment and around 185 acres (75 hectares) at Hollesley Bay.

'At that time,' said Bernard, 'there were fifteen mares and two stallions and they took all the carts and stuff.'

'Not a bad little centre there now,' observed Derek.

'They fund it with rehab on racehorses. They've fenced the fields a treat. Good grass management,' conceded Bernard.

'Lovely horses,' noted Derek, 'You'd go for a walk in the morning and the horses would come to the road.'

The idea was that the Suffolk Punch Trust would provide employment and training opportunities for prisoners in the planned visitor centre.

'We did what we did to try and keep them there. We also sold the Trust the Suffolk sheep. We had to get them back from Featherstone. That was the oldest registered flock of Suffolk sheep. Flock number nineteen,' added Bernard.

In phase three, the dairy herd, equipment and the remaining land at Hollesley Bay was sold and a mothballed nursery was reinstated with investment in equipment and irrigation. Plans were put in place to enhance the amenity areas and provide certificated training. In July 2007, phase four saw the closure of the veg prep and distribution enterprise and the introduction of some building skill courses. Today, according to the Ministry of Justice, HMP and YOI Hollesley Bay 'is an outward looking modern institution which holds sentenced adult males from 18 years and upwards without limit. The farm has gone, and a focus on resettlement and reducing re-offending is at the heart of our agenda,'[20] which seems to imply, erroneously, that with the farm the institution had been inward-looking, old-fashioned and focused on neither resettlement nor rehabilitation.

The prison farm at North Sea Camp, near Boston in Lincolnshire, consisted of around 617 acres (250 hectares) of productive agricultural land.

'We had good land,' conceded Phil.

'I mean the saddest place to close was North Sea Camp because it had all been reclaimed from the sea,' said Bernard.

'But now of course nobody wants that doing,' said Phil. 'As a result of us reclaiming land it was probably falling off the East Yorkshire coast even faster.'

In an agreement with the Environment Agency over the repair and maintenance of the sea wall, the Royal Society for the Protection of Birds (RSPB) initially bought 200 acres (80 hectares).

'The first lot we had no option because the sea wall collapsed. I thought that was a bit sad,' reiterated Bernard.

After the arable cropping had finished, the RSPB purchased a further 200 acres (80 hectares).

'When you see it cropped and everything else,' Derek paused, 'and just back under water.'

'Over one thousand acres and we kept twenty-five,' added Bernard.

All surplus machinery and equipment was sold at auction. The market garden was extended with a new greenhouse and additional polytunnels erected. Eventually the prison service retained about 100 acres (40 hectares) of IACS registered land and managed it in-house, grazing the land with a reduced size sheep flock.

'Other than North Sea Camp, do you feel sad about closing any of the other prison farms?' I asked Bernard.

'No, not really.'

Like North Sea Camp, many of the prison farms consisted of very marginal land that had been brought into production using prison labour. When Brown & Co valued the farm at Featherstone in 1996 at £175,000 they expressed concern that the land might be contaminated.

'There were lots of areas that they thought they would sell and then couldn't,' said Chris Coveney.

The sale of nine farms including Hollesley Bay, North Sea Camp, Misterton and Tudworth raised almost £10m and a further £1.4m was generated through the sale of machinery and livestock across fourteen farms.

'All they saw was that they had a huge pot of money sitting there in land,' said Chris.

'Originally they said it was going to raise millions selling all this agricultural land off but I think that eventually after they had dismantled *everything* I think they only made about £300,000.'

At every sale, a claw-back clause was inserted meaning that if the land was subsequently sold for development the prison service would be entitled to a share in any uplift in value.

'One of the things we did,' said Bernard, 'was that every pound of stuff we sold off: the farm, machinery, livestock, the lot, we reinvested because nobody in the prison service could give approval to dispose of that. I wrote to the Treasury and said, "What we want to do is reinvest it." They wrote back and gave us permission to reinvest every bit of money back in.'

Overall the sales of surplus and scrap machinery raised £844,000 while the sale of livestock achieved £714,000.[21] Some of the money was invested in grounds maintenance equipment including mechanical handling along with the construction of increased storage and training spaces. £900,000 was invested in new gardening and horticulture equipment.

'Staff haven't seen investment like that in farm equipment for over ten years,' claimed Bernard.

'He had a few greenhouses put up here and there,' granted Chris Coveney.

'A new parlour at one place?' I added.

'Not much compared to what they'd destroyed.'

In 2003 the five veg prep units employed 165 prisoners and cost £8 million per annum to operate of which £5.3 million was spent on vegetables to process. Although the farms were able to justify the capital expenditure to build the five units they'd struggled with maintenance costs especially after budgets were devolved to individual institutions. If the units had been inside the individual establishment then the institution would have had responsibility for funding maintenance rather than Farms & Gardens. It was predicted that the vegetable processing equipment would reach its end-of-life by 2008 and it would cost £5 million to replace the units.

The veg preps didn't form part of the modernisation programme but a separate business case recommended their closure. According to the Closing Report, 'This recommendation although more expensive in raw material terms recognised that the end product did not meet today's catering requirements. The units were also coming to the end of their planned life and major capital expenditure would have been required to still produce a product that was not meeting customers' requirements. Approval was given by the Prison Board to close the plants in July 2007' a move supported by the National Audit Office who stated, 'We welcome this development.'[22]

'We could have kept the veg preps going because it was an industry that could have been done within the curtilage of the prison but that required recapitalising,' noted Big Rob.

One of the veg preps was at Leyhill prison which centred around a Grade-II listed mansion that the service had restored at an estimated cost of £25 million following a fire in 1991. Initially, the only effect of the farm modernisation programme on Leyhill was the closure of their milk pasteurising and cartoning enterprise.

'Although we got rid of the glasshouses we built a new, modern unit up on the sports field near the quarters, new glasshouses and polytunnels,' enthused Bernard. Horticulture inside the prison walls was 'reborn with a glasshouse and other equipment purchased.'[23]

During the three years of the modernisation programme it became clear that Leyhill's nursery and visitor centre enterprises were not viable in terms of prisoner employment and training. Plans were put in place to reduce the size of the nursery and to relocate it within the main prison grounds. The future of the visitor's centre and the renowned Tortworth Court arboretum that had been developed by the 3rd Earl of Ducie between 1853 and 1921 was uncertain.

'In June 2001 they sold the old officers school which is now a hotel, to one of the top group of hotels, Four Pillars,' said Bernard. 'A lot of prison land was under what they call Critcheldown so when we sold it we had to sell it back to the people it was compulsory purchased from, the Ministry of Defence and Lord Dewsey at Leyhill. So we offered it back to them and Lord Dewsey didn't want the arboretum so the hotel got the arboretum. He was going to take the nursery and some fields. A lot of places like Critcheldown we had to search out the old owners and pay market rates to original owners or their descendants.'

In 2004, to better define operational as well as organisational boundaries, a new entity, the National Offender Management Scheme (NOMS) was created following recommendations by Lord Carter, a healthcare entrepreneur and management consultant. The first head of NOMS was Phil Wheatley, the existing director general of the prison service. Prison shops were reopened in response to a push for inmate training, something that had to be done 'inside the walls' largely because of convenience. Inmates working on the few remaining farms found themselves spending much of their time attending formal lessons and appointments with counsellors, advisors and panel meetings.

In 2005 Bernard arranged a 'get together' for farm managers.

'You know I didn't tell anyone at headquarters because they were paying for it but they didn't know it. I had to tell Phil that we'd done this because it was appearing in the prison service news!'

A short 'Farm Managers Reunion Newbold Revel 2005' pamphlet was distributed to each of the attendees. Steve Horrocks pointed out the black and white 'Hand milking at Dartmoor Prison, 1956' photo on the front. Inside the strapline read, 'Where the past meets the future' under which was typed: 'As Head Office Farm and Gardens, under the guise of Land Based Activities, will cease to exist

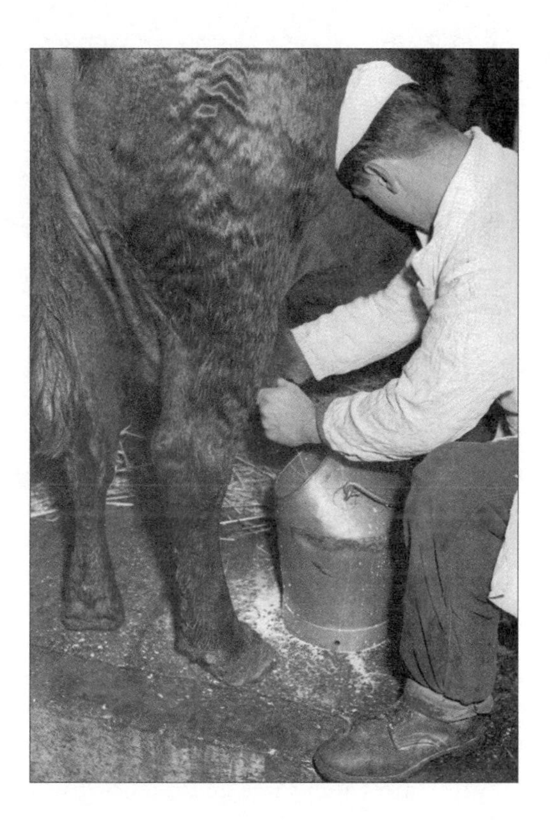

Hand milking at Dartmoor Prison (1956).[24]

by this time next year this may be your last opportunity to catch up with some of your old colleagues. Please take the chance to reminisce about old times and see what is planned for the future. We hope you have an enjoyable day.'

'Believe it or not,' said Bernard, 'we started off with a film of some prisons with two minutes silence and then we did something about what we had done with some of them and what we were doing.'

'Two-minute silence, for the people or the farms?' I asked.

'Make your own mind up! It worked out very well and it was very well attended and we had a two-hour lunch because people wanted to talk. It was a lovely day as well.'

'Yes, the weather was terrific,' agreed Derek.

2005 'Get together' of 65 HMP farm managers showing my dad, Bev Wright, centre second row.[25]

'But if you look at the picture now there is a lot of them not there,' observed Bernard.

My dad with striped tie, had Chris Hastings on his right and Tony Jessup to his left. Ivor Gough, who mentored Lorraine and Jason in addition to chairing union meetings at which significant deals were negotiated for farm managers, stood behind my dad wearing a dark shirt. To his left was Jason alongside Pete Chisholm who had Steve

Horrocks to his immediate left wearing a very straight tie. Behind Jason's left shoulder stood Reg Simpson.

'I'm not sure he's still alive' mused Maurice.

Behind Steve's left shoulder was Jim Partridge who saved the Portland sheep. 'I took John Kingman,' said Derek as he, Bernard,

Farm manager John Kingman standing in the courtyard of the dairy at Dartmoor prison before it became a museum.[26]

Maurice and I pored over the 'Get together' photo. John Kingman, wearing a suit, stood with hands clasped on the front row.

Behind him, on the fourth row, a jocular Bernard, wearing glasses, had Mike Pengelly to his left. Fourth from the left on the back row was Bryan Wakely with Derek Webber in front of him. 'Big Rob' Haslam was photographed fifth row far left, immediately in front of the 'other Rob', Rob Henderson, back row, last on the left. The tallest man on the back row was Hugh Johnstone, the 'diluted' head of Farms & Gardens after it had all been sold.

'We get a card from him,' added Maurice.

'Ken Thomas was there, Henry,' added Bernard.

Henry Sharman was the farm manager at North Sea Camp and Ashfell. He could be seen seated on the front row far right. Tragically in 2012, after he retired, Henry went to Peterborough show and a traction engine rolled back and crushed him.

Eddie Chambers pictured front row in the middle 'died last Thursday,' said Maurice, when I met up with him in November 2014.

At that meeting I asked Maurice about other names and faces that I was unfamiliar with, some of whom had been included in the notes that he and Bev had drawn up when they first thought about writing this book.

'Peter Stevens, he may not be alive. His wife died. Dennis Higman, probably dead, ex-governor Hollesley Bay thirty-five years ago. Lesley Wheeler, regional director, gone. Mike Pengelly, could be blunt and soppy, not sure if he's around, ask Derek. Ian Dunbar, lovely man, died in 2010. Frank Church, dead, gardens manager at Hollesley Bay. McArthur, gone. Arthur Donkins, dead. Nick Carver paralysed, had a bad accident in Thailand.'

Maurice was absent from the 2005 reunion because he'd been on holiday at the time. Jeff Goundrill was also absent. I asked Bernard what had happened to Jeff.

'He left of his own accord but he's done very well for himself out in Cape Verde, runs a landscape business. He's got his own website and stuff,'

'Has he?' queried Derek.

Bernard nodded.

I looked up Jeff and found his facebook page which listed his occupation as HMP 1982–2004. Jeff had written: 'Started a new chapter in our life setting up home and business in Cape Verde. Lifestyle is brilliant and to be recommended, work is hard but satisfying, the landscape business is going well.'

When Big Rob retired, despite his commitment and seniority, he was ineligible for a long service medal because he was a civilian rather than a prison officer.

'I got a coin in a little box as my long service award. I know they cost £8 each,' said Sarah Croft. 'The monetary value doesn't matter, it's just the lack of thought. At least if the coin 'ad been a brooch I could wear it. I'd be proud to wear something that people would ask what it was and I'd be able to say "for working in the prison service". But what can you do with a coin except put it in a drawer?'

When Pete Chisholm retired after 31 years' service, he was given a mug. When I asked Maurice what he received after 34 years in the service he said,

'Nothing.'

For those who are still in the service there's a new policy: prison officers and 'operationals' get a pin after 20 years' service and non-operational staff who have served 25 years will be eligible for a medal. A man of action, Jason said,

'So I've ordered my own! I haven't picked it up yet. If I go to 60 I'll have done 38 years.'

Towards the end of July 2011 I helped my dad rotavate his allotment that backed on to the graveyard in the 'impoverished' market town of Thorne.[27] My dad grew gladioli, popular with mourners, between his plot and those of the deceased. We'd lavished these same gladioli over my grandma Elsie's coffin as she was lowered to lie next to Joe under a headstone engraved with a spinning wheel. As we dug I asked him in passing if he'd like to be buried here.

'No.'

Despite living here for a quarter of a century he felt no affinity for the area or its people, this wasn't his home, it wasn't where he belonged.

'Anyway, I'm not planning on dying.'

Back at his house, knowing that the following day he'd be admitted to Sheffield hospital for an operation to remove part of his pancreas, my dad renewed his shotgun certificate. Not so much a permit to kill but a license to live.

Three weeks later the allotment looked unkempt. In shock after the oncologist rang to say that the operation had gone 'very well' but nevertheless he'd need chemotherapy, my dad and I escaped outside into the back garden where he larked about, posing with an onion on his head. As I left he gathered me to him and hugged me very tightly before sending me on my way with two bags of runner beans and a string of onions that were sure to make me cry.

'I think he is very brave,' I wrote in my diary.

To mark my dad turning 69 I presented him with a photo montage. It included Soi's replacement, a recently deceased rough-haired and somewhat cantankerous terrier named Poppy, his reddish-brown cattle, betting slips, his five grandsons, a picture of him astride 'Mystery' the black pony that his father sold from under him and 'Blossom', his pet name for my mum.

Towards the end of 2012, as my dad's strength waned, I helped him and his friend Albert humanely snap the necks of a dozen, 'Roly-Poly' turkeys that the two of them had hand-reared in Albert's shed. After the feathers had settled, he deftly dressed and trussed what would become my Christmas dinner.

His condition deteriorated so I returned often, visiting him at home and then latterly in hospital. On 9 February 2013 I updated friends on facebook:

> It is like watching a tall ship without compass or earthly sustenance onboard lift anchor to catch a light offshore wind. With gently unfurling sails an unchartered journey begins. But the ship has not disappeared from view just yet. I got a call this morning,
> 'Bring water, gasping,' says my dad.
> I rushed to hospital, ran up the stairs, saw the door to his room was open, legged it along the corridor and there he was, SITTING up in bed! Now, thanks to his new 'friend' morphine, that ship is flying not sailing!

On the ward, although he was supposed to choose from each category (starter, main and pudding) my dad ordered his childhood favourite: ice cream, tinned fruit and jelly. I watched him concentrating hard, as he scratched out whatever it was that would have been served with cucumber so it would be clear that what he *really* wanted was a cucumber sandwich, on white bread *not* wholemeal.

When the woman came to collect the menu I was surprised that she knew him,

'Are you Bev Wright from the prison?'

'Yes.'

'Did you know my husband?'

He did. But he didn't know that Jack had died last year.

'I just want you to know that you were my husband's saviour,' she said, then explained that after Jack lost an arm in an industrial accident he was teased and picked upon until he started working with my dad in the 1990s.

'*Thank you*. You were the only one who encouraged and supported Jack to push himself.'

On 11 Feb 2013 I wrote on Facebook:

> We joked that the only thing my dad hadn't organised was his own funeral. Not anymore. He's done that too!

Back in Devon, Bernard, Maurice, Derek and I studied the 2005 farm managers reunion photograph. I turned to Bernard and Derek,

'Steve Horrocks would like to do another get together and he said he'd organise it.'

Bernard kept his lips firmly closed and stared straight ahead, 'Hmm.'

I continued, 'In the Midlands somewhere.'

There was silence.

Then Bernard laughed.

'That didn't go down very well did it? Unfortunately, there's a lot left under a cloud. Since we closed the farms it's *amazing* how many managers got into problems. No-one lost their job. We moved people around a bit. We gave them new jobs. Some of them some very big jobs. But no-one *lost* a job.'

But some farm staff, like Chris McGown had already been made redundant. Bernard made the process sound thoughtful and generous before adding,

'That was quite honestly because we'd have had to pay a fortune in different things. And no-one was transferred which is why we did the juggle with the stud group, but some people got officer's jobs, went as prison officers. Most of the farm managers became in charge of industries or whatever, but it's amazing how many have *got into problems*. You look how many farm managers were left in 2005 when we finished the farm closures and how many of them have gone since, at a very young age some of them.'

'You mean gone, died?' I asked.

'No. Gone, finished.'

'Retired or resigned,' clarified Maurice.

'Young men who could have stayed on?'

Bernard nodded in agreement.

'Young managers like Steve Horrocks?'

Bernard changed tack. 'I've got the same problem as Maurice for names but the Leyhill bloke has gone, North Sea Camp bloke has gone.'

'Gone,' reiterated Derek, 'young bloke.'

At Steve's retirement party in 2010 Bryan approached Derek and asked, as a close friend of Bernard's, what he'd done to have so much malice from Bernard for all those years? Derek reportedly said to Bryan,

'You knew too much.'

'What did you know?' I asked Bryan.

'Like Bev my background was livestock. Bernard's wasn't.'

When I met up with Lorraine and Chris in 2014 I explained that I'd already spent a day with Steve and he seemed to be happily retired. Steve was very proud of his work on the prison farms, his spare bedroom was wallpapered with maps showing all the farms that he'd worked on.

'What age is he?' asked Lorraine.

'Early 50s,' said Chris.

'Same age as me or bit younger,' noted Lorraine, 'A bit young to be retired.'

There was a short pause in which little was said so I filled it,

'Steve has a few Longhorns he bought off the service.'

Lorraine and Chris simply nodded.

In Doncaster Royal Infirmary my incurable dad was the only person registering the births of Lincoln Red calves from his hospital bed. None of us knew what caused his pancreatic cancer or what effect exposure to work-related aggro or agrochemicals may have had.

When my dad could no longer walk unaided, I wheeled his dressing-gowned self to the only onsite shop so that he could escape the banality of the ward. There he spent all his disability allowance on lottery tickets which to my surprise he trusted me to check. Back at home with my mum we were astonished to find, tucked between the lottery tickets in his wallet, a tiny black and white photograph of a young woman, dressed smartly in a fitted, tweed, two-piece suit.

Flanked by an avenue of towering plane trees, neither of us recognised her or the location.

Next morning, I was the acute ward's first visitor. At first my dad shrugged. Then grinned. It was Julie, his beloved mother. Captured by Billie behind the camera rather than behind bars.

On 3 March 2013 I wrote:

> The Great Escape – been wanting to take my dad out in the car but he is too weak to transport (he can't stand unaided). He was hospitalised on Saturday night (the ambulance picked him up). As I drove in to see him on Sunday morning I had a cunning plan – 'dadknap' him. It worked! On discharge there was no ambulance available for hours so with the help of the nurse who loves his floppy ears (!) we got him into the car. I sat behind him and held him upright so he could look out and mum drove him home. He has made it to spring – seen new buds on trees, snowdrops at the side of the road, a recently trimmed hedge – life, as important to him as any one of us, goes on. Very kindly, Aide from across the road bore him into the house but that night he was carried out by an ambulance crew.

Hi Jayne [Secretary of the Lincoln Red Cattle Society]

It is with sadness that I have to inform you that my dad, Bev Wright, died peacefully yesterday 4 March at 1615.

So it is with great timeliness that I got your emails both about the Great Yorkshire show agreeing to our request for a Trophy for presentation to the Champion Lincoln Red Female and your suggestion about recognising the top breeding Lincoln Red female. Bev would be delighted so long as we can provide an interesting trophy! We will of course tell you when the funeral is in case you or any other members of Lincoln Red Cattle Society want to attend.

Thank you very much for your support. As you know, the Lincoln Red Cattle Society has meant a great deal to my father. Ann and I are both a bit out of our depth with cattle/showing related issues but we will do our best!

Best wishes
Hannah

His memorial service a week later coincided with the spring equinox. I put together a floral spray: budding sprigs nipped from the ornamental beds he'd once tended at YOI Hatfield, a now-shrivelled daffodil in his favourite colour and flowers from a bunch left at the house by kindly Sarah Croft, his former secretary. As I placed it upon his coffin a bemused pallbearer suggested that I might want to hide the onion! I desisted.

Well-attended by family, friends and former colleagues, Brian Cawthorne expressed surprise that Chris Hastings, who'd been photographed next to my dad at the 2005 reunion and worked with him at Lindholme prison, wasn't at the church.

'The only instruction we got from Bev was that everyone was welcome but two weren't,' said my mum.

After my sister read Kipling's poem *If*, Maurice paid tribute to his close friend who he'd last seen just two days earlier. I joked about my dad keeping photos in his wallet of cows and dogs rather than his family then recalled his speech at my wedding.

'Best people,' he'd announced to everyone.

'*You are all best people.*'

For the next couple of weeks, until he was interred in Clanfield church yard where my mum and dad had married, his ashes were kept next to the vacuum cleaner, in an under-stairs cupboard. Like my heart, the box was surprisingly heavy.

14

Going full circle

'Every limit is a beginning as well as an ending.'
George Eliot, *Middlemarch*

'You might like to put this in because I think it's a gem,' said Bernard.

'When the BBC asked me about prison farms, I said, "Well it's like this, we still talk about winning the world cup in 1966 and I can guarantee that people will still be talking about prison farms for a long time to come."'

'It's true, very true,' agreed Maurice. Bernard laughed.

'I often wonder if the circle will be formed?' said Derek.

'They've done it in the States,' said Maurice, recalling how he'd met Ann Widdecombe when she was appointed Minister of State for Prisons in 1995 and she'd told him that the government was thinking of selling off all the farms and he'd said to her,

'In the United States they are buying them back. They *regretted* doing it.'

Prior to the closure of the prison farms there'd been a significant contraction in the number of people working in agriculture nationally. This led senior politicians and Phil Wheatley, who was running the prison service, to argue that there was little point in training prisoners, particularly the majority of whom had come from urban areas, to work with animals, as it wouldn't help them find employment on release. Following the completion of the farm modernisation programme the number of prison farms reduced drastically; when my dad passed away in March 2013 there were only five left: Hewell Grange, near Redditch in Worcestershire; Usk in South Wales; North Sea Camp, near Boston in Lincolnshire; Kirkham in Lancashire and East Sutton Park in Kent which has a horse livery, rare breed pigs and sheep. Collectively, the five holdings equated to about 750 acres (305 hectares), a mere 5% of the land farmed by prisoners in England and Wales twenty years before.

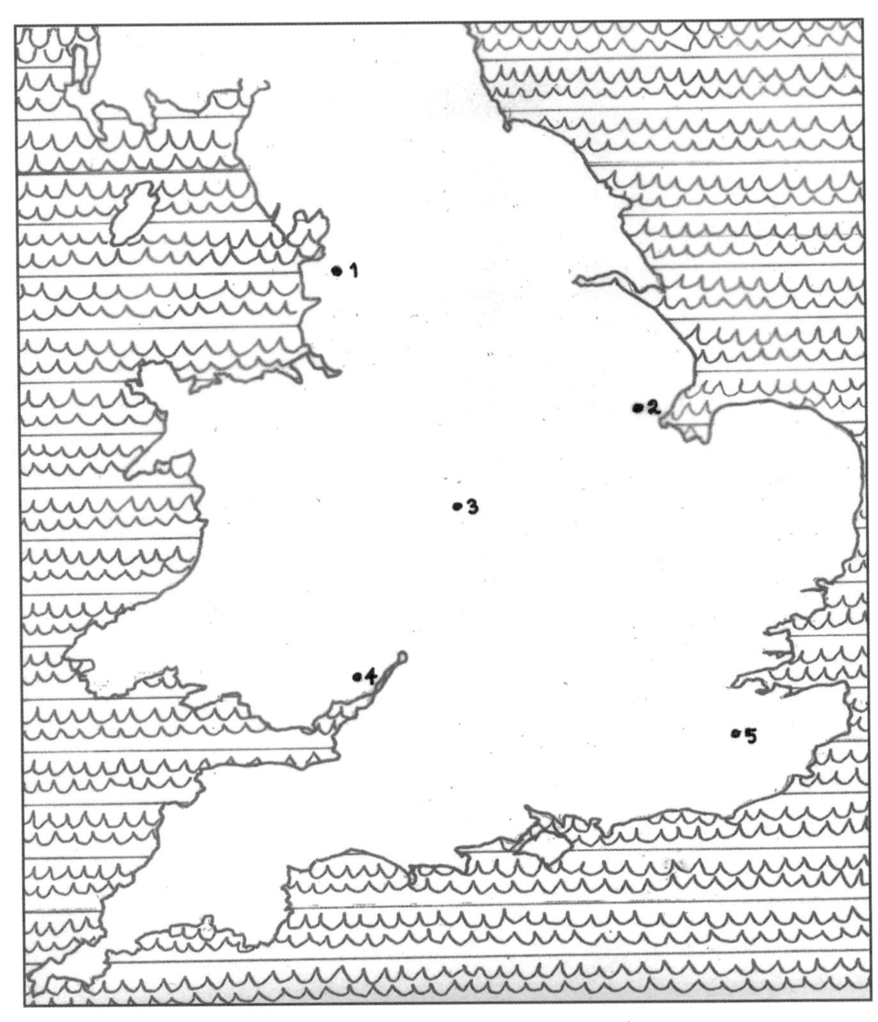

Map of prisons with farms in 2017.[1]

Legend: Prisons with farms in 2017	
1 – Kirkham, Lancashire	4 – Usk, South Wales
2 – North Sea Camp, Lincolnshire	5 – East Sutton Park, Kent
3 – Hewell, Warwickshire	

Hewell Grange retained 148 acres (60 hectares) of IACS registered land because of a lack of alternative work on site for prisoners. The farming operations centre around a dairy herd and pig rearing. Surrounding its Grade-II listed manor house is a Capability Brown designed 'National

Park and Garden' that includes a large walled area of historical interest, especially to the Hereford and Worcester Gardens Trust. There is also an arboretum containing trees of scientific importance and a reed-filled lake surrounded by woodland which is designated a site of special scientific interest (SSSI) for the wildlife it supports, including all three British species of woodpecker. The grassland is grazed by many rare breeds of livestock, including Berkshire, Tamworth and Gloucester Old Spot pigs many of which were rehomed at Hewell Grange as other prison farms were sold or surrendered to their previous owners.

To comply with legislation governing waste water treatment Bernard authorised the installation of two stores at Hewell Grange, 'one for muck and one for silage.'

Overall, he described it as,

'A lovely farm actually,' before adding,

'It was a job to know how to get rid of it.'

Bernard wasn't sure what had happened to the arboretum since he retired in 2008 when the probation and prison services combined to form NOMS but he knew that the walled garden had been retained, some of the greenhouses had been refurbished and a new visitor centre had been built.

As he retired, Hewell Grange was combined with two nearby prisons, Blakenhurst and Brockhill to form HMP Hewell, the first of Britain's 'Titan' prisons designed to hold more than 2500 prisoners. But following a round of cost cutting by the Ministry of Justice, the Brockhill part, which included the modern visitor centre, was closed in 2011 and sold for redevelopment in 2014.

The second commercial farm retained by the service was Cilwrgi farm located about 10 miles from Usk in Wales. The farm is a designated site of special scientific interest (SSSI) with approximately two-thirds of the farm's 460 acres (186 hectares) registered as agricultural land and a third woodland. A further 15 acres (6 hectares) at the rear of the prison is so wet and difficult to access that it's only mown once a year.

As part of the modernisation programme, old, industry-manufactured kennel buildings were demolished and a modern dairy unit erected to house a now thriving milk herd. A variety of outbuildings remain with some used to accommodate a flock of chickens. Commercial horticulture was restarted in refurbished greenhouses and newly erected polytunnels. A fifty-year-old forestry plantation is being harvested and the wood is prepared by prisoners trained to operate the sawmill before it is supplied to various prison industries and workshops. On average between fifteen and twenty-five prisoners work and train on the farm every day.[2]

Of the other three prison farms retained post-modernisation, the largest was North Sea Camp at 617 acres (250 hectares).

'A couple of years ago there was a news programme which went to North Sea Camp,' recalled Bernard, 'it was showing what the prisoners were doing in the polytunnels. There's still interest.'

Inmates help rear beef cattle, commercial white pigs and sheep on about 98 acres (40 hectares). The high-quality meat is accredited through the Red Tractor Beef and Lamb scheme and any surplus rare breed pork is sold through a company called Ginger Pig from Yorkshire who supply specialist London shops.

All the salad and vegetable crops grown on the farm go into the prison kitchen whilst seeds grown in ten polytunnels are sold to an online seed company. A recent Biodiversity Audit found the farm to be 'fully compliant'. And although they didn't win, the garden at North Sea Camp was entered into the Windlesham Trophy Fresher Garden competition for the first time in 2014.

Kirkham is still a major producer of vegetables and the 79 acre (32 hectares) site includes two acres of greenhouses that produce sixty tonnes of tomatoes, twenty tonnes of pepper and aubergines for supply to the prison kitchen, a prison farm shop and other retail outlets. The farm shop is profitable and turns over £40,000 per annum.[3] Land Based Activities employs 106 of the 600 prisoners at Kirkham working on the farm looking after pigs or the Longhorn cattle, in the greenhouses or the farm shop. For comparison, 180 prisoners were employed in the horticultural unit at Kirkham in 1975. Kirkham regularly exhibits at nearby Southport Flower Show and since 2013 they've been the runner-up in the Windlesham Trophy and won best kept prison garden in England and Wales at the Chelsea Flower show. Farm Manager Alan Pitham was highly commended in the 2016 Butler Trust Award for growing food and flowers and rearing rare breed cattle and pigs.

When I met Norma and Deb at NOMS headquarters, I mentioned that I'd found a website called Farming Futures that envisaged six near-future land based jobs including that of high protein insect farming. Whilst 13kg of animal fodder is required to produce 1kg of beef, only 2kg of vegetable feed will produce an equivalent amount of protein from insects like crickets, locusts or beetles.

'Three weeks ago on *Countryfile*,' said Maurice, 'it was on there that they are using insects as animal feed. That's just the beginning.'

But for now sheep and rare breed Longhorn cattle graze Kirkham's pastures with excess cattle advertised for sale through the Longhorn cattle society. HMP Kirkham also has a few British Saddleback pigs and fifty Rhode Island hens. When I visited, a clutch of four elderly pet sheep belonging to a member of staff gazed unerringly towards a dozen or so diminutive black Hebridean sheep, recently arrived from HMP Grendon who appeared overwhelmed by the long, lush grass.

'The only time we ate lamb was when they were culled,' said Wayne, a former inmate at Grendon.

'Was that better than the normal food?' I asked.

'Very strong because it was a rare breed. Sometimes a bit too much to be honest but the lamb curry was nice. Probably because it was cooked by someone else to be honest. But they have quite a lot of agricultural land at Grendon but apart from the lamb we didn't get any of that produce into the prison. It was ridiculous.'

It seems that the once thriving prison farm family has itself become critically endangered; only seven farm managers from the 2005 'get together' are still employed in the service: Chris Coveney, Jason Errington formerly at Ford, Martin Skinner at Moorland, Mathew Pye from Wymott, Justyn Cage at Onley, Dave Jones 'up north' in Wetherby and Phil Thomas based in the Estate Directorate.

Before Big Rob retired, Prison Service Industries and Farms (PSIF) used to own everything,

'The buildings, all the equipment inside and for agriculture, all the tractors and all the land. There was no such thing as an 'SLA' Service Level Agreement but that is how it would be termed nowadays between prison industries and farms by the governor.'

Everything: facilities management, works, maintenance, waste management, fire safety and stores was being privatised. This was a process facilitated by Sarah McKnight, former policy manager at NOMS from 2007 but CEO of ONE3ONE Solutions from early 2013. ONE3ONE, so called because when it was established there were 131 prisons in England and Wales (subsequently reduced to around 110) was appointed by the Ministry of Justice in 2012 to provide purposeful work for prisoners in collaboration with external businesses who could make use of prison facilities, equipment, inmate labour and staff expertise. The chief executive of the Howard League for Penal Reform at the time, Frances Cook was quoted as saying that the decision by the Ministry of Justice to hand prisons over to private companies was 'a mistake of Olympic proportions.'[4]

The amenity side of horticulture, that had been so profitable for Farms & Gardens became part of 'total facilities management' contracted out to two private companies, Amey and Carillion who manage prison grounds across four geographical areas in England and Wales.

'The bit that we said we would keep in Prison Service Prison Industries (PSPI) was market gardening where there is a production element to it and we could justify that it was job training, there were skills to be learnt from it and potentially jobs on release,' said Norma.

Although it seemed cost effective to outsource ground maintenance, there was some concern that external contractors may not be as willing as former Farms & Gardens staff to do whatever was necessary to maintain appearances. So some prison governors, 'given unprecedented operational and financial autonomy, and been trusted to get on and run their jail in the way they see fit' according to former Prime Minister David Cameron, have opted-out of national contracts and chosen their own suppliers.[5] Attempts to privatise amenity services have largely failed; 75% of prison gardens are tended in-house largely because gardening is seen as an activity that fits well with regime hours, is rehabilitative and educational and generates an income for the inmate and the institution. Pottering about in a greenhouse growing a few vegetables and tomatoes 'has its own benefits,' said Jason Errington adding, 'and there's not a lot else for older inmates to do.' Gardening, like farming in the past, is particularly good at accommodating fluctuations in inmate numbers.

'Governors see it as a garden sponge,' quipped Chris Coveney.

In 2014 'pro-farm' Jason Swettenham, a former prison officer and governor took on the role of head of the PSPI Business Development

Group. Tasked with manufacturing and delivering the products and services identified by ONE3ONE, Jason predicted that the number of inmates working on agriculture projects would quadruple over the next five years.

Amazingly, despite Land Based Activities ticking over without a dedicated budget, there are signs of greater coordination between prisons. For example, the prison shop at Askham Grange has started to sell produce from other prisons and mini distribution networks have started to spring up. Faced with competition for their operation from private companies like SERCO, nearby establishments like the South Yorkshire 'cluster' (Hatfield, Moorland and Lindholme) banded together to supply vegetables (except potatoes, carrots and cabbage) to the prison kitchens.

For the last few years the contract to supply all food produce to prison kitchens has been held by 3663. It was assumed that the contract was exclusive, precluding the service from supplying the kitchens with any home-grown produce, however,

'Chris has managed to find a little bit of a chink,' conceded Norma, 'where if it's grown locally or on site then we would be allowed to supply it. The actual volume that we are going to supply is so insignificant anyway, in the scheme of things, 3663 are not really that bothered.'

Heads of Catering have been responsive to an appeal by Chris to supply them with locally grown prison produce but it will require cooperation on a local level.

'I remember Rob Haslam saying to me,' said Norma, 'that they probably wouldn't look at growing root crops because the issue is about how you clean them and peel them and chop them and all of that. They haven't got the time in the kitchen to do all that, it all comes in ready-done. Of course, that's where the veg preps used to come in.'

Chris, who's seen a lot during more than thirty years in Farms & Gardens, says that caterers are coming back on board, recognising the quality and value of prison grown produce and they're especially keen to source relatively expensive, 'exotic' crops like chillies, peppers, spring greens, salad and herbs from prison gardens.

'If you look at what prisoners are being fed now it's all pre-packed almost like aircraft food,' said Bernard.

According to Jeremy Wright, Secretary of State for Justice in 2014, 'Meals must be safe to eat, offer prisoners variety and meet the nutritional, religious and medical needs of all. Currently each prison decides what meals are made available on a day-to-day basis against a specification of requirement set out in Prison Service Instruction 44/2012 Catering Meals for Prisoners.'[6] The type, timing, quality and quantity of food consumed by prisoners has varied over time with breakfast packs, convenience foods such as burgers and pies and cold meals such as sandwiches now commonplace. 'These foods are often poor sources of some important nutrients and most contain high levels of salt' stated an independent report on the quality of food in public institutions in 2007.[7]

And food is still cited as a cause of prison disturbances; in February 2015 the national tactical response unit, which Maurice once headed, was called to privately-owned HMP Northumberland after cold food led to protests by prisoners.[8]

At HMP Lindholme, a £1.5m bakery opened in March 2004 which employed 84 prisoners, many of whom registered to study for an NVQ with at least four securing full-time employment post release. In 2011, Real Bread Campaign member Jane Mason of the Virtuous Bread company began teaching prisoners how to make bread at HMP High Down in Surrey, the site of one of four Clink restaurants that offer 'high end dining' staffed by prisoners on day release. All the bread is made using a sourdough culture as yeast could be used to brew alcohol on the wings.

In Spring 2016 Clink's lunchtime menu included a starter of 'Confit sea trout, samphire, sorrel and a tomato and horseradish crème fraîche' (£5.95) and a main of 'Spring lamb Wellington, trio of cauliflower, whipped potato and raisin purée (£14.95) with a choice of desserts: 'Elderflower and strawberry panna cotta' (£5.95) or home-made Clink ice cream (£6.95).

By comparison the budget for prison caterers to feed prisoners was £1.87 per day, which if it was a Sunday, according to the Food Standards Agency, might include prisoners being offered a choice of chicken bhuna, okra, rice and naan bread or roast chicken and chipolatas with gravy, stuffing, roast potatoes and cabbage followed by apple crumble and custard or fresh fruit.[9] I couldn't help thinking that this was the kind of meal my dad would have enjoyed. I also wondered whether the Clink would ever serve prison farmed insects.

'It's not uncommon in other parts of the world and high end, trendy restaurants,' noted Jason quipping, 'so those bugs that we send with the lettuces are good!'

In August 2013, a social enterprise called Green Shoots Associates, which had the aim of 'creating a sustainable approach to commercial food production', secured funding through the Tribal Group's new futures European Social Fund/NOMS programme for inmates at HMP Dartmoor, to grow oyster mushrooms on coffee grounds in converted prison cells. The mushrooms were sold through various outlets including Boston Tea Party, a commercial café chain. In 2015 Green Shoots announced that it would expand the mushroom growing into Eastwood Park, a women-only prison, HMP Bristol and Guys Marsh. But when I mentioned this to Norma in 2016 she exclaimed,

'News to me!'

Deb, however, recalled,

'They came and spoke at one of the GOOP conferences.'

I thought I'd misheard, GOOP? Deb explained that GOOP stood for 'Green On the Outside for Prisons', that it was a Big Lottery funded initiative that she said had been 'quite big a couple of years ago.'

GOOP seeks to address prisoners' mental health issues through gardening and has attracted funds to install polytunnels and build gardens within prisons.

'They monitored prisoners who were on the gardens party; they'd get questionnaires about if they were happy working outside and if their fitness improved. Unfortunately, as always happens, the funding dries up. Most prisons tend to monitor that locally now. But it's linked in with what they call 'fig' or 'pig'.'

Again, I struggled to understand what Deb meant.

'It's PHIG', the Prison Health Improvement Group.

'You'd get land based activities, as was, involved in that together with mental health, education, careers, that sort of thing, just to monitor improvements in mental health for prisoners working in land based activities.'

Deb emailed me details of Dr Michelle Baybutt at the University of Central Lancashire, the GOOP project co-ordinator. Established in

2008 following a successful pilot at Haverigg in Cumbria, GOOP was initially funded for five years. The projects are 'bottom up', designed to meet the needs of the particular prison and its prisoners rather than implementing 'top down' policies or agendas. Projects typically include establishing an outdoor area for growing food and promoting relaxation, providing accredited training in horticulture and landscaping, maintaining outdoor spaces for the prison and the local community and growing produce for sale to staff, visitors or external businesses such as local cafés.

GOOP attracted follow-on funding from the Big Lottery Fund and there are now twelve horticultural projects operating within prisons in the North West of England all of which have been shown to improve the mental well-being, physical activity and healthy eating of more than eight hundred participants, for example, some inmates have stopped self-harming and reduced smoking.[10] At HMP Risley two polytunnels have been erected, one to grow cut flowers and the other to grow vegetables and at HMP Styal in Cheshire seventy female prisoners are employed on the gardens making it the second largest employer in the prison behind education. The inmates grow their own lunch as well as supplying local outlets including Styal's Clink restaurant.

Michelle was so surprised to hear about the extent of Farms & Gardens in the past that she invited me to come along to the next GOOP network meeting.

'There'll be a site visit to a GOOP prison. There'll be walking, talking, sharing information, stimulating creative thinking.'

'It sounds just like the old *Farm Walk*.'

'That's the best part really!' said Michelle.

Maurice was very amused when I told him that the Farm Walk had been resurrected and even more pleased when I asked him if he'd like to come with me.

As Lorraine had observed, 'It's going full circle.'

While I was with Norma and Deb I mentioned another prison based food initiative that I'd found on the internet. Founded by Joannah Metcalfe, Greener Growth is a community interest company (CIC) that works with disadvantaged members of society, with an emphasis on prisoners, ex-offenders and the homeless. Their aim sounds familiar, to promote sustainability and nutrition by planting and harvesting locally-grown, seasonal fruit and vegetables on vacant or underused land as well promoting biodiversity and nature habitats. According to their website, prisoners at Hollesley Bay turned a 10,000 square foot walled garden into 'a food and fruit resource. Some raised beds were installed and areas cleared to site composting material.'[11]

Offenders, whom Greener Growth preferred to call clients, were issued with a certificate of attendance as well as a 'report card', countersigned by prison management, that detailed the type of work they'd undertaken. The website continued, 'Declan Moore, the prison governor, fully supports Greener Growth's philosophy of Recovery Through Nature.' Phase two of the Hollesley Bay project (part funded by the Humane Earth Foundation) will focus on reviving commercial glasshouses sited at the north-east of the prison perimeter to grow cash crops and food for the prison kitchen. Initially, the existing poor soil has to be enriched. A planting and harvesting regime has been prepared.' Greener Growth stated that it was developing projects with HMP Blundeston, HMP Wayland and HMP Warren Hill.

When I asked Norma she said,

'Again, news to me!' before adding,

'I hope that Chris Coveney knows all about it!'

I subsequently returned to the website and found that a link to an *East Anglian Times* article featuring their work at Hollesley Bay was no longer available. It stated, 'Requests from HMP Warren Hill, HMP Wayland and Norwich prison to roll out our services to their institutions cannot be met until new financing is forthcoming.'

'Marked improvements in Horticulture have been made with a total of £40,000 invested in the area' stated the Independent Monitoring Board's annual report on Channings Wood.[12] Various land based employment opportunities had been created through the refurbishment of redundant polytunnels. 'This has included the repair of eleven polytunnels and the installation of an effective irrigation system. Eight of the polytunnels are being used to grow chillies in partnership with Devon Chilli Farm' which consisted of 'Devon ChilliMan', aka Cliff Hyslop and 'Hot Juan', aka David Floyd.[13] 'Finally after almost six months of planning and frustration with various setbacks the Prison project is very much back on track,' wrote Cliff Hyslop in June 2015.

By August 2015, with the help of four inmates, one of whom had very relevant experience having worked on a tomato farm in Greece for over seven years, two thousand chilli plants were installed in seven polytunnels, each of which was served by an automatic watering system. The watering system was crucial. Over one particularly hot weekend, when inmates would not normally be available to water plants, the system used a staggering 7,000 litres of water.[14]

Back on the wings, 'Chillies' had become the new currency but for the service overall they had little value.

'Financially it wasn't justifiable,' declared Norma,

'Nothing in it for us. Chillies weren't going back into the service. It was for them to sell them on commercially. But the actual activity involved in supervising pots of chillies, there isn't much for prisoners to do, therefore the work activity wasn't there to justify the resource that was being tied up doing it. So that contract came to an end. We said, "Come and take your plants away, we are not that interested."'

When I accessed the Chile Foundry website in March 2016 I found the following:

Sorry but the Chile Foundry is now closed.

I will not be renewing the hosting of the site, so when it is gone it is gone...

Good luck
Dave

Within a short time, the condition of the recently refurbished horticultural facilities at Channings Wood deteriorated significantly.

'The place is just run down,' said Jason, who noted that only seven of the polytunnels were still covered and all the glass in what had once been 'a lovely greenhouse' was smashed.

A return to full self-sufficiency within the prison service is unlikely given a doubling of the prison population and the decision to outsource food supplies to private companies. But like the inevitable turning of the seasons, ideas and initiatives that once flowered and faded have, with the help of an almost extinct 'breed' within the prison service, begun to germinate. Within a broader sustainability agenda there are signs of renewed enthusiasm for inmates to grow seasonally and locally appropriate food that embodies low food miles. I began to think that with political and institutional support and knowledgeable staff my dad's, 'Later, later' might have a future after all.

Thirty years ago, there were 250 prison service industries' staff based at headquarters, a fifth of whom worked in land based activities under the headship of Maurice.

'We had lots of people at head office without anybody being quite sure of what they did,' said Phil.

Now, including land based activities, there are fifty staff for everything.

'Land based activities are down to one,' said Norma before adding, 'Effectively two when the second one comes in.'

This was news to me. By the 'second one' Norma meant Jason Errington who stood between Pete Chisholm and Steve Horrocks when the Farm Managers' Reunion photograph was taken in 2005.

As Maurice, Bernard, Derek and I studied the photograph, Bernard said,

'I suppose the only one that's left is Jason Errington at Ford.'

But unlike Pete and Steve, I couldn't recall having ever heard of, let alone met Jason, despite the extent of the horticultural unit at Ford that generated much of its revenue through contracts with external customers. Some of the money generated from the sale of the farms following the modernisation programme was used to upgrade Ford's horticultural facilities into a modern, well-equipped nursery. Glass in the greenhouse was replaced and mobile benches installed; an irrigation main was renewed and an irrigation lagoon relined; high maintenance polythene tunnels were replaced with a multi span unit and ground maintenance equipment was overhauled.

The fact that Jason Errington was being appointed to take up a position at headquarters equivalent to the position of head of Farms & Gardens formerly held by Maurice and Bernard was remarkable, and largely due to the enthusiasm of Norma's boss, Jason Swettenham.

'Jason is very keen to develop land based activities and start supplying produce back into the prison kitchens, so in many ways we have almost gone full circle!!' exclaimed Chris Coveney.

'It's good that Jason is going to headquarters, a really talented man,' wrote Bernard. Chris reminded me to contact Jason,

'Ask him who his line manager was when he worked at Blantyre House in Kent, I understand that the example he set was instrumental in his rapid success and promotions!!'

When I pressed him for more information his response made me smile,

'Let's just say that you always need to be careful what you say/do to people in the prison service as you never know who will be *your line manager* in the future!!!'

In April 2016 Maurice suffered a second heart incident and was forbidden from exerting himself. After re-starting his heart, doctors advised him to have a defibrillator fitted then decided that his irregular and excessively high heart rate would require an ablation instead. Presciently, Maurice and Mo had recently sold their bungalow and moved into a ground floor flat immediately below Mo's son and daughter-in-law. Mo, in an effort to protect Maurice, told me,

'We might sell the mower.'

Maurice laughed and joked that he might have to do some of the mowing if the gardener didn't do a good enough job! Desperate to dig, to have Devon's red soil under his fingernails, he asked the gardener to build some raised beds for permaculture which he'd seen a lot of when he visited prisons in the USA. What John Glover had said of my dad applied equally to Maurice,

'He was the same as me, he liked to be outside and doing.'

When I met up with John, he'd been retired from Hatfield for several years.

'I was never going to be a foreman. You tell me what to do and I will go and do it. Quite happy. You can't have everyone being ambitious. I'm quite happy with what I've done with my life.'

'You look happy,' I observed.

'I am.'

Maurice, who had no intention of giving up volunteering for the Youth Offending Team (YOT) or chairing the board of governors at the local primary school, was sofa bound when I visited a couple of days after his heart surgery. From there he advised his daughter-in-law that self-seeded potatoes were likely to become diseased if re-planted when she appeared at the door and asked him to identify what she'd dug up.

'But as that one's only been lightly forked, you could give it a wash and eat it?'

Mo looked disgusted!

While I was with him, Maurice described a recent outing.

'The Eden Project have opened a project near Occombe farm near Paignton in Devon for disadvantaged, ex-offenders and it's run by an armed offender who was in Pentonville. YOT had a training day to visit this place and see what was on offer as we send young offenders there now for the same reasons as we did then. I listened to this offender spouting off about Pentonville and one or two other places that he'd been. He was quite open about it. He was talking to the assembled civilians saying how good it was to work on the gardens and how it got them into the habit of working. I was laughing inwardly at this because this was seventeen years afterwards! It just shows what the thinking is now.'

'It must've been odd to hear that from an ex-offender?' I suggested.

'I kept quiet. He was very, very arrogant. There was one of the senior YOT people there who, as an aside, spoke to one of her colleagues. The ex-offender turned to her and said, "*You* are a very rude person." It took me a lot of self-discipline not to have a go at him. Back at the office she said, "I felt that *small*."'

'Don't you tell them what you've done?'

'I don't say a word. Nobody knows. I tell them at YOT but others might think I'm an old stager who wants his two penneth in.' He paused,

'If they asked me, I'd tell them.'

It made me think. I contacted Jason Errington and asked if I could meet him, to hear more about his plans for farming and gardening within the prison service. I'd been told that he was quite young so I was surprised that he remembered my dad, but they'd both run veg preps, my dad at Lindholme and Jason at Standford Hill on the Isle of Sheppey. What about Maurice? After all, he'd left the farms to become an area manager in 1991 and retired from the service twenty years ago in 1996. To my astonishment, Jason said,

'He was on my interview panel when I was first appointed as a farm manager.'

Then I remembered that Maurice, the man who always has a plan, even as an area manager, retained responsibility for the appointment for farm managers. And I realised that I could be like my dad, 'Wright, the righter' as well as the writer. I asked Jason and Maurice if they'd like to meet, to close the circle. A delighted Maurice replied,

'He can ask me anything he likes!'

15

A rare breed blossoms

'When lilacs in the door-yard bloom'd,
And the great star early droop'd in the western sky in the night,
I mourn'd – and yet shall mourn with ever-returning spring.'
Walt Whitman, *When lilacs in the door-yard bloom'd.*

In May 2014, legal action by groups supporting the outstanding rehabilitative work carried out at the two open female prisons, East Sutton Park and Askham Grange in Yorkshire, which is similarly situated in an historic country house, halted their imminent closure.[1] Staff, like Lorraine and Chris, who own homes onsite were immensely relieved as they'd been living with the threat of having their house compulsory purchased for three years.

Over the last six years I have relocated five times but now I have finally settled. I have bought a modern house that lies within the high walls of a kitchen garden formally attached to a Jacobean farmhouse. Its radial design reminiscent of Bentham's 'Panoptican'. Windows on four sides allow the delightful garden with its established herbaceous borders, raised vegetable beds, herbs, soft and top fruit to permeate the interior where I've set up the cherry wood spinning wheel that I inherited from my grandparents. Appropriately enough, the village hosts one of the UK's oldest woollen mills.

Fortunately, I live within an hour of Maurice, who having recently undergone heart surgery was recuperating at home when Jason, the newly appointed head of Land Based Activities (LBA) within Public Sector Prison Industries came to see him.

'I guess that every prison in the country has a got a small parcel of land?' enquired Maurice, knowing that the prison service operates on the second largest government estate. 'So everybody can still work, can't they?'

Post-modernisation, pockets of land attached to penal institutions in England and Wales add up to almost 1,000 acres (400 hectares).

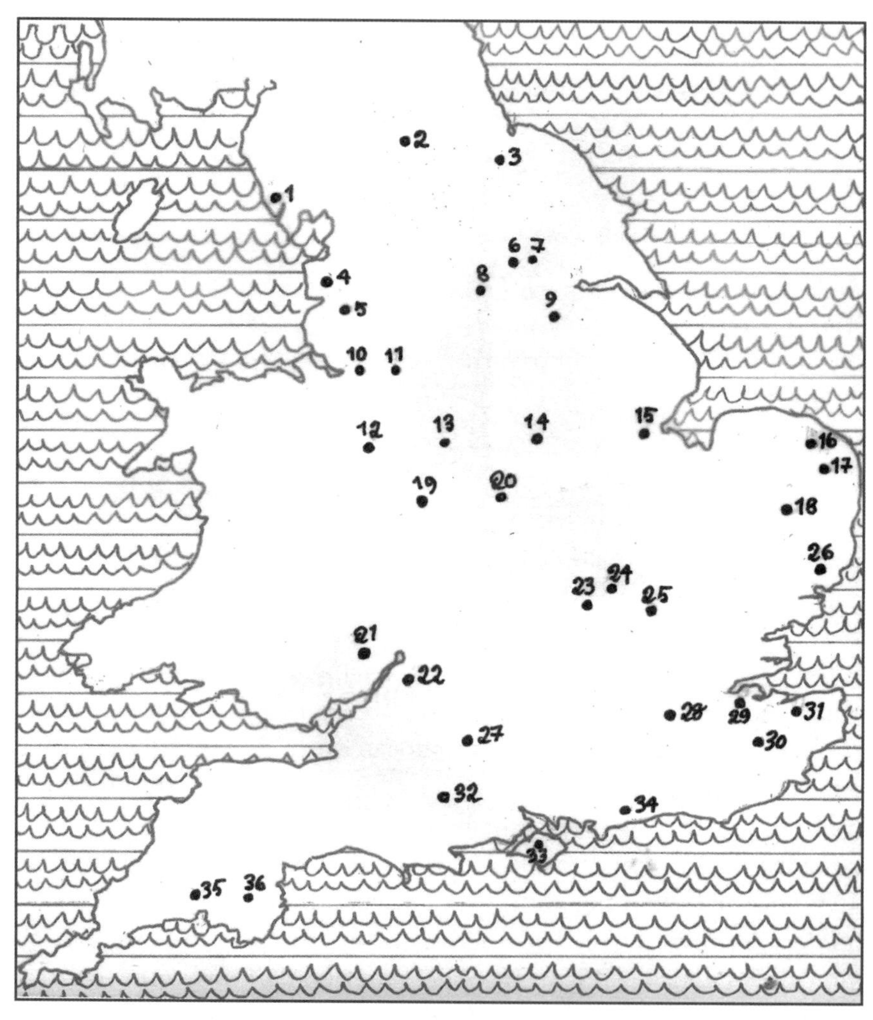

Map of prisons with market gardening in 2017.[2]

Legend: Prisons with market gardening in 2017	
1 – Haverigg, Cumbria	10 – Thorn Cross, Cheshire
2 – Deerbolt, County Durham	11 – Styal, Cheshire
3 – Kirklevington Grange, North Yorks.	12 – Stoke Heath, Shropshire
4 – Kirkham, Lancashire	13 – Sudbury, Derbyshire
5 – Wymott, Lancashire	14 – Whatton, Nottinghamshire
6 – Wealstun, West Yorkshire	15 – North Sea Camp, Lincolnshire
7 – Askham Grange, North Yorkshire	16 – Bure, Norfolk
8 – New Hall, West Yorkshire	17 – Norwich, Norfolk
9 – Hatfield, South Yorkshire	18 – Wayland, Norfolk

19 – Hewell, Worcestershire
20 – Onley, Warwickshire
21 – Prescoed, South Wales
22 – Leyhill, Gloucestershire
23 – Bullingdon, Oxfordshire
24 – Grendon, Buckinghamshire
25 – The Mount, Hertfordshire
26 – Warren Hill, Suffolk
27 – Erlestoke, Wiltshire
28 – High Down, Surrey
29 – Rochester, Kent
30 – East Sutton Park, Kent
31 – Elmley, Kent
32 – Guys Marsh, Dorset
33 – Camp Hill, Isle of Wight
34 – Ford, West Sussex
35 – Dartmoor, Devon
36 – Channings Wood, Devon

So together with the five remaining prison farms, the land available for cultivation is approximately 1,730 acres (700 hectares).[3] In fact, the percentage of prisons in England and Wales without farms but with an area devoted to small-scale production of vegetables, fruit and flowers is comparable to the early 70s. Currently, 102 out of 111 prisons in England and Wales bring nature inside the walls in various ways including therapeutic or sensory gardens, wildlife habitats or edible produce.

In 2016 more than a thousand inmates across thirty-seven prisons spent 1.5 million hours working in commercial horticulture, defined as using polytunnels, greenhouses or open ground to grow vegetables, salad crops, annual bedding plants or nursery stock.[4] Based on commercial horticulture alone, LBA is currently the third largest employer of inmates within the prison service but if, as previously, amenity services were included, they would be the lead employer occupying two thousand inmates. As LBA only employ half the number they did twenty years ago there is potential for expansion especially as the staff to inmate ratio required to supervise horticulture is low, up to forty prisoners can be supervised by two staff. It is an activity that can be established within a year unlike woodwork or textiles and much of the equipment, for example, polytunnels, sheds and gates can be manufactured in-house and supplied to prisons at nil cost.

'In reality, what's happened,' continued Jason, 'is you've taken farms out of it, prison industries haven't actually got enough work to occupy these prisoners. Farms & Gardens as a 'sleeper' has sat there and it has a massive role to play. I mean I walked around a prison with redundant greenhouses and polytunnels yesterday and I said, "You could employ 70 blokes on here comfortably." They've got prisoners who are unemployed.'

'Just sitting around?' asked Maurice.

'Sitting around with nothing to do. You wonder why nobody has thought of this. The farms would not only employ prisoners growing produce and looking after livestock, they'd generate work in woodwork.'

'That's *right!*' Maurice enthused.

'Because instead of having plastic Farms & Gardens crates like we used to, we can make them out of wood and brand them with a stamp and sell them out the farm shops as well.'

Maurice heartily agreed.

'The potential for it is *huge*. If you came around Maurice, you'd be horrified if you saw how it's gone. I don't think that it's particularly anybody's fault, I just think it was a victim of circumstance in a way. I think that if you've got someone who has the gift of the gab and can sell it and can push the right buttons with senior people, I think it will all come back. I can't see it not coming back.'

I asked Jason whether he knew that Maurice was the only person to ever visit all the prisons in England and Wales.

'Did you? Every one?'

'When I left, I'd visited all one hundred and forty-seven. I made the point of doing it.'

'Get that number down for me!' implored Jason.

'I guess,' said Maurice, 'that you have a similar management style to I had?'

Jason wasn't sure what he meant.

'Which attracts people and then they're prepared to listen to you.'

'I must say that wherever I've been, I've been saying that we should get Farms & Gardens going again and I haven't had *any* negativity.'

'No? That's good.'

'Everywhere I go I see that there are these farms with *so* much potential and I know, I can see, that I can make a name for myself. I know I can.'

'Just by resurrecting it,' said Maurice.

'When I speak to people like yourself Maurice it invigorates me to make it work because I *know* it's the *right* thing to do and I want to do it. I've got ten years left in my career and I'd rather do something that I enjoy than something that's going to be a grind.'

'You can turn the whole thing round in ten years,' suggested Maurice, who'd done exactly that.

'I could.'

'You can do it,' said Maurice. He paused, 'It takes a lot of your own personal time.'

'Yeah, you've got to believe in it.'

'You have.'

'I've never not believed in it,' said Jason, 'I've always said that is the way to go. Do you miss it Maurice?'

'I take great interest in it. I'll tell you what, the first year after I retired I really did. The prison service people said, "Well it was because you liked the power." It's not that really. You get so ingrained in what you're doing that it's difficult to totally switch off.'

Jason thought it would be possible to create a community interest company, a charity that would buy prison products, sell them and employ prisoners to run the business. It all sounded very familiar.

'Isn't that what you were proposing in 1988 when Jason first joined the service?' I asked.

'Yes. When I came back from America I wrote a paper that showed how over a period of time you could make the Farms & Gardens self-sufficient by doing exactly what you're saying now. The money that we made each year, which was about £4m, was to be given back to us plus what we asked for which would then become a reducing commitment.'

'So eventually you'd run a standalone business?' enquired Jason.

'Yes, but they were just not interested,' lamented Maurice.

'I thought I was inventing something new!'

Generously, Maurice conceded, 'Well, it *is* still new to the service! If you can do that it would be *brilliant*, it really would.'

Similarly, Jason envisaged mini-distribution networks whereby prisons in local clusters could grow and supply their own fresh produce. I recalled Chris McGown saying that Exeter prison used to work 'hand-in-glove' with Dartmoor and Portland in what he called, 'a little clique on their own.' Jason reported that staff at Rochester supported the idea of home-grown tomatoes being supplied to the prison kitchen and excess produce being collected in a van driven by a prisoner and delivered to nearby Standford Hill on the Isle of Sheppey.

'I've got all the infrastructure there.' But when he called Standford Hill he met with resistance; they preferred to sell their produce through the farm shop rather than supply other prisons. They described LBA as *finished*.'

'That's the sort of attitude I've got to beat. I need to build some bridges in some places.'

'Farms & Gardens, as it was with the animals, won't come back so we've got to go with the future and challenge and modernise,' he enthused.

Having farmed 14,072 acres (5,695 hectares) and been the third largest agricultural holding in the country, as well as the third largest milk producer, sometimes it was necessary to look back to go forward.

'I fancy putting in some chickens, some of the old-fashioned breeds and I want to do plant collections.'

Commercial and rare breed livestock are still present within the prison service in England and Wales albeit on a much smaller scale. For example, Prescoed (formally known as Usk) has 120 dairy cattle and a herd of Pedigree Welsh Black cattle grazing its 420 acres (170 hectares) while Hebridean ewes at Grendon, Spring Hill and now Kirkham produce fat lambs for the kitchens.

'*Back to rare breeds again!*'

'You know regional things.'

'Yes! That's *exactly* what I did! Wymott had some regional poultry at one time, years and years ago,' said Maurice. Wymott, a Category C prison in Lancashire, currently has a flock of pedigree Suffolk sheep who supply the occasional Sunday roast.

'Well I was thinking Sussex chickens in Ford, that sort of stuff.'

'Yes, that's *exactly* what we were doing! keeping native breeds in their county of origin.'

'It's PR, the community thing.'

'That's right, that's what allowed us to bring the school kids in. We let them look at all the rare breeds. I knew that it'd be difficult to bring people inside the prison, inside security and that.'

'Some jails you could,' granted Jason.

'Kirkham have got a *huge* greenhouse and a few animals, shorthorns.'

'Longhorns,' I corrected.

'Shorthorns, longhorns, I'm not a farmer,' laughed Jason.

Maurice and I shared his mirth but unfortunately, at prison service headquarters and amongst some industries staff, a negative stereotype of farmers still persists.

'One of the things that always bugs us Maurice is that wherever we go, whatever we do, we'll always be a 'spud picker'.'

'That *is* the *image,* isn't it,' conceded Maurice, who started out as a pig farmer.

'The image of a farmer with his wellies on. You can't shake it off. Even with my colleagues at London, who I get on very very well with, they call me a 'spud picker' and a 'sprout plucker' and all this sort of stuff.'

Maurice nodded.

'And I've had it said to me, "Well you're a semi-skilled industry" and that, *that* niggles me because my family are all in horticulture, my dad and all his brothers were horticulturalists and knowledge-wise they'd 'knock anyone in the tin hat' the amount, the depth of knowledge that you have to have to be in LBA.'

'Of course,' agreed Maurice who as head of Farms & Gardens managed a multi-million budget, 13,590 acres (5,500 hectares), 17 large farms, an 80-person management team and a temporary workforce of 3,500 prisoners, but still faced prejudice about his management ability.

'Surpasses in my opinion some of the other occupations but we're *never seen* as that are we?'

'No, no.'

'And that's something.' Jason laughed. 'You did very well. I don't know how you did it but you got to be Yorkshire area manager,' he paused, 'you must've had difficulties.'

'I did. Management difficulties with my colleagues,' Maurice understated. 'But in terms of running the area it wasn't that bad because of the management that I'd done. I'd been around a long time; I'd served in loads of prisons so that wasn't too difficult. So long as you were able to switch on to the political aspects that helped.'

Jason nodded. 'I passed all the exams to go operational and become a prison governor. I did incidents and adjudications and the JSAC [a role play assessment] but the scheme was pulled. They called it a 'cross hierarchical move', you could move from non-op to op but all the way through that I had prison officers saying, "But you're a farmer, what do you know about running prisons?" I'd say, "I've probably had more to do with prisoners than you've ever done, I've done 25 years in the prisons." But they don't see it and they never will. It's just a badge you have to wear isn't it?'

Maurice, one of the most highly qualified operational staff in the whole service and one of the most modest people I've ever encountered, agreed.

After talking incessantly for more than an hour we paused for a comfort break. Maurice left Jason and I sitting in his front room eating Mo's freshly baked rock cakes.

'I know I haven't got to invent anything,' said Jason, 'It's *all* been done. *All* I've got to do is to convince people that it's the *right* thing to do. And they don't take a lot of convincing. What Maurice has done is exactly what I'm trying to do. I'm not doing it new. You know Maurice and Bernard, I like to think that I'm the same, they're good at communicating and that's why it was successful and that's why I think that I can do it, communicate *the vision*.'

We heard Maurice returning, I smiled, he was happily singing.

'What I need to do is to get what caterers spend on produce and find out how much money we are spending on outside companies on things that I could provide. I don't have that data. One of the things that I've proposed already is that what we need to have on a smaller scale is the old Farmplan.'

Maurice asked whether Farmplan was still available. It is, and it has the same distinctive red-on-yellow colour scheme as its sister company, the *Farmers' Weekly*. An online forum discussed the merits of Farmplan aggregating data as part of its new GateKeeper service, with contributors concerned about farmers being charged to access it or their data being sold.

Jason said, '*You need to know* what the business is doing.'

'Farmplan was such a good system. So they don't do any internal transfers or anything?' Maurice asked.

'No.'

When the head of finance had produced a spreadsheet with the farm shop sales from Wymott, Kirkham and East Sutton Park on it there were no input costs.

'All of what we do now Maurice, there's no trading account.'

'*Isn't there*!'

'I need to be able to say that I've made this much from this much money so give me this much and I will make you that much. I've got to show the value of it.'

Although Farms & Gardens have historically been profitable there's not always been government support for promoting external sales. As long as the service doesn't compete with local suppliers, surplus produce can be sold to wholesalers after kitchens and farm shops have taken what they want. In 2016 income from commercial horticulture approached £1m almost 90% of which was generated through a combination of internal 'soft charge' credit, local agreements with the staff canteen, income from farm shops like the one established at Kirkham in 1996, or through commercial contracts of which there are currently twelve covering livestock sales, seed production and annual bedding plants for local authorities. Jason estimated that Farms & Gardens could double every £1 invested in it,

'We've got free seeds and free labour and our running costs are not specific to us. I'm going to have a conversation with Farmplan to see if we can tailor the package that we buy off them.'

It all sounded very positive but in the back of my mind I remembered Chris Coveney saying that Farms & Gardens 'were too open' compared to industries, who didn't have the equivalent of Farmplan, and how their transparency had contributed to their demise.

'One of the issues is that we haven't got anyone (like Mo) who can do the data input. I said, "Well get an offender to do it." I know there's a risk with that but that's the answer,' said Jason.

Maurice agreed, 'We had prisoners working in some of the farm offices and in the States inmates lived on the farm, slaughtered and butchered their own animals and drove the produce between prisons.'

'I did 'reducing reoffending' at Ford,' explained Jason, 'it was my job to put prisoners working in the community. I was trying to make links with companies. I was knocking on the door trying to get them work but you say to the prison service, "Will you employ a prisoner as a driver?"

"No, we can't do it."' Little had changed.

'In the back of my mind, you must remember this Maurice,' said Jason, 'we used to do amenity costings?'

'*Yes, of course, yes,*' he laughed.

'What we need to do is almost invent an amenity costing sheet.'

Maurice was stunned.

'If we cut the grass, because obviously we don't want the prison to fall into disrepute and be untidy, we need to evidence what we're doing. And you can see it coming back!'

'Well that costing scheme, you can actually get it from the local authority.'

'Can you?' asked Jason.

'They've got a list of jobs and rates per hour.'

'That's what you did?'

'Yes.'

'It's funny how it's gone round,' mused Jason.

'I'm just going to rope Jason in to move that manure,' I said after another hour had passed.

'I'm sorry I can't be much help,' said Maurice.

'You can do your usual,' I suggested.

'I can open the gate.'

'Directing,' I teased. 'We need a *senior* manager.'

'Bring the car down!' shouted Maurice as we went out the door past the pig-shaped garden ornaments. Later, when I listened back to the audio recording I expected our absence to be marked by silence but instead I could hear Maurice humming a tune.

'There's a bit of weight in it,' shouted Jason as we heaved the bags out of the back of my car onto Maurice's garden wall.

'What've you got growing?' I asked.

'Not a lot. Spuds, peas. Only put them in last weekend otherwise they come up too early.'

'Frost and that,' said Jason.

When we reconvened in Maurice and Mo's front room Jason said, 'Maybe over the years we didn't do ourselves any favours. I think we probably outgrew ourselves in a way; the perception of the staff at Ford was that it was a nursery that just happened to be attached to the prison. They saw themselves as a separate entity. When I went in and said, "We've to go to the security meeting, you've to be at the board meetings, when they need stuff moving we need to get on a tractor and move the stuff for them," they didn't like that. I think that at some prisons, the farm was the farm and the prison was a bit of inconvenience and it made it difficult for them to operate.'

'But that was the wrong way to go. You *have* to be an integral part of it,' extolled Maurice.

'That's right. You have to have them want you.'

'If the governor needs you and sees you as an asset then that's going to help. You have to go to meetings and be part of the establishment,' he insisted.

'Bernard Feist wasn't like this but since he left there's been a bit of a defeatist attitude that we've accepted,' said Jason.

'That this has happened and we can't do anything about it?' asked Maurice.

Jason replied with fighting talk, 'I'm *determined* to make a difference. *Everywhere* I go I'm *pushing on an open door* with regard to growing and supplying our own food. Eighty-five thousand prisoners have got to eat.'

Now the service spends approximately £15 million every year purchasing fresh produce from external suppliers of which a quarter, according to a wider government procurement strategy supported by DEFRA, should be grown in the UK.[5]

'We need to badge it as *self-sufficiency*,' exhorted Jason, 'We can save the tax payer money.'

'Corporate social responsibility and ethical consumerism are big business,' I added while Maurice nodded in agreement.

'The core business is that we've prisoners who all need to be fed. To support that the main reason we are there is to rehabilitate prisoners and that has got to be our ultimate aim. Education, training and the work ethic, *all* that has got to be at the core of what we're about. The work has got to be relevant, it's got to be interesting, not putting screws in bags.'

Between 2012 and 2022 the number of inmates employed in prison industries is expected to double to 18,000 which presents a significant opportunity for Land Based Activities. Following a recent six-month pilot scheme that saved nearly £500,000, the Ministry of Justice announced that inmates would be manufacturing a variety of items for the Ministry of Defence including fence posts, refurbished hydraulic jacks and sandbags (rather than mailbags). 'By providing this new service, prisoners will be giving something back to their country, while learning important new skills and the value of a hard day's work,' said former Secretary of State for Justice, Chris Grayling.[6]

'I'm being mischievous,' Maurice twinkled, 'but does it give them skills?'

Nationally, the careers service reports that more than 40% of land based jobs are unfilled compared to a quarter in other trades. Until recently recruitment to Land Based Activities has been hampered by jobs only being advertised via the official prison service website rather than in local papers. In 2015–2016 sixty-eight recruitment campaigns resulted in only eight people being hired. Now adverts are being placed in trade magazines like *Horticultural Weekly* and once again they are specifying that technical, agricultural or horticultural rather than generic skills are required.

Although sixty-two prisons offer City & Guilds qualifications in horticulture, it is not clear whether ex-offenders will be eligible to apply.

'LBA is a sleeping giant and we have to do something about it. We need the staff,' said Jason.

Having trained as an NVQ assessor in case she was laid off, Lorraine has little spare time to ride her horse; when she's not instructing female inmates on how to look after pigs, she's busy assessing them. Outside staff are working as hard, if not harder, than ever.

'The outside wall is the outside wall and we don't want anyone going over it,' stated Jason, 'so at some prisons we need to put up anti-dash fencing that can be built in engineering. I need to get support from the centre to make the job work, otherwise I can go from place to place and talk and talk and pass my ten years and achieve nothing, but that's not what I want to do. In the past, they've ploughed money into engineering and woodwork year on year.' Certainly, some prisons have unused, sophisticated engineering equipment.

'I'm asking for money for LBA, the work is there, you haven't got to take a gamble.'

'The government are saying that they want inmates to be active either in education or work,' said Maurice.

'And with the emphasis on home-grown food and food miles and occupation and everything, it's the right time,' said Jason.

'It is.'

'This year I bid to have a pot of money, a small pot, so I can go into prisons and say, "We will support this and that." I asked for £30,000 and they gave me £20,000.'

'That's peanuts!" said Maurice.

'It is peanuts but I thought, it's a start! I've got to convince London to give me more staff. Textiles have a team of eight and engineering have got a team of five. LBA is the second biggest employer in the prison service and I've got the smallest team, there's just Chris Coveney and I. I will be saying, "You want me to grow the business? Give me the people and I can do this, this and this,"' said Jason.

I turned to Maurice, 'We'll do what we can won't we?'

He laughed. 'I wish you all the best, I hope you succeed I really do.'

'It won't be from lack of trying.'

'I know it won't,' agreed Maurice.

Former Head of Farms & Gardens Maurice Codd with the author and Jason Errington, Head of Land Based Activities.[7]

'We should be growing our own food and I'm spreading the word already but it will be an uphill battle.'

'I wish you success. Watch this space!'

'I'll definitely keep in touch.'

'You know where we are,' I said.

'We can meet up and have a meal,' suggested Maurice.

'That'd be good.'

'And you can save your daily allowance!' I teased.

We all laughed.

Prison caterers, particularly those in the north, are enthusiastic about sourcing local, fresh, quality produce and are especially keen to see high cost bespoke produce such as okra or herbs grown on-site.

'We need to treat caterers as proper customers. We need to plan cropping. Kirkham is good,' noted Chris Coveney when Maurice, Jason and I met for a second time at a GOOP network meeting at HMP Kirkham in September 2016.

'We've been stitched up by food supply companies, they make it cheap for a couple of years and then they put up the prices. We need to address the 'misinformation' about contracts and say that caterers can buy or use prison grown produce and we need to be able to supply fresh meat,' said Chris.

'One of the things that I've come up against is that when you were doing it, you used to skim some of the catering budget to prop up the farms. Am I right?' asked Jason.

'No,' laughed Maurice.

'Well, let me word that another way then. You had a value that you put in per prisoner for produce into the kitchens?'

'Yes.'

'And that value, that money, if you hadn't been providing it would've been given to the caterer to buy food?'

'That's right, yes.'

'The caterers when the farms finished got that money?'

'Yes.'

'They don't want to lose that money. The utopia for them is for me to give them all the produce.'

'*Free*?'

'Yes. *And* they still have a budget.'

'*You can't do that!*' said an incredulous Maurice.

Laurie Gornall, head of Land Based Activities at Kirkham seemed disappointed that anyone else other than Maurice, Steve Horrocks, Dave the newly appointed manager at Lancaster farms and myself stayed behind after the GOOP meeting to sample the home-grown roast beef with all the trimmings served by inmates in the staff canteen.

'Where do you want to go? What do you want to see?' he asked after we'd finished. Without hesitation Steve replied, 'The cows' and Maurice and I smiled as we knew this was the first time he'd been back to Kirkham since retiring in 2012.

On our way to see the Longhorn cattle, Diane the recently appointed Farm Manager, whose background in arboriculture and conservation made her a perfect choice for Kirkham, pointed out greenhouses brimming with aubergines and tomatoes. She ticked off a member of staff who'd left his fork leaning against the outside of a shed. Inmates, whose working day is punctuated every hour and a half with a break for tea or lunch, wandered around pushing wheelbarrows. Laurie indicated raised beds near a potting shed installed by GOOP that was used mainly by elderly inmates and Maurice stopped to chat to someone he recognised who was nearing retirement.

As we approached the field of cattle, a tractor driven by an inmate dropped off the farm foreman who lamented that some visitors didn't appreciate that the wildlife area wasn't meant to be 'neat' nor that the outdoor reared Saddleback pigs thrive in mud. Knowing nothing about the ins and outs of livestock rearing, Dave stood wide-eyed as Steve and the foreman inspected a lone Longhorn bull and discussed the merits of hiring rather than buying a bull. As they entered the field, like a magic carpet, the Longhorns rose and floated toward their familiar chatter. Seeing Steve grab the flank of a pale, young heifer whose potential as meat he could well imagine, Diane suggested he might like to come back and help them prepare their animals for showing. He smiled broadly and when I left he gave me a huge hug.

When I asked Mo whether Maurice had enjoyed his visit her response surprised me.

'It made him feel sad. He misses it.'

Working outside is no longer seen as a punishment but a privilege. At Preston almost one hundred and fifty prisoners are on the waiting list for gardening which is particularly attractive to older and less able-bodied prisoners. Last year Preston received the Windlesham Trophy for a new garden category introduced by Chris Coveney, 'Best use of recycled material'. Preston has embraced 'Outdoor Learning'; in the morning inmates are taught maths and English in a shed that doubles as a classroom and an office. In the afternoon, inmates tend plants in the polytunnel or get involved in landscaping. Having found that many of the prisoners have never tasted fresh, easy to grow vegetables like beetroot, staff are appealing for funds to install a 'hot plate' in the shed. To further their 'skills for life' and promote healthy eating habits, inmates will be able to prepare their own lunch (simple dishes like mushroom soup).

Cat. C horticulture, where inmates can work inside the walls is the 'growth area' quipped Chris but ironically, as caterers come back on board it is security that has become a major obstacle. For example, at Wymott tomatoes withered on the vine due to a lack of water as staff struggled to get security clearance to even open the tool shed.

Meanwhile 'Blossom', as my dad affectionately called my mum, keeps the graveside allotment ticking over and ensures the substantial stone trough flanked by metal milk churns that decorate her front garden are filled with brightly-coloured annuals. Her near neighbour, John Fisher still works across the road at Hatfield prison.

At the time that my dad died Hatfield was 'meeting majority of targets'. Along with the other prisons in the South Yorkshire cluster, Moorland and Lindholme, it was earmarked for privatisation. But, faced with mounting criticism of private operator SERCO, the decision was taken to retain the South Yorkshire cluster in the public sector. In 2014 Chris Dyer moved from Northallerton, a closed prison in North Yorkshire to become the new governor,

'He asked us to tell him what we were about,' said John Fisher.

After a lengthy and detailed consultation process Chris Dyer created a new corporate identity for Hatfield, a vision based on a set of values and clear standards to operate by and a new corporate colour scheme: blue, lilac and white.

Following an unannounced inspection in August 2015 that saw Hatfield achieve 'exceptional performance', the highest rating, Michael Spurr, chief executive of NOMS said: 'Hatfield is a safe and well-run prison, where prisoners are being given excellent support to turn their lives around upon release. The Governor and his staff deserve huge credit for their crucial role in rehabilitating offenders, including providing high quality education, training and employment opportunities.'[8]

'Chris transformed Hatfield,' said John.

As there is no longer a 'works' or 'stores' department, if the governor requires a new plug socket he pays Amey, a private contractor to install it.

'It's the same people doing the work.'

Resettlement is at the heart of the agenda at Hatfield which currently houses two hundred and sixty-six end-of-sentence inmates aged eighteen to seventy-four. Each inmate spends thirteen weeks at nearby 'Hatfield Lakes', situated adjacent to Lindholme prison, where they are assessed before being sent to Hatfield to undertake two levels of work: 'enhanced stage one' – relatively low paid work designed to build trust and work habits, for example working with a local authority or the council, and 'stage two' – paid outwork in jobs vetted by the service in which the inmate earns a 'proper' wage. Somewhat ironically John told me that one of the inmates he supervises earns three times what he does.

To further resettlement opportunities for inmates, the former staff club house where my dad and I used to play snooker is being renovated and turned into a shabby chic furniture store run by *Refurnish*, a Doncaster-based social enterprise and registered charity. *Refurnish* aims to prevent landfill by refurbishing old electrical goods and furniture whilst providing work and training opportunities for disadvantaged people.

The prison has retained its own laundry facilities and John Fisher told me that the welders course has re-opened. Once again inmates can undertake an NVQ in horticulture: two greenhouses, each costing £30,000, have been installed, one at Hatfield and the other at Hatfield Lakes. Five polytunnels have been erected on the old sports field and an area behind the garden wall of the houses opposite is being used to cultivate rhubarb.

The contract with 3663 to supply food to the prison kitchen has ended and, although a new company has taken over, fresh garden produce is once again being supplied to the caterers. Prisoners are also making their own bread.

'With yeast?' I asked.

'Yes,' affirmed John, 'if inmates want alcohol they'd rather buy it.'

The horticultural renovation at Hatfield has been overseen by Chris George, 'a garden guy who's in charge of activities. He's like Bev but on a smaller scale,' said John Fisher adding, 'It was short-sighted to sell it all off, it'll cost more to replace it.'

When Hatfield was governed by John Clark and my dad managed Tudworth and Misterton Carr, the sale of milk, pigs, meat, 'and those red cows,' as John Fisher called them, generated an annual profit of £700,000.

'I'm a bit upset that the farms have gone,' said Wayne, 'because I've never been able to go and work with pigs.' Effervescent and affable, Wayne was one of two prisoners asked to set up a farm shop when they transferred to Hatfield.

'I came here on the 20th April and I was given a set of keys.'

'You were expected just to get on with it?' I asked.

'It was a bit scary. I didn't know anything about produce.'

'Did you have any retail experience?'

'Slightly. I'd worked in a warehouse. I was a bingo operator and I did care assistant so I had that bit to me. I was asked to start doing signage. I went down to the polytunnels. Thought, 'this is nice', what is it?'

Open seven days a week, 'Thyme Served' is run by inmates, unsupervised.

In addition to plants and edible garden produce, the farm shop stocks hanging baskets, eggs from chickens kept at Hatfield Lakes and furniture made at Durham prison. I wasn't surprised when John said, 'It gives the prisoner a sense of work ethic.' Intended to build trust, it also sounded as if there was the potential to generate real currency for use on the wings. At the end of each day, 'money will be placed in a tin and they lock it.' John collects the tin and, without checking it, locks it away overnight and returns it to the inmates operating the farm shop the following morning.

'If other prisons have public outlets then they need to be opened up because the amount of people who have come in here and gone, "We've never met a prisoner before. Are you a prisoner? Oh, you don't seem like one." Their expectations change. It gives you such a confidence boost that the public don't think you are a monster,' said Wayne.

The 'Thyme Served' Farm Shop that opened at HMPYOI Hatfield in 2016.[9]

'I love the shop. I love what it stands for. And knowing that the lads are really proud, that customers come back and go, "Oh you know what, we had that for our Sunday dinner and it was great." And working with the public has taught me a lot; that I know more than I think I know.'

Wayne contrasted his experience at Hatfield with other prisons that he'd spent time in since being sentenced in 2001.

'At Leeds there was just grass, no flowers, nothing, not even a sports field. At Swaleside, next to Standford Hill on the Isle of Sheppey there were large grounds but nothing except a beautiful floral display at the gatehouse. They had one greenhouse and one polytunnel but years ago they'd had everything you could think of. You could see where the beds had been taken out and grassed over. At Stocken there were flowers everywhere. The house was obviously owned by someone else and they sold off all the farms. They used to have pigs. We had topiary bushes and raised beds and the lads were doing level two horticulture and it looked fantastic. Grendon was quite a depressing place. They've got a horticulture course but you do it in a classroom and the only place with flowers is the bit that the public can see. It used to say, 'Welcome to Grendon' in flowers but nothing else. If you went on to the gardens you did it for twelve months but you just mowed grass.'

'What about the chapel?' I asked.

'No. I was the orderly and it was a lovely lady called Sylvia who bought in the flowers.'

'When I came here to the assessment site I ended up on the gardens but all we did was hoe a bit of soil and cut a bit of grass but we did see that they had a polytunnel and they were growing something.'

'I try the produce and it is completely different. When the tomatoes come in we try them because we have to be able to tell the customers that these are sweet or delicate or stuff like that. I mean the cauliflowers, you just have to look at them to see whether they are decent or not. We've got two lots of potatoes and the 'gourmet roasting potatoes' really need to be gourmet roasting potatoes. We've had a couple of customers come in and boil them and they've gone really mushy but I've gone, "Well I did tell you that they were roasting potatoes."'

'Realistically,' said Wayne, 'we should be self-sufficient for the prison service because let's get it right, the rubbish they buy and it *is* disgusting rubbish. They are dictated to about who they have to buy from. This stuff is phenomenal, the taste is completely different and it's near on free because all you have to do is let some stuff go to seed and next year the stuff is completely free for yer. I think all prisons should go self-sufficient and only buy in what they need to. At the end of the day half the stuff here is frozen and most of them don't know how to peel a potato because it all comes in ready peeled. It is *disgusting* to be honest.'

'It's a massive learning curve for people. I want an allotment where I can grow my own veg. Even though I haven't done it here I want to do it because that tastes way better than the supermarket stuff and it's not that hard. I think with the way that things are going there's many families that struggle out there and some of the lads are in here because they've struggled. The only way they can manage is by committing crime and they don't know anything else. If they can know how to grow their own stuff and how to keep things for storage then it's going to take some of the pressure away.'

John Fisher smiled, 'It's gone full circle.'

'Prison works if you look for it,' said Wayne. 'I think prison jobs have gone the wrong way and they have to get back outside. I really do.'

Time outside is time well served.

Outside time a rare breed blossoms.

NOTES

Chapter 1 – Home on the farm

[1] In the UK there were 5 million cows in 1875 and 15.2 million in 1974 (Zayed, Y, 21st January 2016. *Agriculture: historical statistics.* Briefing paper number 03339. House of Commons Library)

[2] Private collection, Ann Wright

[3] Author's private collection

[4] Focus on Farming Survey (2001) reported in BBC news 'Most farmers 'against euro'' Monday 11th June 2001 available at https://is.gd/CpoLXt (accessed December 14th, 2016)

[5] The minimum wage for agricultural workers in the late 1960s was £14 16s per week and a two-bedroom house cost about £2,000. Agricultural Wages (Hansard, 17th November 1970 available at https://goo.gl/OB2PkK (accessed 15th April 2016)

[6] Private collection, Ann Wright

[7] A sack of corn weighed two and a quarter hundred weight or 114kg

[8] Percentage available at https://goo.gl/K52nFo (accessed 7th April 2016)

[9] National Farmers Union, *UK Agricultural Review – Farming in Crisis,* June 2002

[10] In 1939 15% of the UK's population was employed on almost half a million farms, Office for National Statistics.

Chapter 2 – New recruits

[1] Former governor and regional director Bill Driscoll, from *Prison Britain III – Fresh Start,* BBC Radio 4, 5th August 1997 in Liebling, A., Price, D. and Shefer, G. (2012) *The Prison Officer.* Second Ed. Routledge: London, p.169

[2] HM Prison Service (undated) *Farm Conference History 1956-1975 Volume One* p.111

[3] DIS Policy. *Farms and Gardens: Historical Background* (19/2/1971) Draft copy supplied by Maurice Codd

[4] Mr Darroch quoted in HM Prison Service (undated) *Farm Conference History 1976–1995 Volume Two* p.245

[5] Author's private collection

[6] *Farm Conference History 1956-1975,* op. cit., p.200

[7] Mr Nash, newly appointed governor of Wymott, Farm Management Conference 12th–14th July 1977 op. cit., *Farm Conference History 1976-1995* p.227

[8] Liebling, A., Price, D and Shefer, G (2012) *The Prison Officer: Second Edition*. Routledge: London p.168

Chapter 3 – Hooves and shoots

[1] Butts, M (April 1932) On Gardens: Gardens and gardening, rev. of Gardens and Gardening: Studio Gardening Annual, *The Bookman*, 82, 487, 40

[2] Bentham, J (1838) in The works of Jeremy Bentham collected by his executor, John Bowring

[3] Miss Alice Bacon, Minister for State, Home Office (1966) Borstal, Gaynes Hall. Hansard https://goo.gl/5XNvij (accessed 15th June 2017)

[4] *Farm Conference History 1956-1975* op. cit., p.23-24

[5] National Justice Museum, Nottingham. AAPSM:1993:0137. Reproduced by permission of the Ministry of Justice.

[6] National Justice Museum, Nottingham. AAPSM:1997:0888. Reproduced by permission of the Ministry of Justice. Undated but circa 1905.

[7] Map courtesy of Brian Dunce

[8] National Justice Museum, Nottingham. AAPSM:1995:0476. Reproduced by permission of the Ministry of Justice. Undated.

[9] National Justice Museum, Nottingham. AAPSM:1993.0410. Reproduced by permission of the Ministry of Justice. Undated. Reproduced in Home Office Prison Department (undated) *Farms and Gardens in the Prison Service* p.1

[10] *Farm Conference History 1956-1975* op. cit., p.90

[11] National Justice Museum, Nottingham. AAPSM:1998:0230. Reproduced by permission of the Ministry of Justice. Undated

[12] Hollesley Bay Colony Farm Walk 1968 in *Farm Conference History 1956-1975*, op. cit., p.96

[13] Hollesley Borstal template available at https://goo.gl/Dnr8xx (accessed 27th March 2016)

[14] Farm Walk Hollesley Bay Colony 1958 in *Farm Conference History 1956-1975*, op. cit., p.22

[15] ibid. p.23-24

[16] Farm Walk Lowdham Grange 1956 ibid. p.1-8

[17] National Justice Museum, Nottingham. 'Sunday Pictorial Pic, Dartmoor': AAPSM:1998.0013. Reproduced by permission of the Ministry of Justice. Undated.

[18] DIS Policy, op. cit.

[19] Farm Management Conference held at Wye College (University of London) near Ashford, Kent, 9th-11th July 1969 in *Farm Conference History 1956-1975*, op. cit., p.105

[20] *Farm Conference History 1956-1975*, op. cit., p.113

[21] Photo courtesy of Howard Morse

[22] ibid., p.117

[23] *Farms and Gardens in the Prison Service*, op. cit., p.12

[24] 'Featherstone Project', Farm Management Conference 1980 op. cit., *Farm Conference History 1976-1995* p.266

[25] ibid.,

[26] *Farms and Gardens in the Prison Service*, op. cit., p.6

[27] Prison Service News [PSN] (Nov 1990) 'John Sandy retires: 34 years' love affair draws to a close', p.4

[28] Map courtesy of Brian Dunce

Chapter 4 – Escape to the country

[1] Alexandre Dumas, *The Count of Monte Cristo*, first published in English in 1846 by Chapman and Hall

[2] National Justice Museum, Nottingham. AAPSM:1993:0413. Reproduced by permission of the Ministry of Justice. Dated March 1970.

[3] Nick Knight, Report of the 1991 Farm Management Conference op. cit., *Farm Conference History 1976-1995* p.354

[4] ibid.

[5] DIS Policy, op. cit., paragraphs 11-12

[6] Farm Management Conference, 10th-12th July 1973 op. cit., *Farm Conference History 1956-1975* p.172

[7] National Justice Museum, Nottingham. AAPSM:1998:0020. Reproduced by permission of the Ministry of Justice. Dated March 1956.

[8] James, T (2006) *Over the Wall and Away: More escapes from Dartmoor Prison.* Orchard Publications: Chudleigh, Devon.

[9] ibid.

[10] ibid. p.13

[11] Reproduced with permission of Punch Ltd., www.punch.co.uk

[12] Prison Reform Trust (1991) *The Woolf Report: A summary of the main findings and recommendations of the inquiry into prison disturbances.*

[13] Prison Reform Trust (2015) *Strangeways 25 years' on: Achieving Fairness & Justice in Prison,* lecture delivered by The Rt. Hon. Lord Woolf at Inner Temple Main Hall on 1 April 2015 available at https://goo.gl/phnoEE (accessed 20th May 2016)

[14] Woodcock, J (December, 1994) *'The Woodcock Enquiry' Report of the enquiry into the escape of six prisoners from the special security unit at Whitemoor prison, Cambridgeshire, on Friday 9th September 1994.* London: HMSO

[15] Prison Service News (July 1991) Vol 9 No 87 Front Page

[16] NOMS Service Annual Report 2014/15: Management Information Addendum (30th July 2015) available at https://goo.gl/BdY1yp (accessed 3rd May 2016)

[17] Warrington Guardian 20th March 2014 'One escape every two weeks in the past two years at Thorn Cross' available at https://goo.gl/tPJJiL (accessed 3rd May 2016)

[18] HM Treasury (January 1985) *Staff Inspection Report on the Farm Managers and Foremen in H M Prison Service.* Unpublished document, p.13

Chapter 5 – Self-sufficiency

[1] National Justice Museum, Nottingham. AAPSM.1990.0100. Reproduced with permission of the Ministry of Justice. Dated 1932.

[2] Kipps, M and Thomson, J (January/February 1988) Taking the gruel out of porridge: or A review of prison diet. *Nutrition and Food Science*, 88, 1, p.2-5

[3] ibid. Kipps et al., (1988) citing 1984 Household Food Consumption and Expenditure, Ministry of Agriculture, Fisheries and Food, p.15

[4] Farms and Gardens Section Farm Management Conference, 1969 op. cit., *Farm Conference History 1956-1975* p.110

[5] Schoenthaler, S.J and Doraz, W.E (1983) Types of offences which can be reduced in an institutional setting using nutritional intervention: A preliminary empirical investigation. *Int. J. of BioSoc. Res.* Vol. 4(2) cited in Thompson, A (November/December 1990) Diet and Delinquency. *Nutrition and Food Science*, p.9-11

[6] Gesch, C. B., Hammond, S.M., Hampson, S.E & Crowder, M.J (July 2002) Supplementary vitamins, minerals and essential fatty acids on the antisocial behaviour of young adult prisoners. *British Journal of Psychiatry*, 181, 22-28

[7] National Audit Office (2006) *HM Prison Service: Serving Time: Prisoner Diet and Exercise*. Report for the comptroller and auditor general. HC939 Session 2005-2006. London: Stationary Office p.1

[8] Gray, G.E (1986) Diet, crime and delinquency: a critique. *Nutrition Reviews/Supplement*, May 1986, pp. 89-93

[9] *The Woolf Report* (1991) London: HMSO Cm 1456. 'Tumim' report (January 1993) *Doing time or using time. Report of a review by HM Chief Inspector of Prisons for England and Wales of Regimes in Prison Service Establishments in England and Wales*. London: HMSO. Lygo, R (1991) *The Management of the Prison Service*. London: Home Office.

[10] Goodger, A (2003) A brief introduction to training prisoners within the British justice system in practical catering skills. *Nutrition & Food Science*, 33(1), 6-8

[11] *Farm Conference History 1956-1975* op. cit. p.110

[12] *Staff Inspection Report*, op. cit.

[13] Farm Management Conference 12th-14th July 1977 op. cit., *Farm Conference History 1976-1995* p.232

[14] DIS Policy, op. cit., paragraph 32

[15] *Farms and Gardens in Prison Service*, op. cit., p.8. Reproduced by permission of the Ministry of Justice. Undated.

[16] ibid. p.13. Reproduced by permission of the Ministry of Justice. Undated.

[17] National Justice Museum, Nottingham. AAPSM:1997:1075. Reproduced by permission of the Ministry of Justice. Undated.

[18] E.R. Farm and Gardens in the Prison Service, Date on or just before 1987 according to Maurice Codd. 2 page document. Source unknown. Document supplied by Howard Morse

[19] Farms Review video (1992) produced and supplied by Howard Morse

[20] Prison Department Prisons Board Farm and Gardens Policy Note by Controller (Administration), 13 Dec 1974. PB(74)43

[21] Kelly, J and Bates, C (18th February 2016) 10 ways the UK's eating habits have changed. https://goo.gl/zbmJ2o (last accessed 17th March 2016)

[22] NHS 'The new guidelines on vitamin D – what you need to know' (21st July 2016) available at https://is.gd/PP5oGC (accessed 30th April 2017)

[23] Crow, N (November 1995) System kitchens: improving catering quality and value for money in HM Prison Service. *Facilities*, 13(12), 21-25. MCB University Press p.22

[24] Kipps, M., Thompson, J and Thomson, A (March/April 1988) Modern Prison Diets. *Nutrition and Food Science*, p.13-15

[25] Mr Alastair Thompson, Catering Manager for the Supply and Transport Branch at Corby, *Meeting the Needs of the Prison Dietary* in Farm Management Conference 25-27 March 1986 op. cit. *Farm Conference History 1976-1995* p.320

[26] PSN (May 1992) Nasi Goreng and faggots replace gruel and molasses at Gloucester Prison p. 8

[27] Farm Management Conference 10th-12th July 1973 Royal Agricultural College, Cirencester op. cit. *Farm Conference History 1956-1975* p.182

[28] David Kent, Head of S & T, letter to establishments dated 12th August 1996. Unpublished document

[29] *Meeting the needs of the prison dietary,* op. cit.

[30] *Serving Time*, op. cit.

[31] David Kent, letter to establishments, op. cit.

[32] Food Standards Agency (2008) *Safe food and healthy eating for all. Report 2007/08.* London: The Stationery Office

[33] *Serving Time,* op. cit.

[34] Daniels, L (2008) *Final report: Example menus for adult men in prison.* Report prepared for the Food Standards Agency

[35] HMP/YOI Littlehay: Independent Monitoring Board Annual Report for February 2009-January 2010

[36] ibid.

[37] HMYOI Northallerton Independent Monitoring Board Annual Report for March 2009-February 2010

[38] Cockerton, P (Feb 1st 2013) Prison Food Shock: Pork found in 'Halal' meat served to Muslim prisoners. *Mirror* https://goo.gl/Xvsxqp (accessed February 4th 2016)

[39] £62,657,000 according to Jeremy Wright, Friday 22 March 2013 Written Answers to Questions. Prisons: Food see https://goo.gl/4LX6Te (accessed 4th February 2016)

[40] Jeremy Wright, Secretary of State for Justice, 29th January 2014. Written Answers to Questions. Prisons: Food see https://goo.gl/6XPd0e (accessed 15th June 2017)

[41] Edwards, J.S.A., Hartwell, H.J., Reeve, W.G and Schafheitle, J (2007). The diet of prisoners in England. *British Food Journal*, 109, 3, 216-232

Chapter 6 – Therapy

[1] Extract from *Black Sheep* by Susan Hill, published by Vintage Books © Susan Hill 2013. Reproduced by permission of Sheil Land Associates Ltd.

[2] DIS Policy, op. cit., paragraph 33

[3] Planning and Services Manager, Farm Management Conference 12th-14th July 1977 op. cit., *Farm Conference History 1976-1995* p.227

[4] National Justice Museum, Nottingham. AAPSM:1993:0420. Reproduced by permission of the Ministry of Justice. Dated March 1970.

[5] *Farm Conference History 1976-1995* op. cit., p.228

[6] ibid. p.243

[7] Sempik, J and Aldridge, J (2006) Care farms and care gardens: Horticulture as therapy in the UK in Hassink, J and van Dijk, M (Eds.) *Farming for Health*. Springer pp.147-161

[8] ibid.

[9] Annual Independent Monitoring Board Report HMP/YOI East Sutton Park 1st November 2014 to 31st October 2015, p.10

[10] Longley, D (1991) op. cit., *Farm Conference History 1976-1995* p.369

[11] PSN (December 1986) The 'cowman' who commands respect, p.9

[12] Bob Leckie, Butler Trust Award winner 2016 at https://goo.gl/ai0Yko (accessed 15th June 2017)

[13] ibid.

[14] ibid.

[15] Report of the 1991 Farm Management Conference op. cit., *Farm Conference History 1976-1995* p.372

[16] 'Pollett Review' (1996) *Review of the agricultural and horticultural activities in HM Prison Service October 1995 – January 1996*. Unpublished document. p.42

[17] DIS policy, op. cit., paragraph 13

[18] ibid., paragraph 14

[19] Farm Management Conference 11th-13th July 1978 op. cit., *Farm Conference History* 1976-1995 p.243

[20] Darby, P (2004). A farming revolution. *PSN*, October/November 2004, no. 233 p.20

[21] Ormerod, E (2008) Companion animals and offender rehabilitation – experiences from a prison therapeutic community in Scotland. *International Journal of Therapeutic Communities*, 29, 3, 285-296.

[22] ibid., p.287

[23] Dr. Phil Thomas quoted in Faith Alive (undated) p. 7 -11

[24] Lawrence, J (1971) Nothing Barred. *Reveille* 14th-20th Aug 20, p.11

[25] National Justice Museum, Nottingham. AAPSM:1997:1074. Reproduced by

permission of the Ministry of Justice. Undated.

[26] *Farm Conference History 1976-1995* op. cit., p.243

[27] Prison Service Agri Business Review (PSABR) (January 1997). Unpublished document

[28] HMP Blantyre House Annual Report of the Independent Monitoring Board 1st July 2010-30th June 2011

[29] PSABR, op. cit.

[30] HMP Blantyre House Annual Report, op. cit.

[31] Personal communication. Letter from Amy Cullen (2014)

[32] McNicholas, J. & Collis, G.M. (1995). The end of a relationship: Coping with pet loss. In I. Robinson (Ed.), *The Waltham book of human-animal interaction: Benefits and responsibilities of pet ownership* (pp.127–143). Oxford: Pergamon Press

[33] Annual Independent Monitoring Board Report HMP/YOI East Sutton Park 1st November 2014 to 31st October 2015, p.10

[34] Bragg, R., Wood, C., Barton, J and Pretty, J (2015) *Wellbeing benefits from natural environments rich in wildlife: A literature review for The Wildlife Trusts*

[35] Peter Stevens quoted in *Oxford Mail* (Jan 4th 1973) Prisoners step out on the 'open' farm, p.9

[36] DIS policy, op. cit.

[37] For example, Fletcher, R F (2008) Offenders in the post-industrial labour market: from the underclass to the undercaste? *Policy & Politics*, 36, 2, 283-297

[38] DeViggiani, N (2003) (Un) healthy prison masculinities: theorising men's health in prison. *Unpublished PhD thesis*, University of Bristol

[39] Chorley, M (25th March 2012) GPs devise new treatment to beat depression. It's called gardening. *Independent* available at https://goo.gl/gsQ1x (accessed 3rd May 2017)

[40] Rice, J.S & Remy, L.L (1998) Impact of horticultural therapy on psychosocial functioning among urban jail inmates. *Journal of Offender Rehabilitation*, 2,3/4, 169-191

[41] Elger (2009) quoted in Meek, R and Lewis, G (2012) The role of sport in promoting prisoner health. *Int. J of Prisoner Health*, 8, ¾, 117-130

[42] Fazel, S., Hope, T., O'Donnell, I., Piper, M and Jacoby, R (2001) Health of elderly male prisoners: worse than the general population, worse than younger prisoners. *Age and Ageing*, 30(5) 403-7

[43] Community Forest Trust (2016) Measuring the social return from investment in the Natural Health Services. Available at naturalhealthservice.org.uk (accessed 4th May 2017)

[44] *Serving Time*, op. cit.

[45] Moneymaker, J.M and Strimple, E.O (1991) Animals and inmates: A sharing companionship behind bars. *Journal of Offender Rehabilitation*, 16, 3/4, 133-152

[46] Carpentieri, J.D (25th August 2001) Jail House Flock, *The Guardian*

[47] BBC Panorama 'Tough Justice in Britain – Texas Style' 12th October 2015

[48] Amy Cullen, op. cit.
[49] ibid.

Chapter 7 – A rare breed

[1] Thomas Jefferson, Letter to Ebenezer Hazard, 18 February 1791 available at https://goo.gl/pcSfsF
[2] Suffolk spelling
[3] Photo courtesy of Howard Morse
[4] Sunday Times (20th June 1971) 'Farms without bars'.
[5] DIS Policy, op. cit., paragraph 26
[6] Photo courtesy of Howard Morse
[7] Wilding, C (undated) *Defra Review of Policy on Genetic Resources for Food and Agriculture*, p.31
[8] Moss, S (3rd November 2015) Joe Henson obituary. *The Guardian* p.35
[9] Feist, B (July 1994) Rare breeds in secure conditions. *The ARK: Rare Breeds Survival Trust*, Vol XXI, Number 7 pp.254-255
[10] National Justice Museum, Nottingham. AAPSM:1995.0111. Reproduced by permission of the Ministry of Justice. Undated.
[11] PSN (June 1992) 'PSIF Euro export first!' Vol 10, No 97, Front Page
[12] Coast-to-Coast video by Guy Phillips supplied by Howard Morse
[13] ibid.
[14] ibid.
[15] BBC News (18th July 2012) 'Sheep filmed swimming to shore in Morecambe Bay'
[16] Scunthorpe Evening Telegraph (January 30 1997) p.19
[17] British Lop Pig Society available at https://goo.gl/lXh7Kx (accessed 15th June 2017)
[18] Source unknown. Newspaper article 'Kirkham's Lops are the tops'. Cutting provided by Howard Morse
[19] Carter, L (Winter/early Spring 2011) An open prison with an open mind. *FarmersMart* p.65
[20] Anonymous 'S.S' (no date) 'Bullocks, bulls and cows…' Your Letters. Letter written to ICPO volunteer Sr Agnes by UK prisoner in an open prison. p.14
[21] Horrocks, S (2009) All creatures great and small in PSN (July/Aug 2009), number 265, p.23. https://goo.gl/zsEipE (accessed 15th June 2017)

Chapter 8 – On show

[1] Lewis Carroll (1865) Alice's Adventures in Wonderland
[2] National Justice Museum, Nottingham. AAPSM:1997:1076. Reproduced by permission of the Ministry of Justice. Undated.
[3] National Justice Museum, Nottingham. AAPSM:1997:0397. Reproduced by permission of the Ministry of Justice. Undated.
[4] Lord Carter, Hansard (25th April 1988) British Food and Farming Year HL Deb vol 496 cc5-6

[5] Farm Management Conference 1969 op. cit., *Farm Conference History 1956-1976* p.111
[6] Dowell, B (2015) Classic Ronnie Barker prison comedy Porridge "to be revived" by the BBC available at https://goo.gl/LilEQV
[7] Morse, H (1992) Video from the 1992 Royal Show. Courtesy of Howard Morse
[8] Morse, H (1988) Video footage of Berkshire pigs at Smithfield Show. Courtesy of Howard Morse
[9] PSN (June, 1991) 'Chelsea '91' p.6-7
[10] HM Prison Leyhill Chelsea Flower Show 1991 'The edible garden' leaflet
[11] PSN (Feb 1991), vol 9, no 82. p3. 'Leyhill skills merit Chelsea Show entry'
[12] HM Prison Leyhill Chelsea Flower Show 1992 'Here we go round the mulberry bush' designed by members of the civilian and inmate Farms and Gardens team. Leaflet.
[13] Prison Service Communications 1995. HM Prison Service: A prison service to be proud of. HM Prison Service at Agricultural and Flower Shows May-August 1995. Pamphlet.
[14] Copyright 'D Low'. Private collection, Ann Wright
[15] Photographs by Bev Wright. Collection of the author
[16] Photo courtesy of Jayne Burrows, Secretary of the Lincoln Red Cattle Society
[17] Photograph courtesy of livestock photographer, Anthony Mosley
[18] Farmers Weekly (3rd April 2006) 'Needham bull takes Lincoln Red title'

Chapter 9 – Where there's muck ...

[1] Farms & Gardens Section: Position at 20th October, 1952. Unpublished document supplied by Maurice Codd
[2] Farm Management Conference 1970 op. cit., *Farm Conference History 1956-1975* p.123
[3] DIS Policy, op. cit., paragraph 32
[4] Farm Management Conference 11th-13th July 1972 op. cit., *Farm Conference History 1956-1975* p.161
[5] PSABR, op. cit., p.19
[6] *Farm Conference History 1976-1995*, op. cit., p.209
[7] ibid. p.235
[8] Author's private collection. Dated 1982
[9] *Staff Inspection Report*, op. cit.
[10] Farm Management Conference 10th-12th July 1973 Royal Agricultural College, Cirencester op. cit., *Farm Conference History 1956-1975* p.182
[11] *Staff Inspection Report*, op. cit.
[12] *Pollett Review*, op. cit.
[13] National Justice Museum, Nottingham. AAPSM:1993:0412. Reproduced by permission of the Ministry of Justice. Dated March 1970.
[14] Lander, N (3rd/4th October 1992). The convicts who reap what they have sown. *Financial Times Weekend* p. vii

[15] The Prisons Board included the Director General, Director of Personnel, Director of Security and Director of Finance
[16] Home Office Prison Department Directorate of Industries and Farms (April 1983) The reorganisation of the directorate of industries and farms [Reorganisation]. Draft Copy. Unpublished document
[17] ibid., p.3
[18] ibid., p.3
[19] Codd, M (1984) Address to farm management conference. Private collection
[20] Feist, B (18th March 2016) Personal communication: email
[21] Tony Gilchrist, Senior Farms & Gardens Manager (1986) op. cit., *Farm Conference History 1976-1995* p.326
[22] ibid., p.372
[23] Clive Bendy, Training Manager PSIF (1991) ibid., p.368
[24] *Staff Inspection Report* op. cit.

Chapter 10 – Making the grade

[1] Henry David Thoreau (1854) *Walden; or, Life in the Woods.* Boston: Ticknor and Fields
[2] *Farms and Gardens in the Prison Service,* op. cit., p.13
[3] Simon & Corbett (1992/1994) Centre for Criminal Justice Research, Brunel University cited in PSABR report 1997, op. cit.
[4] Pollett Review, op. cit., p.28
[5] Prison Reform Trust (Summer 2015) Prison: the Facts. *Bromley Briefings*
[6] *Farms and Gardens in the Prison Service,* op. cit., p.13
[7] DIS Policy, op. cit., paragraphs 16-17
[8] *Farms and Gardens in the Prison Service,* op. cit.
[9] DIS Policy, op. cit., paragraphs 16-17
[10] David Longley (1991) op. cit., *Farm Conference History 1976-1995* p.369
[11] National Justice Museum, Nottingham. AAPSM:1993:0417. Reproduced by permission of the Ministry of Justice. Dated March 1970.
[12] Farms and Gardens Section: Organisational chart and duties of the staff [1952/53] [O.& M. Report]. Unpublished document supplied by Maurice Codd
[13] Bacon (1966), op. cit.
[14] National Justice Museum, Nottingham. AAPSM:1998:0247. Reproduced by permission of the Ministry of Justice. Undated.
[15] PSIF Farms video illustrating PSIF Farms and Gardens section activities, undated, video courtesy of Howard Morse
[16] Amy Cullen, op. cit.
[17] Rask, J (2005) *The incidence of hidden disabilities in the prison population.* York: The Dyslexia Institute
[18] Liebling et al., op. cit., p.166
[19] National Justice Museum, Nottingham. AAPSM:1995:1202. Reproduced by permission of the Ministry of Justice. Dated 1969.

Chapter 11 – A fresh start

[1] Home Office (1979) Committee of Inquiry into the United Kingdom Prison Service: Report, Cm 7673 [*The May Report*]

[2] Farm Management Conference (1980) op. cit., *Farm Conference History 1976-1995* p.266

[3] For example, Fitzgerald, M and Sim, J (1980) Legitimating the prison vision: A critical review of the May Report. *Howard Journal of Penology and Crime Prevention*, 19, 2, 73-84

[4] Faulkner, David (2014) *Servant of the Crown: A Civil Servant's Story of Criminal Justice and Public Service Reform*. Hook, Hampshire: Waterside Press

[5] *Farm Conference History 1976-1995*, op. cit., p.267

[6] ibid., p.264

[7] This seems to differ from Liebling et al., (2012) who claimed that the first time an outside company reported on the organisation of the Prison Service was 1990 when regional directors were abolished and a new area manager structure introduced.

[8] *Staff Inspection Report*, op. cit.

[9] Black, J (1993). The prison service and executive agency status – HM Prisons plc? *International J of Public Sector Management*, 6, 6, 27-41, p.31

[10] After Tadnoll, Mike went on to work at Hewell Grange, one of the few prison farms still operational.

[11] Lydon, H and Wright, B (1991) 'Inmate activities and the role of the specialist' op. cit., *Farm Conference History 1976-1995* p.355

[12] Photo courtesy of Howard Morse

[13] Lydon and Wright, op. cit., p.355

[14] Liebling et al., op. cit., p.193

[15] Mennicken, A (2013). 'Too big to fail and too big to succeed': Accounting and privatisation in the prison service of England and Wales. *Financial Accountability & Management*, 29(2), May 2013, 0267-4424

[16] Nottingham Post (21 September 2015) Huge fall in Nottingham home burglaries available at https://goo.gl/4Qu7U2 (accessed 20th May 2016)

[17] PSABR (January 1997), op. cit.

[18] Liebling, A., assisted by Arnold, H. (2004) *Prisons and Their Moral Performance: A Study of Values, Quality and Prison Life*. Oxford: Oxford University Press. p.69

[19] Prison Enterprise Management Conference, 29th-31st March Keele University 1995 op. cit., *Farm Conference History 1976-1995* pp.377-386

[20] Mennicken, op. cit.

[21] Stephen Shaw, quoted in Selby, M (10th December 2003) Sir Stephen Tumim. Obituary. *The Guardian* available at https://goo.gl/ww2qw1 (accessed 14th June 2017)

[22] *Tumim Report* (January 1993), op. cit.

[23] *Pollett Review* (1996), op. cit.

[24] ibid., p.4
[25] ibid., p.1
[26] ibid., p.31
[27] ibid., p.1

Chapter 12 – Nails in the coffin

[1] Extract from *Swineherd* by Eiléan Ní Chuilleanáin © 1986 reproduced with permission of Eiléan Ní Chuilleanáin.
[2] PSN (July 1992) Director General's vision of responsibility. Vol 10, no 98, front page. Article supplied by Howard Morse
[3] PSN (Feb 1991) Untitled, vol. 9, 82, p.3
[4] Liebling et al., op. cit., p.199
[5] Ivor Gough quoted in Lander, N (1992), op. cit.
[6] Deloitte and Touche press release (Oct 22nd, 2002) 'Farmers earn less from producing food as low profits bite' cited at https://goo.gl/Y68enK (accessed 28th March 2016)
[7] Jeffrey, S (2000) 'Plummeting incomes add to farmers' woes'. *The Guardian*, Oct 12 cited by www.corporatewatch.org (accessed 28th March 2016)
[8] Data from John Nix farm management pocketbook cited in Feist, B (undated) 'Closing report on the Farm Modernisation Programme' [*Closing Report*] supplied by Bernard Feist
[9] Ministry of Justice (January 2013) *Story of the Prison Population 1993-2012 England and Wales* available at https://goo.gl/iLH7JO (accessed 21st March 2016)
[10] *Pollett Review*, op. cit.
[11] ibid., point 1.2
[12] Lewis, D (1997) *Hidden Agendas: Politics, Law and Disorder.* Hamish Hamilton: London. p. ix
[13] Brown and Co. (December 1996) *Valuation of Agricultural Property prepared on behalf of HM Prison Service.* Unpublished report.
[14] Agricultural Development Advisory Service (ADAS), the advisory arm of the Department of Agriculture before it became the broader focused, Department for Environment, Food and Rural Affairs (Defra) in June 2001
[15] ADAS (1996) Assessment of produce quality, pricing and financial and operating systems
[16] PSABR, op. cit.
[17] 'Points raised Hannah email 19/10' by Bernard Feist
[18] *Closing Report*, op. cit.
[19] Horticulture Matters (May 2013) A report by partners in the Horticulture Industry available at https://goo.gl/HKo7lI last accessed 5th February 2017
[20] ibid.
[21] *Closing Report*, op. cit.
[22] *DIS Policy*, op. cit., paragraph 13

[23] *Closing Report*, op. cit.
[24] Farming UK (2007) European Festival of the Plough available at https://goo.gl/XqGAK1 (accessed 22nd September 2016)
[25] *Closing Report*, op. cit.
[26] Hardwick, N (2012) reported in HMP East Sutton Park – Safe, Decent and Effective available at https://goo.gl/pR4yxK (accessed 2nd April 2016)
BBC News online 'First prisoners moved to Downview as Holloway closes' (3 May 2016) available at https://goo.gl/4Uh5Om (accessed 19th May 2017)

Chapter 13 – Dispersal

[1] Extract from *A Year's Turning* by Michael Viney, published by The Blackstaff Press © 1996. Reproduced with permission of Michael Viney.
[2] Oulton, C (1996) Prison Closure Threat to Rare Sheep. *The Independent online* available at https://goo.gl/zIiqe2 (accessed 3rd June 2016)
[3] *Closing Report*, op. cit.
[4] Darby (2004), op. cit.
[5] ibid.
[6] ibid.
[7] ibid.
[8] Source unknown. Newspaper cutting. 'Prison sells 300 cows in battle to cut costs'. Courtesy of Howard Morse
[9] 'Growing for Life' available at https://goo.gl/vwjSxd (accessed 15th June 2017)
[10] ibid.
[11] *Closing Report*, op. cit.
[12] ibid.
[13] Probert, S (2007) Former prison farm up for rent. *Birmingham Post*, 24th May 2007
[14] RSPCA Birmingham Animal Centre available at https://goo.gl/OKp2ql (accessed 15th June 2017)
[15] *Closing Report*, op. cit.
[16] North West Auctions Limited: Lancaster Auction Mart Dispersal Sale of The Lancaster Herd of 155 Pedigree Holstein Cattle on Thursday 11th August 2005 @ 11am. Private collection Steve Horrocks
[17] Probert (2007), op. cit.
[18] *Closing Report*, op. cit.
[19] National Justice Museum, Nottingham. AAPSM:1997:0405. Reproduced by permission of the Ministry of Justice. Undated.
[20] Ministry of Justice available at https://goo.gl/HNQoms (accessed 12th April 2016)
[21] *Closing Report*, op. cit.
[22] *Serving time*, op. cit.
[23] *Closing Report*, op. cit.
[24] *Farms and Gardens in the Prison Service*, op. cit., inside front cover; Farm Managers' Reunion pamphlet (2005), front cover. Reproduced by permission

of the Ministry of Justice. Undated. Courtesy of Steve Horrocks

[25] Author's private collection and courtesy of Howard Morse

[26] PSN April (undated but probably 1971) p.6-7. National Justice Museum, Nottingham. AAPSM:1997.0951. Reproduced by permission of the Ministry of Justice

[27] Yorkshire Life (7th May 2012) The South Yorkshire market town of Thorne nicknamed 'Little Holland' available online at https://goo.gl/PVB874 (accessed February 12th 2017)

Chapter 14 – Going full circle

[1] Map courtesy of Brian Dunce

[2] Independent Monitoring Boards (2016) HMP North Sea Camp Annual Report 1st March 2015-29th February 2016

[3] NFU (23rd July 2015) 'Farming used to grow sense of worth in prison' available at https://goo.gl/gOGKcb (accessed 22nd April 2016)

[4] Frances Cook, Chief Executive of the Howard League for Penal Reform quoted in News release, 8th November 2012

[5] Cameron, D (8th February 2016) Prison Reform: Prime Minister's Speech

[6] Wright (2014), op. cit.

[7] Nutritional Guidelines for Food Served in Public Institutions prepared for The Food Standards Agency by The Caroline Walker Trust: Final Report

[8] Metcalfe, W (2nd February 2015) Cold prison food almost sparks full-scale riot after inmates have tense stand-off with guards. *Mirror newspaper*

[9] The Caroline Walker Trust, op. cit.

[10] Impact Report: Greener on the Outside for Prisons [GOOP], University of Central Lancashire (May 2015) available at https://goo.gl/Z89N0B (accessed 5th February 2017)

[11] Greener Growth: Hollesley Bay available at https://goo.gl/lRIEtw (accessed 12th January, 2015)

[12] Independent Monitoring Boards (2014) HMP Channings Wood Annual Report September 2014 to August 2015, p.7

[13] Hislop, C (2015) Devonchilliman – may be in prison? available at https://goo.gl/QEehBG (accessed 27th March 2016)

[14] Hislop, C (2015) 2,000 Chilli plants drink 7,000 Lts in a weekend at Channings Wood prison available at https://goo.gl/TGNn6G (accessed 27th March 2016)

Chapter 15 – A rare breed blossoms

[1] Bowcott, O (4 May 2014) Planned closure of two women's prisons halted by legal action. *The Guardian* available at https://goo.gl/Ghnbgd (accessed 2nd April 2016)

[2] Map courtesy of Brian Dunce

[3] 'Prison Land' unpublished document supplied by Bernard Feist in 2014

[4] Errington, J (September 2016) Public Sector Prison Industries: Commercial

horticulture status report. NOMS document. p.3

[5] ibid.

[6] UK Government Press release: Prisoners to supply armed forces with kit (1st February 2015) available at https://goo.gl/oGwGXK (accessed 12th May 2016)

[7] Author's private collection

[8] HM Inspectorate of Prisons (2016) HMP/YOI Hatfield – a safe, decent and purposeful resettlement prison available at https://goo.gl/5U5LGb (accessed 28th May 2016)

[9] Author's private collection

TiMELiNE

1852 First farm established at Dartmoor prison
1908 First Borstal established at Rochester includes a farm
1935 North Sea Camp Borstal and farm built on land reclaimed from the sea
1938 Hollesley Bay Colony opens with world's largest Suffolk Punch horse stud
1939-45 WWII 'Dig for Victory' campaign
1947 13 farms, 5,000 acres (2,000+ ha), 1,000 inmates employed
1953 First prison farm conference
1955 22 farms, 52 gardens, 8,115 acres (3,200+ ha)
1968 Cabinet directive stipulates that prison farms must be cost-effective
1971 35 prison farms, 12,000 acres (4,800+ ha)
1971 Management by Objectives piloted in Farms & Gardens
1975 Prison service becomes self-sufficient in pork and bacon
1978 £1.3m profit and Farms & Gardens award 228 proficiency certificates to inmates
1982 Maurice Codd takes over from Peter Stevens as Head of Farms & Gardens; HM Inspectorate of Prisons established; prison population approx. 44,500
1984 Prison food better than household food; Preston win first Windlesham Trophy
1985 First Butler Trust Awards; the Treasury commissions a staff inspection report on prison service farm managers and farm foremen; catering officers dispense with butchery skills
1986 Farms & Gardens help Rare Breeds Survival Trust house 40 rare, heritage breeds
1987 Farms & Gardens create a national distribution network to supply 90 prisons with home-grown vegetables, milk, meat and

jam; prison sentences shortened and less inmates allowed to work outside on the farms

1989 Farms & Gardens exhibit widely at agricultural and horticultural shows

1990 Woolf inquiry recommends penal reform; all capital expenditure frozen

1991 Maurice Codd is appointed Area Manager and Bernard Feist becomes Head of Farms & Gardens; Chris Train retires as the longest serving HMP Director General

1991 Maidstone win the Windlesham Trophy; Leyhill exhibit at Chelsea Flower Show; the Criminal Justice Act 1991 dismantles the state prison system and enables private sector administration of prisons

1992 14,000 acres (5,600+ ha), 17 large farms, an 80 person management team, 3,500 temporary workers and an annual turnover of £35 million; HMP Farms & Gardens the 3rd largest farming operation in the UK, able to feed 47,000 inmates

1992 Farms & Gardens win 25 awards at the Royal Agricultural Show and export rare breed pigs to France and Japan

1993 Home Secretary Michael Howard replaces Kenneth Clarke and delivers his 'Get tough – lock them up' speech; UK Prison Service and Scottish Prison Service become executive agencies with prison catering and education contracted out

1995 Following prisoner escapes Michael Howard sacks Director General Derek Lewis and replaces him with Richard Tilt who requests an assessment of land holdings and capital; David Ramsbotham is appointed HM Chief Inspector of Prisons

1996 Farms & Gardens employ 1,047 inmates; Pollett review of prison service agricultural and horticultural activities; Brown & Co value prison agricultural land

1997 Prison Service Agri Business Review recommends stopping pig production, closing three farms, phasing out potato growing, ending dairy farming within five years, discontinuing 'peripheral activities' except jam making

1998 Sudbury win the Windlesham Trophy and retain it in 1999; Home Detention Curfew introduced for prisoners serving short sentences

1999 HMP East Sutton Park opens a farm shop

2001 21 farms, 5,500 acres (2,200+ ha), number of inmates employed falls below 250; the Suffolk Punch horse stud is sold

2003 'Farm modernisation programme' – sale of machinery, livestock and land raises £1.5million of which £900,000 is reinvested in horticulture; HMP Hewell farm shop closes; HMP Kirkham establishes a 25 acre (10 hectare) conservation site; Phil Wheatley replaces Martin Narey as Director General

2003 Ofsted criticise Lindholme prison for not offering accredited horticultural or agricultural training

2004 The House of Commons Affairs Select Committee decides that the prison experience should be 'normal'; workshops are re-opened with emphasis on training, learning and skills; Dartmoor prison farm closes; HM Prison Service becomes National Offender Management Service (NOMS)

2005 Cows at Lancaster prison sold; first Farm Manager 'get together'; inaugural Keith Bromley Award for Education & Skills Training

2006 12 farms and 10 dairy units sold, 2,770 acres (1,100+ ha)

2007 UK prison food report advises more use of seasonal, local produce

2008 Ofsted inspection notes pride looking after small animals and prison grounds

2009 HMP Kirkham farm wins Butler Trust Award and HRH Princess Anne asks to see the rare breed Longhorn cattle

2010 Michael Spurr replaces Phil Wheatley as Director General; Butler Trust Award to 'Greening on the outside of prisons' project

2013 5 prison farms remain

2014 Sale of HMP East Sutton Park prison and farm halted after legal action

2015 Prison population exceeds 85,000; no dedicated budget for land based activities; faced with competition from private companies, prisons create mini distribution networks to supply vegetables to prison kitchens

2016 Bob Leckie, Land Based Activities manager at HMP/YOI

	Thorn Cross wins a Butler Trust Award and the Keith Bromley Award for Education & Skills Training; Jason Errington appointed Head of Land Based Activities; Heads of Catering start requesting locally grown produce; **more than 1,000 inmates spend 1.5 million hours growing plants**
2017	Her Majesty's Prison and Probation Service (HMPPS) replaces NOMS; **100+ prisons bring nature inside the walls; income from farm shops, livestock sales and supplying the prison kitchens approaches £1million**

ACKNOWLEDGEMENTS

I could not have written this book without the support of my dad's colleagues and friends, many of whom were present at his memorial service and whose accounts formed the basis for this book. In particular, I feel privileged to have inherited my dad's friendship with Maurice & Mo. This book is testimony to Maurice's humility, generosity and prodigious memory.

Chris and Lorraine Coveney who, like Maurice, have Farms & Gardens at their core, are an absolute inspiration, unstinting in their enthusiasm and support for all who are lucky enough to know them. Thanks to all the contributors, especially those still involved in promoting or benefiting from land based activities in the prison service, such as Jason Errington, Amy Cullen and Wayne.

I am grateful to Howard Morse for sharing his audio-visual archive and to HMPPS, Bev Baker at the National Justice Museum, livestock photographer Anthony Mosley and Jayne Burrows, secretary of the Lincoln Red Cattle Society for permission to reproduce photographs. Thanks to Jim Clancy at Streamline Photography and Design for patiently preparing the images and typesetting the manuscript. I am much obliged to Wayne Cook, who prior to his retirement handed over responsibility for printing to Peter Hart, so that *Outside Time* could, appropriately enough, be printed by prisoners at HMP Coldingley.

Thank you to my family and friends for your ongoing support. Andrew, your goading worked. Patrick, your feedback is appreciated! Annabel and Martin Shaw, I owe you a copy for providing me with a space to write. Trusted friends Grainne Saunders and Stephanie Hicks made kind and constructive comments on an earlier version whilst nature and travel writer Miriam Darlington merits special acknowledgement for sound mentoring and professional advice. I am indebted to my lovely octogenarian friend Brian Dunce, who knows much about everything; I hope that your fine paintings and drawings get the wider recognition they deserve. A credit is also due to Alex Lay and Gillian Fallon for whittling the wording on the cover.

I would like to present a long-service award to Fionnguala Sherry-Brennan for her tremendous professionalism and commitment. Your patience, kindness and outstanding editorial support made anything and everything possible.

Finally, I owe much to my greatest champion, my dad, who catalysed a journey of appreciative enquiry for my mum and I that helped heal the broken hearts he left behind.